D0928122

FIGURES OF THOUGHT IN ROMAN POETRY

FIGURES OF THOUGHT
IN
ROMAN POETRY

GORDON WILLIAMS

YALE UNIVERSITY PRESS 1980 NEW HAVEN AND LONDON

Designed by James J. Johnson
and set in Monophoto Bembo type by
Asco Trade Typesetting Ltd., Hong Kong.
Printed in the United States of America by
Halliday Lithograph, West Hanover, Mass.

Published in Great Britain, Europe, Africa, and
Asia (except Japan) by Yale University Press,
Ltd., London. Distributed in Australia and
New Zealand by Book & Film Services, Artarmon,
N.S.W., Australia; and in Japan by Harper & Row,
Publishers, Tokyo Office.

Library of Congress Cataloging in Publication Data

Williams, Gordon Willis.
  Figures of thought in Roman poetry.

  Includes bibliographical references and indexes.
    1. Latin poetry—History and criticism.   2. Figures
of speech.   I. Title.
PA6047.W43   871'.01'08   79–23725
ISBN 0–300–02456–8

CONTENTS

PREFACE

Some explanation is needed for two features of this book. First, technical terms of rhetoric are often used, including some that have been invented by me. Rather than construct a glossary of such terms (in which definitions would need to be very brief and could be unhelpful out of context), I have recorded in the Index, under the name of each term, the place in the text where that term is defined. Secondly, I have written the book in the hope that it will be read also by those whose main interest is in literatures other than those of Greece and Rome. With such readers in mind, I have supplied English translations for all passages of Latin quoted. These translations make no claim to elegance; their function is to be as literal as possible and even to adhere as closely as possible to the Latin word-order so that a reader who is unsure of his knowledge of Latin may still be able to find his way about the Latin texts that are generously quoted throughout the book.

My most grateful thanks must go to two friends and colleagues, Thomas Cole and John Herington, both of whom, at times that were most inconvenient to them, nevertheless very kindly read the whole book through for me and made many excellent suggestions for its improvement. The reader for the Yale University Press also made a number of very helpful observations. All of these have been incorporated in the text, with this note as the sole mark of acknowledgement and my gratitude.

G. W.

New Haven
June 1979

INTRODUCTION

This book is about the technique of poetry. Its thesis is that for a comparatively short time—from the major poetic composition of Catullus (around 60–55 B.C.) to the death of Horace in 8 B.C.—Roman poets fully exploited a technique of composition that was characterised by several important features; these ran counter to rhetorical theory as it has come down to us (mostly from later periods) and so have gone unrecognized. The most far-reaching of these was a virtual denial of the fundamental distinction between form and content. In rhetorical theory that distinction permitted total prescription of the technique of composition by dividing it into two separate areas: language was subject to ordering by exhaustive description of vocabulary, syntax, and figures; content was likewise subject to ordering by the rules of *inventio*: the technique by which all the latent or inherent possibilities in a given idea or cluster of ideas could be 'discovered' and exploited. It was from the elaboration of this latter set of rules that what has recently been called the technique of 'generic composition' was evolved, and this was done, in my view, in a period later—even considerably later—than the one of which I am talking; for details of this technique I need only refer to the work of Cairns (1972). But once that comfortable distinction between form and content was disregarded, conventional rhetorical analysis was impotent and the way was open to the poet to apply to ideas the same configurations that had been applied traditionally to language. An idea, that is, could be regarded as a semantic unit, analogous to a word, and could be subject to configurations with other ideas just as had been done previously with words. Consequently, for instance, new techniques could be devised for managing transitions of thought, and the poet could say one thing while expecting his reader to understand that he meant something else, which might be related to what he said in one or more of several different ways.

That brings me to the second important feature of poetic composition in this short period. For, if the poet could say one thing and mean another, it follows that a particular view was being taken of the nature and function of poetry. It was understood to be an act of communication between the poet and a reader who was privileged in the sense that he had—or was assumed by the poet to have—a special access to the poet's process of thought. In some respects that privilege consisted in being a member of a restricted coterie to which the poet also belonged, and there are certain aspects, especially of the poetry of Catullus, that are only accessible to privileged information of this sort. The relationship, for instance, between Propertius 1.21 and 22 can be regarded as the poet's way of extending that privilege to a wider circle of readers for the purposes of publication (see Williams (1968) 177–78). But in the main the reader's privilege consisted in his having, in virtue of education, social position, and sympathetic understanding, a capacity to divine the subtleties of reading that a particular poem or passage required. That divination might well not come on a first reading or even on a second. In fact, this poetry was of the kind that reveals more of itself on each reading. What the reader needed most, therefore, was the capacity to recognise where judgment could only be provisional, or needed to be suspended altogether until the whole poem had been read, or read for a second time. That is, it was not a poetry of immediate impact, it was not a rhetorical poetry; it was a poetry of meditation, it was a private act of communication with an individual reader who responded to the fullest extent of his literary capacities. It was not a poetry intended for public performance to a large audience with whom its success would have to be measured in terms of its immediate impact. I have explored that contrast between these two types of poetry in two earlier books: *Tradition and Originality in Roman Poetry* (Oxford 1968) and *Change and Decline: Roman Literature in the Early Empire* (California 1978). There I have tried to show how the Roman view of the nature and function of poetry changed during the age of Augustus: Horace, who died in 8 B.C., was the last of the poets who represented the tradition that had been established mainly by Catullus; while Ovid, who was already poetically active by about 20 B.C., can be seen to have viewed poetry as a rhetorical composition, however subtle, whose value lay in its capacity to manipulate an audience by making immediate impact, as if the poet were an orator or musician. What I have tried to do in the present book is to exemplify, by interpretation of many passages, the nature of the demand which poets of the earlier period were prepared to make on their readers through the application of figures to ideas.

The reason why this has not been done before can be explained in terms of the enormous authority exercised by rhetorical theory. Poetry of the period I am discussing was simply not comprehensible in terms of rhetorical theory, and so it was misunderstood (as can be seen from ancient commentaries) from a time soon after its composition. To put it briefly and crudely, the whole thrust of rhetorical theory was to assimilate the condition of poetry to that of prose (particularly oratory) so that it could be subjected to the sort of ordering, both interpretatively and prescriptively, that had been worked out for prose over many centuries. This authority was the more plausible in its impertinent impositions, in that, for reasons I have examined in *Change and Decline*, poetry after the age of Augustus willingly assimilated itself to the condition of prose (with the addition of metre), and this was the tradition both of poetic composition and of exegesis that was handed on to the Middle Ages and the Renaissance. It is only fairly recently that the imposture has been seriously questioned; and, as far as Roman poetry is concerned, the process of questioning has hardly started.

Consequently I have been faced with difficult problems of terminology. The trouble arises from the fact that ancient rhetorical theorists certainly acknowledged the possibility and indeed the existence of figures of thought; but, for reasons that I explain in chapter 2, they confined their analysis to simple structures for the most part, like rhetorical question or aposiopesis, and devoted their attention otherwise to figures of speech. Depending to some extent on the scheme of analysis outlined by Roman Jakobson in his essay on aphasia in *Fundamentals of Language* (New York 1956), I have distinguished the major modifications produced by configurations of thought as being either metaphoric or metonymic (or synecdochic) in mode. What may cause difficulty here arises from the fact that ancient theorists used the words 'metaphor' and 'metonymy' to describe modifications of meaning that are produced by the fact that a sign or group of signs is connected to an unexpected or unusual referent. The resulting modification is intelligible to the reader because a relationship of similarity or of contiguity links the normal or expected referent with the new referent. The capacity to recognise the relevant relationship of similarity or contiguity must pre-exist in the reader; he will not find it resident in the literary context. However, when analogous modifications are applied to ideas, or groups of ideas, there are certainly relationships of similarity and contiguity to be recognised, but there are no simple or easily identified referents. Instead of finding basic facts of experience or language contradicted (as happens normally when 'metaphor' or 'metonymy' are interpreted literally), the reader must sense by a variety of clues from the actual literary context that the poet is saying one thing and meaning another. The various forms which 'saying one thing and meaning another' might take in configurations of ideas could be covered by a variety of ancient terms such as irony, *emphasis*, euphemism, *praeteritio*, *dubitatio*, *apostrophe*, and others. In the main I have not attempted to apply these close distinctions; one easily gets into a scholastic nightmare of labelling in which the important issues simply disappear from view. So I have kept to the basic broad distinctions of metaphorical and metonymic modes.

I have done this even in analysis of connexions of thought. This might appear inane, since clearly all connexions of thought are capable of being categorised as either metaphorical in mode (involving associations of similarity) or as metonymic (that would include, for instance, all logical connexions). However this aspect of transition in poetry is only worth analysis where unexpected and surprising associations form the basis for the connexion; it so happens that such passages have often been judged to be lacunose by editors or they have been subjected to editorial surgery by means of transpositions of lines to 'improve' the connexion of thought. In such cases it has seemed worthwhile to me to analyse the nature of the transition in terms of these two modes. This type of configuration does not, of course, come within the concept of 'saying one thing and meaning another'; instead the poet appeals to a capacity in the reader to grasp the inner sense of an unexpected association of ideas that often resonates beyond its immediate context. Equally outside that concept is another technique which I have included because of its importance in the period that concerns me. This is what I have called 'thematic anticipation': a theme that will become significant later is introduced at a much earlier stage in such a way that the reader must recognise in the prior context a signal to suspend judgment. This is a figure of great importance for sustaining the energy of a complex poem. It often has a close structural similarity to the poetic use of analogy (basically a metaphorical mode) that I have called 'arbitrary assertion of similarity'. In both cases the reader is being warned to suspend judgment, and the 'suspension of judgment' is one of the most striking features of the meditative poetry of the late Republic and early age of Augustus.

I have departed from traditional terminology in various ways that I have tried to explain above. I have also, whenever it suited me, invented new terms for features that I wanted to identify. Some of these have already been mentioned; these and others—such as the distinction between 'primary' and 'secondary' language, the 'index of proportion-ality', or the 'objective framework'—will be explained at appropriate points in the course of the argument. I hope that it is not necessary to apologise either for these (I have invented as little new terminology as possible) or for the constant necessity to analyse passage after passage of the poetry of the period. It is only by such close textual examination and by gathering similar passages together that we can free ourselves from the tyranny of traditionally imposed interpretations.

SOME UNSOLVED PROBLEMS IN THE *ODES* OF HORACE

The odes that will be examined in this chapter have one characteristic in common: the text appears to say one thing, while the reader is required to understand something else that is not expressed explicitly in the poet's words. If my analysis of these poems is correct, then it should be possible to define the relationship between what is said in the text and what must be understood by the reader in terms of a poetic procedure that might have been familiar to contemporary readers in the ancient world. But it is a further characteristic of the problems in these particular odes that they seem not to have been understood in antiquity (much less in more modern times), and it may well be that the capacity to understand this poetic technique was lost from a time relatively soon—perhaps as little as half a century—after the odes were composed. Such a hypothesis is not as startling as it seems at first sight, for there was a change in attitudes to literature and in the concept of its function in society which can be seen in the work of Ovid, who was already composing a decade before the death of Horace.

1. *Horace* Odes *1.16*

This ode is addressed to a girl who is not identified, except by the periphrasis *o matre pulchra filia pulchrior*, 'o daughter more beautiful than your beautiful mother'. She is invited to destroy the poet's lampoons either by burning them or by throwing them into the Adriatic. This setting certainly recalls the poem of Catullus (36) in which, by a verbal trick, the *Annales* of Volusius are substituted as an offering to the fire-god for Catullus' lampoons, vowed by Lesbia as a sacrifice if the poet were

I

restored to her and ceased to write such poetry.[1] But the reminiscence does no more than provide immediate understanding of the dramatic situation, and the structure of the ode is quite different from that of Catullus' poem, in which, as usual, Lesbia has no dramatic existence except as one element in the poet's thoughts. In Horace's poem the girl's presence as a character is felt throughout.

The ode is one of those, composed of an uneven number of stanzas, in which one block of sense is connected to another equal block of sense by a transitional stanza.[2] In the opening three stanzas, the poet seems first to apologise for his lampoons (which he penitently designates as *criminosis*, 'vituperative') and then to launch into a general reflection on anger and its power over men's behaviour: it is more powerful than religious frenzy, and is not daunted by swords, storms, fire, or the thunderbolts of Juppiter himself. The tone of apology and conciliation, which seemed to be initiated in the opening stanza, seems naturally also to extend over the following stanzas, and the impression created is that the poet is setting his own anger in a general explanatory and apologetic context.[3] This impression is not at first contradicted by the transitional stanza (13–16), which gives a mythological account of the origin of anger in mankind: in a version of the legend, probably invented by Horace for his particular purpose here, Prometheus is said to have run out of material when creating living creatures so that, when he came to man, he had to go back and take elements from the already created animals; among those elements was the lion's capacity for rage and violence.

But, in the final three stanzas, the reader suddenly becomes aware, at the words (22) *compesce mentem* ('cool it!'), that now the poet, far from apologising for his own anger which inspired the composition of the offending lampoons, is really attacking the girl for her display of anger. As often in Horace's *Odes*, this final section of the poem deeply complicates the thematic structure. The attack starts from what seems a conventional mythological example (17–28):

1. See Williams (1968), pp. 221–24.
2. See ibid., pp. 122–23.
3. Nisbet and Hubbard (1970), pp. 202–04, regard the poem as a simple *dissuasio* to the girl throughout—'the only person of whose anger we are aware'. Against this view, see further below.

irae Thyesten exitio gravi
stravere et altis urbibus ultimae
 stetere causae cur perirent
  funditus imprimeretque muris

hostile aratrum exercitus insolens.
compesce mentem: me quoque pectoris
 temptavit in dulci iuventa
  fervor et in celeris iambos

misit furentem: nunc ego mitibus
mutare quaero tristia, dum mihi
 fias recantatis amica
  opprobriis animumque reddas.

'Anger laid low Thyestes in terrible ruin, and it has been the ultimate cause for the total destruction of great cities and for the enemy, insolent in victory, to plough the land where the walls stood (21). Curb your temper: I too, in the sweet time of youth, was assailed by passionate anger and driven headlong into impetuous lampoons. Now, however, I am looking to replace wrath with gentleness—provided that you, since I have recanted my insults, become my girl and return your affection to me.'

The difficulty here resides in the opening myth, and the quandary of commentators is well summarized by the remarks of the most recent editors: 'There is some difficulty about Horace's version of the story. The anger referred to must be that of Thyestes; there would be no point in saying that Atreus' anger destroyed Thyestes. Yet it is Atreus who usually illustrates the evils of vengeful anger.... It is not clear how the difficulty should be resolved. Horace might have made a mistake either about identity (like ps-Acro ad loc) or about chronology; but this may not seem likely for a well-educated man who had seen these stories performed on the stage. Or perhaps Varius introduced a new form of the legend in which Thyestes' anger played a more significant part (suggested by Vollmer on Stat. *silv.* 5.1.57). Alternatively, one might look here for the construction by which one member of a pair may be put for both or even for the other member; it may be relevant that both brothers are mentioned by Philodemus (*ira* 14.10 ff.).'[4]

4. Ibid., pp. 211–12.

These are desperate remedies, from the idea that Horace might have got his mythology wrong to the suggestion that Atreus and Thyestes could be treated like the twins, Castor and Pollux. The difficulty starts from the wish to confine the anger in the poem either to the poet or to the girl. A series of considerations shows this to be wrong. First, the function of the transitional stanza is to assert that a capacity for anger is a basic element of every human being's constitution—a fact that is being displayed in the girl's conduct and that was, in the past, displayed in the poet's lampoons. The weight of the poem is thereby shifted from conciliation to attack. Secondly, this attack is underlined by the deliberate contrast (22–25, *me quoque* . . . and 25, *nunc ego* . . .) between the poet's past exhibition of anger and his present desire to curb it—on one condition: that the girl become his lover again. The apparent confession in lines 22–25, *me quoque* . . ., is no 'disarming rhetorical trick';[5] the poet certainly places his exhibition of anger in a rhetorically remote past, a youth from which he has now progressed to an alleged maturity, but the contrast remains only a wish dependent on a condition. Consequently the contrast serves to convey a threat: what happened in the past can happen again. Thirdly, the threat is supported by the clear ring-composition of the poem, which begins with *criminosis iambis* and ends with *recantatis opprobriis*. That ring-composition carries two messages, one to the reader, the other to the girl: the reader must infer that the cause of the rift between the poet and the girl was that the girl abandoned the poet for someone else, and that this act of desertion evoked the poet's jealousy and recrimination; for the girl, however, the ring-composition asserts the ever-present threat of further lampoons if she does not accede to the poet's demand.

The mention of Thyestes, then, must be deliberate. The anger of Thyestes was specifically thirst for revenge:[6] Atreus banished Thyestes from Mycenae after Thyestes seduced his wife. From exile, Thyestes arranged to have Atreus murdered by his own son; he, however, was killed by his father who failed to recognize him. Atreus then recalled Thyestes from exile and served him a dinner of his own children. The girl, injured by the poet, is shown to be similarly vengeful; and the fact that the poet mentions Thyestes rather than Atreus means that he is thereby reserving the supreme role of Atreus for himself. But he does

5. Ibid., p. 213.
6. Ibid., p. 211.

not say so; instead, he moves into a more obvious—and consequently obfuscating—example of anger bringing on its own destruction: the entry of Carthage, for instance, into the second Punic war, which ended with the fall of Carthage itself. In this way the poet's threat is obscured again and does not become clear before the last word of the poem. The myth of Thyestes anticipates and encapsulates that threat. The reader must realise the significance of not mentioning Atreus, but he will not be in a position to do that properly until he has read the whole poem. It is a poem, then, that constantly defeats expectation and reserves its surprise to the end. Some of this effect is achieved by using only part of a myth and requiring the reader to construct the relationship of the unspoken part of that myth to the thematic movement of the poem as a whole. This will be examined further in the next chapter.

2. *Horace* Odes *1.28*

This great ode is constructed by expanding two types of epigram quite frequently composed by Hellenistic poets:[7] the first is the type in which a dead man is addressed in his grave by a passer-by—except that the speaker here (as becomes clear more than half-way through the poem) cannot pass by (1–20); the second is the type in which a dead man speaks from his grave—except that here the dead man, as yet, has no grave (21–36). In the first section of the poem, Archytas, the great philosopher, scientist, mathematician, and Pythagorean of the fourth century B.C., is addressed in language that seems at first honorific (1–16):

> Te maris et terrae numeroque carentis harenae
>   mensorem cohibent, Archyta,
> pulveris exigui prope litus parva Matinum
>   munera, nec quicquam tibi prodest
> aerias temptasse domos animoque rotundum   5
>   percurrisse polum morituro.
> occidit et Pelopis genitor, conviva deorum,
>   Tithonusque remotus in auras,
> et Iovis arcanis Minos admissus, habentque
>   Tartara Panthoiden iterum Orco   10
> demissum, quamvis clipeo Troiana refixo
>   tempora testatus nihil ultra

7. On this aspect of the poem's construction, see Williams (1968), pp. 178–84.

nervos atque cutem morti concesserat atrae,
iudice te non sordidus auctor
naturae verique. sed omnis una manet nox　　　　15
et calcanda semel via leti.

'The tiny gift of a little dust on the Matine shore confines you, Archytas, measurer of sea and land and the unnumbered sand, and it is no help to you that you assailed the regions of the sky and traversed the round heavens with a mind destined to die (6). There perished even the father of Pelops, dinner-guest of the gods, and Tithonus who was wafted to the skies, and Minos who was privy to the secrets of Juppiter, and the regions of Tartarus hold the son of Panthus who was sent down to Orcus a second time (10), although, on the evidence of the shield which he lifted down and thereby proved his memory of the siege of Troy, he had conceded to black death nothing but sinews and flesh—he who is, in your judgment, no mean authority on nature and truth. But the same long night awaits all men (15), and the path of death that must be trodden once and once only.'

The address to Archytas may begin as honorific, but it soon becomes pitying, condescending, and, finally, downright satiric. The explanation for this change of tone does not become clear till lines 21–22, when the speaker reveals that he himself is dead and thus the equal of Archytas who is imprisoned in his tiny grave. Like Cornelia in the funeral elegy of Propertius (4.11), this dead man has become instantly acquainted with the facts of death. Also, like the ode just examined, the structure of this ode requires the reader to suspend judgment till he has read the whole poem. And the withholding of enlightenment is deliberately prolonged by certain devices. When a reader comes to the words (7) *occidit et* . . . ('There died even . . .'), followed by a catalogue of famous men, he instantly recognises the literary territory: he is entering on one of the most conventional topics of *consolationes*—the comforting of the bereaved by the assimilation of the dead person to a series of distinguished names showing that death comes to all and that consolation should be derived from that very fact. The trouble here is that Tantalus, Tithonus, Minos, and Euphorbus-Pythagoras are all conspicuous examples of men who did not die in the sense in which that verb is being used by the speaker.

Again here the latest commentators may serve to illustrate the difficulties of those who confront this text: 'Tantalus was on dining-out terms with Zeus and ate his ambrosia, which ought to have ensured immortality . . . . It is curious to find Tantalus in this list of privileged persons who died; as one of the great sinners he usually plays a more monitory role, and the positive horrors of his punishment are stressed. Tithonus—in this context even stranger than Tantalus; according to the legend he was given immortality, though not eternal youth . . . . Even the story that Tithonus was turned into a cicada does not help us here; *occidit et* must mean "also died". . . .'[8]

Thus the speaker's statements on Minos and Euphorbus-Pythagoras also are accepted as intended to be taken as literally true; but when lines 15–16 are reached this comment is made: 'Yet *semel* surprisingly contradicts 10 f. "Panthoiden iterum Orco / demissum". Horace there accepted that Pythagoras received special privileges; he did not bluntly deny the possibility of visiting Orcus twice, but rather said that even in this extreme case death catches up in the end. One might consider emending *semel* to *simul*, in the sense of "for all alike"; cf. Pind. I. 7.42 θνάσκομεν γὰρ ὁμῶς ἅπαντες, anon. *anth.P.*7.342.2 πάντας ὁμῶς θνη-τοὺς εἰς Ἀίδης δέχεται. Then one would understand not *manet* but *est*, which on grounds of Latinity might be preferable. Yet it must be ad-mitted that *simul* would most naturally be taken as "simultaneously", which is absurd.'[9]

So desperate a remedy must recommend that what the speaker (not 'Horace') says about Pythagoras should be reconsidered. But the difficulties over Minos and Tithonus are only evaded by remedies almost as desperate. For on Minos the comment is made: 'Editors do not observe that Minos belongs to the *communis locus*; cf. Peek *GV* 709.7f. ἀλλ᾽ οὐκ εὐσεβίη τις ἀλεύεται ἄσστροφα Μοιρῶν / δόγματα· καὶ Μείνως ἤλυθεν εἰς Ἀίδην, 1249.19 (from Itanos in Crete) θνήσκει μὲν γὰρ ἄναξ Μίνως [ὃς ἐδέσποσ]ε Κρήτης'.[10] And on Tithonus: 'The crucial piece of evidence does not seem to have been deployed; see ps.-Dion. Hal. *rhet.* 6.5, p. 282.6 ff. (hints for funeral speeches) εἰ μὲν νέος ὢν τοῦτο πάθοι ὅτι θεοφιλής· τοὺς γὰρ τοιούτους φιλοῦσιν οἱ θεοί. καὶ ὅτι καὶ τῶν παλαιῶν πολλοὺς ἀνήρπασαν, οἷον τὸν Γανυμήδην, τὸν Τιθωνόν, τὸν Ἀχιλλέα . . . This rationalisation of the story protects Horace's text but not his logic. *remotus in auras* refers to a special privilege of Tithonus (cf. *conviva deorum* and *Iovis arcanis* . . .

8. Nisbet and Hubbard (1970), p. 326.
9. Ibid., pp. 329–30.
10. Ibid., p. 327.

admissus); the phrase implies a belief in Tithonus' immortality. Horace seems to have conflated an archaic legend ("Tithonus was immortal") with a topic of Hellenistic consolations ("Tithonus died young").'[11]

But none of this can be right: two isolated inscriptions can no more make it reasonable to regard Minos as an example of mortality than the anonymous rhetorician can persuade us that Horace made a silly blunder over Tithonus. This approach not only tends to view Horace's text as a mere patchwork of second-hand 'sources', but it also attributes what is said here to Q. Horatius Flaccus instead of to the ghost of a sailor drowned at sea and washed ashore. The strategy of the poem must involve the addressees and explain their choice. In the second half of the poem the sailor's ghost addresses a sailor who is in a passing ship; this enables the speaker to threaten his addressee with the same fate that has overtaken him. The addressee of the first half of the poem is an equally dramatic choice. By line 22 the reader knows that the speaker has the best of reasons for speaking authoritatively about death: he is dead. And his message has no shred of comfort. The apparent 'consolation' is no consolation at all; he has dogmatically asserted the mortality of those who were most commonly thought immortal. Each phrase that represents the commonly accepted view— (7) *conviva deorum*, (8) *remotus in auras*, (9) *Iovis arcanis . . . admissus*, (10–11) *iterum Orco / demissum*—should be read in mental inverted commas: the tone is bitterly ironical. Archytas was chosen as the addressee because he was the most perfect target for such irony: the speaker's news would fall like lead upon his ears, and the culminating irony of the 'death' of Pythagoras is devastatingly timed.

Here again the poet makes his speaker say one thing but requires his reader to understand something else. There are signals: outstandingly (6) *morituro* sounds a disturbing note addressed to a Pythagorean. But the familiar territory of the *consolatio* which then appears, lulls the reader into an acquiescence from which he is rudely shaken only by lines 15–16. Again, then, understanding is postponed and the reader must suspend judgment while he reads on. What he is finally required to understand is the significance in this particular context of the novel statements about well-known mythical characters: they are substituted for a general statement that, whatever revered experts may say to the contrary, death is final and complete for all men; this device enables

11. Ibid., pp. 326–27.

the poet to postpone a pithy form of that statement to a climactic moment (15–16).[12]

3. *Horace* Odes *1.2*

The problem in this political ode that needs examination concerns the poet's use of the myth of Ilia and the overflowing Tiber (13–24):

> vidimus flavum Tiberim retortis
> litore Etrusco violenter undis
> ire deiectum monumenta regis
>   templaque Vestae,   15
>
> Iliae dum se nimium querenti
> iactat ultorem, vagus et sinistra
> labitur ripa Iove non probante u-
>   xorius amnis.   20
>
> audiet civis acuisse ferrum
> quo graves Persae melius perirent,
> audiet pugnas vitio parentum
>   rara iuventus.

'We have seen the yellow Tiber, its waves violently flung back from the Etruscan bank, proceed to throw down the monuments of the king [Numa] and the temple of Vesta (16), as he boasts himself an avenger to his excessively nagging wife Ilia, and leaves his course to flow over the left bank, to the disapproval of Juppiter, a river infatuated with his wife (20). The next generation shall hear how citizens sharpened swords that ought to have wreaked destruction on the dangerous Parthians; they shall hear of battles, a generation thinned by the vices of their parents.'

The problem is posed and answered by the latest commentators thus:[13] 'What is Ilia complaining about so excessively? The answer escapes most commentators; yet at the most literal level it can only be "because she was thrown into the river". She was drowned because she broke her Vestal vows; so she might reasonably encourage the river to flood the temple of Vesta'. But this is to give an answer in terms

---

12. For further interpretation of this poem, see chapter 2.
13. Nisbet and Hubbard (1970), p. 26.

of the most literal mythology. Even so, it can be refuted from its own
context, for the poet has explicitly portrayed Ilia as happily married
to a husband whose one wish is to please his wife, regardless of consequences and even contrary to the will of Juppiter. But it also produces
a very trivial content for the great contrast which dominates the whole
context. The poet's own generation have been eyewitnesses (13, *vidimus*)
of destruction; the next generation will only hear (21–23, *audiet . . .
audiet . . .*) at second hand the terrors of a civil war that has thinned
their numbers. Here a further feature of the poet's shaping of the myth
is relevant. This poem of Horace is the first evidence for Ilia's marriage
to the Tiber. In previous accounts she was married to the Anio. That
river is a tributary which enters the Tiber from the south-west a few
miles north of Rome. There is no reason to doubt that Horace invented
this form of the legend for his own purposes here, though it does not
affect the argument if, in fact, he chose a form of the legend which
already existed in sources that have been lost. His purpose can only
have been to connect the flooding of the Tiber (a frequent occurrence
in Rome before this time) with destruction of the city, in such a way
as to interpret the flood as an act of vengeance (18, *ultorem*). The Anio
clearly would not have suited that purpose. Further, the parallelism
between (13) *vidimus* and (21) *audiet* shows that the content must also
be related: that is, the myth makes an unexpressed statement about
the civil wars. Pomponius Porphyrion already in the early third century
supplied the explanation: Ilia was angry over the murder of Julius
Caesar in 44 B.C., either because he was a relative of hers since they were
both descended from Aeneas, or because he was *pontifex maximus* and
she a Vestal (disgraced, it is true, but later vindicated both by recognition of the divine cause of her pregnancy and by the founding of
Rome by her son)—or both reasons may be relevant. This explanation
supplies the needed connexion with civil war: the murder of Julius
Caesar started a new phase in civil war which only ended at the battle
of Actium in 31 B.C.; or, to put it slightly differently, the peace from
civil war which Julius Caesar achieved in 45 B.C. was destroyed by his
murder a year later.

The explanation has been rejected for several reasons. First, because
the description of Ilia's nagging as excessive 'would be intolerably
offensive to Caesar's avenger and heir'.[14] But this will not stand. Ilia's
nagging is excessive because it goads the Tiber into taking on the part

14. Ibid., p. 27.

of avenger when that task had been properly executed by Octavian at the battle of Philippi in 42 B.C. and completed at Actium in 31 B.C. (after which the last two assassins were put to death). The second half of the poem, in fact, shows Octavian designated not only as avenger of Julius Caesar but also as saviour of Rome. Secondly, 'it is hard to see why Ilia should wish the destruction of the temple with which her priest was associated'.[15] But she did not. The river was boastful and uxorious; it went too far (even threatening Vesta) and incurred the disapproval of Juppiter. Here the opening of the poem is relevant in implying that Romans are now obedient to the commands of Juppiter, conveyed by storm, lightning, and flood. Once again, the river was not the designated avenger.

In fact, the river episode sets up a context of *ultio* which is only satisfied in the second half of the poem; (13) *vidimus* puts this aspect of the situation in the past, while (21) *audiet* modifies it into the form that is now relevant to the poet.

This is another of those odes that are composed of an uneven number of stanzas, and in which two blocks of sense are connected by a central transitional stanza.[16] In that stanza (25–28), the poet asks what god the people should call upon to prop the falling empire and what prayer the holy virgins should use on Vesta, who does not listen to their hymns. The questions are finally modulated into the form (29–30): 'To whom will Juppiter assign the task of expiating our crime?' If we ask why Vesta has not been listening, the answer must be 'because Julius Caesar was murdered by Romans'—an answer which has been provided by the unexpressed meaning of the myth of Ilia. But the poem has a deep and immediate seriousness. The theme of Julius Caesar's murder is satisfied when the poet finally identifies a figure as the saviour (it turns out to be Augustus in the last word of the poem), and this figure (43–44) 'suffers himself to be designated the avenger of Caesar'. But the poem goes on to end with a two-stanza prayer (45–52):

> serus in caelum redeas diuque
> laetus intersis populo Quirini,
> neve te nostris vitiis iniquum
>   ocior aura

15. Ibid.
16. See note 2 above.

> tollat; hic magnos potius triumphos,
> hic ames dici pater atque princeps,
> neu sinas Medos equitare inultos
>   te duce, Caesar.

'May your return to heaven be delayed and may you be pleased to remain among the people of Rome and may no breeze prematurely snatch you, who are hard upon our vices, to the skies; here, rather, enjoy great triumphs; here be pleased to be called Father and Leader; and do not permit the Parthians to ride unpunished, while you are our commander, Caesar.'

Here the reference to Romulus and his mysterious ascent to heaven marks the addressee as a second founder of Rome; the vices are primarily those of civil war, but the words seem to combine a reference to the attempted moral legislation of 28 B.C.; the triumphs refer to the great triple triumph of 29 B.C.; and the reference to titles, like the reference to Romulus, suggests the conferring of the title of Augustus in 27 B.C. The last words of the ode are particularly significant: the vengeance which so far has been vengeance for the murder of Julius Caesar is here converted into vengeance to be exacted on Rome's great traditional external enemies, the Parthians.

The ode, then, starts from literary reminiscence of prodigies which Virgil connected with the murder of Julius Caesar. But the movement of ideas in the poem is designed to connect the murder of Julius Caesar with the continuation of civil war in 44–31 B.C., in such a way that the murder is conceived as replaced and carried on by the new outbreak of civil war. But in fact the murder has been avenged and the civil wars have been ended by the same man. Yet it was just at this stage, twenty-three years earlier, that Caesar's murder brought renewal of civil war. Hence the poem ends with the prayer for Augustus' continued rule in Rome, and for his continuance of the measures he has initiated. The poem seems also to be asserting that vengeance must no longer be exacted on Romans for crimes committed in civil war; the time for that is past.[17] This was certainly part of Augustus' ideology, as can be seen not only in the way in which Republican stalwarts were drawn into magistracies in the 20s, but also in the extraordinary postponement of the building of the temple of Mars Ultor, vowed by Octavian on the field of Philippi in 42 B.C. That temple was not dedicated until 2 B.C.,

---

17. On this, see especially Steele Commager (1959), pp. 42–54.

and when it was dedicated the theme of vengeance was somehow confused or conflated with that of vengeance exacted on the Parthians.[18] Augustus must deliberately have postponed the building of that provocative temple, omitting it from his programme of 28 B.C. in order to play down the theme of vengeance exacted on Republicans at Philippi and Actium and to permit old hatreds to fade in an atmosphere of reconciliation.

The poem ends with another genuine piece of Augustan ideology, neatly knitted into its fabric: the conversion of the vengeance to be exacted on the Republican assassins of Julius Caesar into a national crusade against the Parthians.[19] The political situation of the ode is precisely that of 27 B.C., and the Parthian crusade functions as an expiation for civil war.

This interpretation of the ode depends on recognizing that the reader must infer the nature of Ilia's complaint (17) and, indeed, work out the significance of the myth of Ilia and Tiber, with its puzzling introduction of the theme of vengeance (18, *ultorem*). But, once again, the reader is not really in a position to do that until he has read at least the next stanza; and, in fact, the particular significance of the murder of Julius Caesar does not become fully clear before the last word of the poem. The ode is unified, from beginning to end, by the theme of vengeance. This too is a poem which gains with each re-reading.

4. *Horace* Odes *1.12*

This great celebratory ode starts from a Pindaric motto and an elaborate Pindaric opening of three stanzas on the power of poetry.[20] There follow five stanzas (13–32) celebrating Greek gods and heroes in a more or less Greek spirit. Then four stanzas (33–48) survey Roman history, and the poem ends with a prayer of three stanzas (49–60) to Juppiter in an explicitly Roman spirit (thus creating an internal ring-composition with the Greek praise of Zeus in 13 ff.).

The final prayer concerns the power of Augustus: may he continue to reign, second only to Juppiter, being to the earth what Juppiter is to the heavens. His military achievements are pictured in terms of

18. See Weinstock (1971), pp. 128–32.
19. On this motif of expiation, see below pp. 118 ff. and 160 ff.
20. On the structure of this ode, see Williams (1974).

the world-conqueror, Alexander the Great. The poem ends by sliding away into a *diminuendo* that is general and remote from the excessively factual and contemporary.[21]

Such a final prayer is often, as in *Odes* 1.2, preceded by a climax; so here (33–48):

> Romulum post hos prius an quietum
> Pompili regnum memorem an superbos
> Tarquini fascis, dubito, an Catonis   35
>   nobile letum.
>
> Regulum et Scauros animaeque magnae
> prodigum Paulum superante Poeno
> gratus insigni referam Camena
>   Fabriciumque.   40
>
> hunc et incomptis Curium capillis
> utilem bello tulit et Camillum
> saeva paupertas et avitus apto
>   cum lare fundus.
>
> crescit occulto velut arbor aevo   45
> fama Marcellis: micat inter omnis
> Iulium sidus velut inter ignis
>   luna minores.

'After these I am hesitant whether I should recall first Romulus or the quiet rule of Numa Pompilius or the arrogant *fasces* of the Tarquin or the famous death of Cato (36). Gratefully, in poetry that promises fame, I shall remember Regulus, and the Scauri, and Paullus, spendthrift of his great life as the Carthaginian overcame, and Fabricius (40). This last, together with Curius of the unshorn hair and Camillus were bred perfect for war by harsh frugality and an ancestral farm with a homestead to suit (44). The glory of the Marcelli grows like a tree in the hidden lapse of time: the Julian sun shines amid all others like the moon among lesser stars.'

Here the odd mention of Cato, out of place by four centuries or more, has puzzled commentators. It inspired Housman to one of his worst conjectural emendations: *an catenis* / *(nobile!) laetum* / *Regulum* ('or Regulus who rejoiced—o noble thing!—in his chains'). Only

---

21. On this technique, see below pp. 182 ff.

slightly better was Hamacher's *an catenis / nobilitatum / Regulum*. Even the latest commentators toy with conjectures, in a clear reluctance to accept the text,[22] and the inexplicability of Cato's appearance seems to have been a factor in their negative judgment on the poem.[23]

But these four stanzas are not a survey of Roman history, as they have usually been taken to be. They express a thesis. The climax is reached in a stanza which celebrates the marriage of Marcellus and Julia in 25 B.C. The poet, however, is not interested in the marriage as such. The following prayer to Juppiter for the continued reign of Augustus shows that the marriage is treated as the climax of Roman history because it represented Augustus' attempt to provide for his own succession[24]—a fact the reader is left to infer from the evasive juxtaposition of the marriage with the celebration of the power of Augustus. The same evasiveness, together with the same implication of supreme power, can be seen also in Virgil's lament over the dead Marcellus (*Aeneid* 6.868–86), and there too the young man appears as the climax to Anchises' vision of Roman history. Both poets were facing the same problem at about the same time.

Two other elements in the poet's historical thesis are clear. First, a view of Roman history as a series of hard-won victories over external enemies. Secondly, an emphasis on old-fashioned morality and especially on the idea that the true Roman character was moulded by a frugal life of farming. Both of these ideas correspond with basic features of Augustus' own ideology. His triple triumph of 29 B.C., deliberately delayed so that the emphasis would not be on Actium as a battle in the civil war but on the conquest of external enemies, was a living symbol of the thesis expressed, for instance, in the *res gestae*,[25] that the *pax Romana* depended on the forcible subjection of the world beyond Italy. Augustus' emphasis on morality and character, his idealisation of the past and the *mos maiorum*, the moral legislation of 28 B.C., 18 B.C., and A.D. 9, the rebuilding of the temples, and edu-

22. Nisbet and Hubbard (1970), pp. 156–57.

23. 'Yet though Horace shows some ingenuity in linking diverse elements, he does not succeed in fusing them; they exist in unhappy juxtaposition, each occupying its own section of the poem. . . . But perhaps one's main quarrel with the poem is its essential implausibility. We cannot apply the naive assurance of this ode to our own world nor to the complex and familiar facts of Augustan politics' (pp. 145–46).

24. On this aspect of the poem, see Williams (1974), pp. 150–54.

25. Chapter 13; see the commentary of Brunt and Moore (1967), pp. 53 ff.

cational reform are all symbolized in the poet's swift pictures of the simple lives of the heroes from earlier Roman history. Only one conspicuous element in Augustan ideology seems to be missing from the poet's historical thesis: the 'restoration of the Republic', as it is loosely called in modern times.

Augustus gave his own account of this in his *res gestae* (34.1):

in consulatu sexto et septimo, postquam bella civilia exstinxeram, per consensum universorum potitus rerum omnium, rem publicam ex mea potestate in senatus populique Romani arbitrium transtuli.

'In my sixth and seventh consulships [28 and 27 B.C.] , after I had quelled the civil wars, and when, by the consent of all the people, I had supreme control of all the affairs ⟨of state⟩, I transferred the state from my own control to the hands of the senate and people of Rome.'

What Augustus expresses here somewhat evasively is filled out by the account of Cassius Dio (53.1–2). In 28 B.C. Augustus resumed the sharing of joint power with his fellow consul; at the end of that year he took the customary oath that he had done nothing contrary to the laws; and he abolished the unjust and illegal regulations of the triumvirate. It is not necessary here to go into all the detailed niceties of constitutional theory and practice that are involved in these statements. What is clear is that Augustus regularised what had been the extraordinary, if not downright illegal, situation that had existed throughout the triumviral period from 42 to 28 B.C. by returning to strict constitutional practice—or the careful appearance of it. He prepared for this in his consulship of 28 B.C., the first complete year that he was back in Rome, and then made a formal restoration of all state business to the senate and people of Rome in 27 B.C. The sense of this is that Augustus was now prepared to regard himself as having ruled in the period 42–28 B.C., if not illegally, then by a right that lay outside the *mos maiorum*; and it was precisely the *mos maiorum* that he was professing to restore (and it was his obedience to that principle that dictated his refusal of the *cura morum* in 19, 18, and 11 B.C.).[26]

It is legitimate to doubt whether Augustus or contemporaries expressed this process by the phrase *rem publicam restituit* or *res publica resti-*

26. *res gestae* 6.1.

tuta; at least they would have said *rem publicam senatui populoque Romano restituit.*[27] But historians are certainly wrong to doubt that the claim to have done this was a part of Augustan ideology. It is sometimes denied on the ground that, if the claim had been made, writers would not have treated Augustus as the effective ruler. The preface to Vitruvius' *de architectura* is used as evidence for this assertion: '. . . its unabashed acceptance of the personal dominance of Augustus is unmistakeable. Moreover, and this is the essential point, its obsequious flatteries could certainly be disregarded and considered as of no historical significance *if* they had been written under any conditions *except* those supposed by modern scholars, namely a recently-proclaimed "restoration of the Republic". Had such a thing been proclaimed, Vitruvius' words would have been grossly undiplomatic—and would not have been written. The same considerations apply, with rather less force, to a number of passages in Horace and Ovid. . . .'[28] The writer then goes on to quote, among other passages, precisely the lines on the power of Augustus (49–58) from the prayer to Juppiter in the present ode. But the point of view is mistaken, as this very ode demonstrates— though the same writer claims that the restoration of the Republic appears in no contemporary poet.[29] It was an entirely Roman, and certainly Augustan, view of Roman history to regard it as the history of a society bound by the *mos maiorum*, in which, however, each age was dominated by a great leader or series of leaders who gave shape and character to their age by their way of confronting its problems.[30] This was the ideology behind Augustus' restoration of the statues of great Romans in the Forum, and it was expressed in the edict: 'His purpose in doing this was that the people could demand from him as long as he lived, and from the leading men of following ages, a confor- mity to their [i.e. the great Romans of the past] exemplar' (Suetonius *Aug.* 31.5). To be great, to give the people leadership, was not incon- sistent with constitutional behaviour. That is also the message of the *res gestae*. And it is outstandingly the message of this ode. The list of great Romans in the historical survey expresses the same view (33– 48), and it is further expressed precisely with regard to Augustus in

27. See the careful examination of the phrase by Judge (1974), pp. 280–90.
28. Millar (1973), p. 66.
29. Ibid., p. 63.
30. See especially Judge (1974), pp. 303–04.

the prayer to Juppiter. To return power to those to whom it belonged was to honour the *mos maiorum* and was not inconsistent with allowing those same people to honour Augustus as the supremely gifted leader and even to thrust that power which was in their giving back on him. To profess love of the constitution and yet accept the burden of one's historical destiny (within that constitution, of course) is a combination of motives familiar in history.

Horace expresses the love of the *mos maiorum* and of the constitution precisely in the surprising mention of Cato. Where the reader expects to find the name of L. Junius Brutus, who expelled the tyrants and founded the Republic, there occurs the name of the champion of the Republic, the man who committed a noble suicide rather than submit to the arbitrary clemency of Julius Caesar. A complex process of thought is demanded of the reader; for, when he reaches the name of Cato, he knows that he should be reading L. Junius Brutus, but that very fact makes him realise that, when he read the name of Tarquin immediately before, he should have understood also the name of Julius Caesar. That is, the name of Tarquin creates the field of unconstitutional rule, to which that of Julius Caesar also belonged; while the name of Cato in this context creates the field of opposition to unconstitutional rule to which L. Junius Brutus also belongs. We could go further and claim that the understanding is also enjoined that the poet, in avoiding the name of Brutus and choosing that of Cato, was explicitly dissociating himself from the violent act of M. Junius Brutus in assassinating Julius Caesar which simply led to a further period of civil war (see the previous ode).

The laudation of the *mos maiorum* and of constitutional rule coheres in this poem with laudation of Augustus as a supreme ruler, second only to Juppiter, and with the unconstitutional celebration of Marcellus as, in some sense, Augustus' successor. In the same way, readiness to blame Julius Caesar coheres, in the vision of Anchises in *Aeneid* 6 (834–35), with laudation of Augustus as supreme ruler or, rather, Leader (791 ff.), and with a discreetly worded laudation of Marcellus as his successor (868 ff.). The allusion to the 'restoration of the Republic' in *Odes* 1.12 is unmistakeable, and its technique provides another example of Horace's saying one thing and requiring the reader to understand another; and, again, it is an understanding that can only come from reading the whole poem. It is a poem of great importance for understanding contemporary attitudes toward Augustus, but it is also of great technical interest for the way in which the poet alludes to the 'restoration of the Republic', without actually mentioning it. It is time now to consider how the various techniques in these poems of saying one thing and meaning another may be classified, and what is the relationship between what is said and what is not said.

CHAPTER II

THEORETICAL CONSIDERATIONS

If the solutions to the series of problems in Horace's *Odes* offered in the last chapter are correct, then some account should be capable of being given of the poet's procedure in each case, based on ancient rhetorical analysis. The trouble here is that, although ancient rhetorical theory recognised the distinction between figures of thought and figures of speech, theorists regarded figures of thought as being concerned simply with configurations of thought, such as aposiopesis or rhetorical question, by which the content was not altered, only the presentation. Consequently they treated under figures of speech phenomena such as metaphor and metonymy, which could involve important and interesting alterations of the content of the ideas.[1] Further, since these were considered as phenomena of vocabulary, and since the theorists' major interest was in definition, not only were these figures treated as mere deviations from what was regarded as a linguistic norm, but, as far as possible, analysis was confined to single words: that is, the ideal examples in all cases were those in which an abnormal word had been selected in place of a normal word, or a word was used in an abnormal way. There is another factor to be taken into account: interest was concentrated on prose, and poetry was regarded simply as prose with the addition of metres;[2] this meant that, for the purpose of interpretation, poets were assimilated to the condition of orators, and this explains the disappointingly simplistic interpretations which are usually to be found in the surviving ancient commentaries.

Theoretically, however, it was open to poets to use the tropes and

---

1. See Longinus 8.1 and the commentary by Russell (1964).
2. See Russell (1967), pp. 130 ff.

figures, identified by the rhetorical theorists, in ways that could not be analysed in terms of some simple deviation from a conceptual linguistic norm, but which involved parallel manipulation of language and ideas. Essentially, to put it crudely, this involved the poet's saying one thing and the reader's being required to understand something else; this meant that the reader's imagination had to work in co-operation with the poet, and it also normally meant that a poem's meaning would not be clear on a first reading. The situation was complicated by the fact that Ovid, and all poets after him, invented or returned to a method of composition whose aim was to render the impact of the composition as immediate and as complete as possible on an audience rather than a reader. Devices which postponed or complicated understanding had to be abandoned in favour of devices which generated immediate, generally emotional, response.[3] The consequence seems to have been that poetry of the late Republic and early Augustan Age was imperfectly understood, or even misunderstood, from a time not long after its composition.

1. *The Four Problems in Horace's* Odes

The solutions to the four problems presented in the last chapter will now be re-examined to see whether an analysis in terms of ancient rhetorical theory can be given. In *Odes* 1.16, the anger of Thyestes is mentioned, but the whole context (lines 17–28) entails a reference of the role of Atreus to the poet in such a way that the mention of Thyestes becomes a threat. This is more than a metonymic substitution of Thyestes for Atreus, since the reader must supply the part of Atreus without losing sight of that of Thyestes. The figure involved is rather that of synecdoche: a part of the myth is told and the reader must supply the rest. This does not, however, complete the analysis, and a further process is involved. For, though the relationship of Atreus to Thyestes is metonymically associative, the further relationship of Atreus/Thyestes to the poet and the girl is analogical; and so the passage as a whole presents a type of metonymy (synecdoche) set within a figure related rather to that of metaphor or simile.

In *Odes* 1.2, within the myth of Ilia and the Tiber, the complaint

---

3. On this problem, see the Introduction and Williams (1978), especially chapter 5, 'Thought and Expression'.

of Ilia causes the river to flood. The reader must infer the nature of that complaint from the context. This, again, is a type of synecdoche in which the myth is partly told, but another part of the myth must be inferred by the reader both from the manner of telling (especially the emphasis on *ultio*) and from the way in which the myth is related to its context. Here the myth is a complex symbol for a particular phase of the civil wars, and the relation of the myth to its context is metonymic.

In *Odes* 1.28 the reader must infer from a later part of the poem that the assertions of death in the cases of Tantalus, Tithonus, Minos, and Pythagoras have a meaning quite different from what the overt form of the *consolatio* suggests. There is *ironia* here in that the speaker says one thing and mean another, and that fact could be signalled by a change of tone. But it is also a type of synecdoche in that only a part of a familiar story is presented—but with unexpected, even contradictory, features—and the reader has to construct a new whole within a context that is not complete until much more of the poem has been read. The relationship of the myths to the major context purports to be paradigmatic, and so to function as a form of metaphor within the context. This poem, however, needs further analysis,[4] but that will suffice for the moment.

In *Odes* 1.12 the suicide of Cato seems to function as a simple metonymy for Brutus' expulsion of the Tarquins and his foundation of the Republic. But further analysis shows that recognition of the metonymy of Cato for Brutus entails re-examination of the mention of Tarquin and the further recognition, not complete until the metonymy of Brutus is appreciated, that Tarquin is metonymically related to Julius Caesar. This double metonymy in which, out of a complex relationship of four terms A/B and C/D, only A and D are mentioned and in which the relationship is only recognised after D has been understood, is better classified as a synecdoche in view both of the amount of reconstruction required of the reader and the way in which all four terms must be held simultaneously in mind. Again here the relationship of the synecdoche to the poem as a whole is that of an unspoken paradigm: the action of Cato is an analogy to that of Augustus.

4. See sections 2 and 3 of this chapter.

2. *Metaphoric and Metonymic Modes*

Ancient rhetorical theorists recognised the basic distinction between metaphor and metonymy. Cicero (*orator* 92–94) defined metaphor as a substitution by similarity, and metonymy (*immutatio*) as a substitution derived from association (*ex re aliqua consequenti*). The author of the treatise *ad Herennium* (4.43) put the case of metonymy (*denominatio*) more directly as deriving 'from things which are related and contiguous, and enabling something to be understood which is not mentioned by its own name'. This basic distinction between metaphor as a substitution by similarity, and metonymy as a substitution by contiguity is also the basis of modern analysis—though, instead of the contrast between similarity and contiguity, some may substitute one between analogy and association or one between what is paradigmatic and what is syntagmatic.

Quintilian treats synecdoche before metonymy;[5] and, though systematically synecdoche is to be seen as a form of metonymy, yet synecdoche is the figure that offers a poet greater possibilities because of the disproportion it permits between the thing substituted and that for which it is substituted. It is precisely because the term 'synecdoche' describes a potentially complex relationship between a text and the reader's understanding that it is the only trope which represents in its name the reader's point of view, not the author's. The basic idea is that of understanding something in connexion with something else, and the 'something else' can only be what is understood by the reader by inference from the context. The relationship is more simple and direct in metonymy. There is another very important feature which Quintilian only mentions in relation to synecdoche: he defines it as 'capable of giving variety to style by making us understand many things from one, the whole from the part, the genus from the species, what follows from what precedes, or all of these *vice versa*; it is more freely employed by poets than by orators' (8.6.19). For this last reason Quintilian allows himself very little time on synecdoche (as distinct from metaphor), but the potentiality of the figure for poets is clear.

Particularly interesting is the category which he passes over so quickly and of which (unlike the others) he gives no examples: the

5. Synecdoche in 8.6.19–22 and metonymy in 8.6.23–27.

understanding of what follows from what precedes and of what precedes from what follows (*e praecedentibus sequentia, e sequentibus praecedentia*). One of the reasons why the speaker's apparent *consolatio* in *Odes* 1.28 should be understood not just as an *ironia* but also as synecdoche is precisely that it is substituted for something which the poet will express directly later. For when he says (15–16) 'but one long night awaits every man and a path to death that must be trodden once and once only', he is, as it were, spelling out the implied message of the *consolatio*; he could have said this immediately and have had done with the subject—to the great loss of the poem, for reasons that will be discussed below. What happens in *Odes* 1.2 and 1.16 is not so clear-cut, since in neither can something said later be pointed to as contained in the preceding synecdoche, but both share the feature with *Odes* 1.28 of not revealing the poet's meaning until the rest of the poem (or at least a part of what remains) has been read. That is, in each case the synecdoche has two aspects: the first is that something is substituted for something else, and the second, that understanding of the relationship between what is said and what is not said can only be inferred by the reader from what follows. The problematic passage of *Odes* 1.12 also contains this feature within its own compass in one respect; for there the synecdoche must be understood by the reader within the words (34–36) *an superbos | Tarquini fascis, dubito, an Catonis | nobile letum*. If, by the time he has come to *letum*, the reader has not grasped the synecdoche, there is nothing further in the poem that will of itself enlighten him, though it is possible that a second or third reading may well do so. What the reader of *Odes* 1.12 will only discover by reading on is the paradigmatic relationship of what is conveyed by the synecdoche to the theme of this whole section of the poem: that is, that it represents one of the ideals of Augustus in as much as a similarity is implicitly asserted between Augustus and Cato in the relevant respect of love for the constitutional *mos maiorum*.

The poetical force of synecdoche can be seen in Quintilian's quoting (8.6.22) of Virgil *Eclogues* 2.66, *aspice aratra iugo referunt suspensa iuvenci* ('see, the oxen are bringing home the ploughshares suspended from their yokes'). Here, as he says, the reader is required to infer the approach of night. He does not quote the next line—*et sol crescentis decedens duplicat umbras* ('and the declining sun is doubling the lengthening shadows')—and so does not consider the further function of the figure. For it is a synecdoche not just for the approach of night, but also for the peaceful, relaxing aspect of night, and this the poet uses, in pathetic fallacy, to contrast with the burning turmoil of the unhappy lover. So, as with a number of the examples from Horace, the figure functions as a synecdoche in respect to itself, but paradigmatically in respect to the wider context. A similar synecdoche (*Aeneid* 2.268–69), which also functions as a pathetic fallacy, Quintilian treats as an example of periphrasis (8.6.59), since, instead of saying 'the first watch of the night', Virgil says, 'It was the time when the first stillness begins and creeps over mankind as the most desirable gift of the gods'. Both examples could also be classed as symbols (*signum*), and, in fact, on the former Quintilian is 'not sure whether this is suitable for an orator, except in argumentation when it is the symbol of something' (8.6.22). Quintilian does not quote it, but he might well have approved Cicero's image from his poem on his own consulship: *cedant arma togae* ('let arms yield to the toga'), where the poet certainly yields to the orator.

Quintilian goes on to treat metonymy as closely related to synecdoche (8.6.23–27); he regards it as a figure more suited to poets than to orators, in spite of the fact that he exemplifies it only by quite obvious substitutions of one word or name for another. Since his view of metonymy is so simple, it follows easily that he regards antonomasia as closely related to metonymy (8.6.29). More interesting is his treatment of allegory (8.6.44–59), but rather for the possibilities inherent in the figure than for anything he actually says. He distinguishes two types of allegory. The first he explains as an extended metaphor or a coherent series of metaphors. The example he gives of this is Horace's ode 1.14. He quotes just over two lines from its opening and comments: 'and the whole of that passage of Horace in which he speaks of a ship instead of the state, of waves and storms instead of civil war, and of a harbour instead of good-will and peace'. What does not appear from this critique is the ingenuity and originality with which Horace adapted the metaphorical type of allegory to his own novel situation. Alcaeus, whose use of the allegory of the Ship of State[6] was Horace's model, was a member of the ruling oligarchy, displaced by the tyrant Myrsilus. He and his friends naturally regarded the state as their

6. Fr. 6 L.–P.

property and properly within their control; so they are naturally pictured sailing on the ship and in a storm which is represented as happening at the same time as the poem is being written.

But Horace had nothing to do with the Roman state; that was in other hands. Further, his point of view had to be conditioned by two factors: first, he was writing, as in *Odes* 1.2, at a time when he could represent safety as well within Rome's grasp; but, secondly, he was himself distant and detached from the civil wars of 36–31 B.C., from which the state emerged through the battle of Actium. The reader is left, as often with Horace, to infer the setting from an ostensible dramatic monologue. Commentators claim to find difficulty in deciding what the ship is supposed to be doing;[7] but there can be no real doubt: the ship has been through damaging storms and is well within sight of the harbour, but a new storm (*novi fluctus*) threatens to sweep her out to sea again (and so into renewed peril). The poet has solved the problem of representing himself in relation to the state by stationing himself as an observer on shore, and his dramatic anxiety is well caught by lively and emotional language (*o navis . . . o quid agis?*), by the way he calls the ship's own attention to her damage, and by the advice which he offers. The whole adaptation is dominated by a lively feeling for the essence of personal lyric poetry.

In the final stanza, when the poet might be expected to strip off the disguise and reveal the allegory, he retreats instead into language of very personal emotion (17–20):

> nuper sollicitum quae mihi taedium,
> nunc desiderium curaque non levis,
>   interfusa nitentis
>   vites aequora Cycladas.

'You who were lately the cause of frustrating anxiety to me, who are now my heart's desire and the object of my deep care, keep far from the waters that boil among the shining Cyclades.'

This is the language of love:[8] *sollicitum . . . taedium* refers to the long years of civil war, but both are words that express the anxiety of the lover and the boredom and frustration of constant refusal;

---

7. For example, Anderson (1966).
8. For the technique of substituting related fields, see chapter 7.

desiderium and *cura* express the yearning and emotion of love. From the one line to the other there is a movement from erotic frustration to anticipated consummation. The idea of representing the citizen as a lover may have been suggested by a passage of Alcaeus where he seems to figure the ship of state itself by the further image of an ageing prostitute who is rejected in favour of a gay party with a younger woman.[9] The important fact, however, is that, when the poet purports to reveal his own point of view, he does it in language that is no less figurative than the allegory itself. Then he ends the poem by slipping back into the image of the allegory, but in a remote picture of treacherous waters that has no connexion with Rome and makes no pretence— indeed, firmly refuses—to make itself a working element in the allegory. Such a sliding away at a moment when reality threatens to get too close is a feature of political poems in *Odes* 1–3 (pp. 187 ff.). The reader nonetheless cannot doubt the poem's setting: it is the same as that of *Odes* 1.2, in the years after 31 B.C. and especially during the crisis of 28 B.C. that preceded the settlement of 27 B.C. But nothing of this is made explicit: the density of the poem itself compels the reader's understanding to infer not only its historical setting, but also— and before that—its dramatic setting together with the poet's own attitude—for both of the latter provide the evidence for the first. Here the figuring of the poet's emotions as those of a lover is particularly effective, because elusive, in a way that demands the reader's co-operation. The degree to which the reader's mind and imagination are given room to work distinguishes this use of the allegory from that of Alcaeus and is characteristic of Horace.

There seems to be no other complete allegory in Horace's *Odes*, but in 3.4 there is a partial allegory, in that, for the whole of the second half of the ode, the poet departs into the myth of the battle of the Giants against Juppiter. The poet never returns from the allegory; instead, as in 1.14, the poem ends on a *diminuendo*, with a brief picture of Pirithous, only remotely connected to the major myth, imprisoned in the underworld (pp. 182 ff.). The myth of the Giants' battle is clearly an allegory for opposition to Augustus and also refers to the period around 28 B.C. The reader, however, is left to infer the meaning of the myth from the confrontation of the second half of the ode with the first.

9. See Page (1955), pp. 189–96.

With this ode we have moved in the direction of Quintilian's second type of allegory. He says (8.6.46): 'On the other hand, there is allegory without metaphor in the *Bucolics*'; he then quotes Virgil *Eclogues* 9.7–10, and continues: 'In this passage, except for the proper name, the ideas are expressed by words used in their literal sense. But the shepherd Menalcas is not to be understood, but the poet Virgil.' Here Quintilian is certainly wrong in his interpretation—at least in the simplistic way in which he puts it. But the type of figure that he identifies here will be important later in this investigation (see chap. 7), and is worth defining here. It depends on the semantic equivalence of two distinct fields of ideas: the poet speaks of one field, but, by a sort of imaginative counterpoint, he can be understood also to be speaking of the other field. The relationship of the two fields, however, is never univocal; the proportionality[10] of their relationship must be sensed by the reader from clues provided by the poet. Furthermore, it is not true, as might appear at first sight, that the mode of their relationship approximates more to that of metaphor than of metonymy.

It can easily be seen that there are situations in which figures like ellipse, irony, periphrasis, and even personification can seem more closely related to metaphor or more closely related to metonymy; there are also situations in which a figure may work in one aspect as a form of metonymy, in another as a form of metaphor. In fact, Cicero remarked that Aristotle did not distinguish between metaphor and metonymy (as, for instance, in *Poetics* 1461[a] 16 ff.).[11] What is important here is not the uncertainty of definition, but the theoretical scope which the figures allowed to Roman poets (as distinct from orators and prose-writers). The major feature common to all the tropes is that they allowed the poet to say one thing (or a part of it) and to mean another, related to what he said by one or other of the two modes of similarity or contiguity, but sometimes by a mixture of both. To put it over-simply, metaphor and metonymy were two modes of inducing a connexion of

10. Here and elsewhere, I use the word 'proportionality' analogously to the way it is used by Aristotle in *Rhetoric*, chapter 21: it suggests the range of uncertainty in the relationship between two complex fields where there can be no simple translation from the one to the other, and where, in addition to the relationship that concerned Aristotle, the reader needs an index of the proportionality between the two fields as such, a sort of index of relative scale, to provide a bridge from the one to the other.

11. Cicero *orator* 94.

ideas in the mind of a co-operating reader: the one controlled ideas whose association depended on similarity, the other, ideas whose association depended on contiguity. In the case of the former type, distance—that is, the distance of the metaphoric from the main contextual field—was important, and the appropriate literary value was the imaginative stimulus of discovery and surprise. In the case of the latter, there was something of the force of a riddle, a sense of mystery and of depth, of things unsaid, of a gap in which the reader's mind could work. This latter type is more purely cerebral than the former and is appropriate only to sophisticated poetry intended for reading rather than for public performance (which is why Quintilian so insistently urged restraint by speakers in using all these tropes). But both belong essentially to categories of discursive thought: the reader's pleasure is cognitive. And even the simple distinction between the two types can be seen to break down in practice: for example, a myth used paradigmatically belongs to the defined field of metaphor, but the working out of the counterpoint between the myth and its context involves an intellectual activity that is closer to the understanding of a metonymy than the apprehension of a metaphor. That is, in complex figures such as allegory or extended *paradeigma* where the *paradeigma* has been substituted for the contextual ideas, although such figures certainly belong to the metaphoric mode and probably appear so from the writer's point of view, the reconstruction of the unspoken contextual ideas or of the field analogous to the allegory must seem to require an application of logic and systematic analysis that belongs more to the mode of metonymy and especially of synecdoche. It is as if at their extreme points the two modes curve back towards one another.

A further important point can now be added. If we include simile among these tropes, it will be seen that the use of such tropes can vary in their relationship to the contextual field between two extremes that extend from parallelism to substitution: that is, they can, on the one hand, stand beside and expand or illustrate contextual ideas; or, on the other hand, they can take their place (in which case the contextual idea has to be inferred and reconstructed). As an example of the latter (and more interesting) use, the problem in *Odes* 1.28 can be used again. There the opening address to Archytas amounts to saying: 'You were as great as anyone could be, yet a few grains of sand are enough for you now' (and that idea—together with the added implication 'and so for any man'—prepares the theme[12] of requesting symbolic burial in the second half of the poem). But instead of spelling out the explanation immediately ('for death is the absolute end of everything'), the speaker enters on what seems to be a traditional *consolatio* comprising a list of great men who have died. The reader is perhaps lulled into forgetting that this is addressed to someone for whom outstandingly death was not the end of everything—quite the opposite, it was the beginning of a new life. Yet, even to ordinary men the list is odd: it is a list of men notorious either for not dying or for their existence beyond death. But with the surprise appearance of Pythagoras, the reader (the ordinary man) becomes indistinguishable from Archytas, the special addressee; for Pythagoras has the same significance for both. Then the climax comes swiftly in the dogmatic assertion, 'death is the end of everything for everyone'. What happens here is that the mythical list (including Pythagoras) has been substituted for a bald statement: 'You were wrong about metempsychosis, and so was anyone who imagined life after death'. This assertion was prepared for in the honorific listing of Archytas' achievements, which appears at first to be merely another traditional theme of *consolationes* ('your grand achievements were no help against death'); but that, too, turns out to be an *ironia* when the reader realises that Archytas' researches were totally mistaken on what was to him the most important question. The speaker merely implies that failure in the way he expresses Archytas' high regard for Pythagoras (14–15); and the failure of Archytas does not become objectively authoritative for the reader till it is revealed that the speaker too is dead (21–22) and therefore knows all the facts of death.

The literary value of the mythic *ironia* and syncedoche in the strategy of the poem is that it postpones, it allows the drama to build up, it raises questions. The poet does not use the apparent *paradeigmata* to argue; rather, they provide an alternative language into which he can transfer to create an appropriate sense of depth and mystery, requiring the reader to suspend judgment and gradually to apprehend an unexpected movement of ideas by a process that is not strictly logical. The suspense of judgment is a particularly important feature of the technique, for the process is cognitive, but it is also *e sequentibus*

12. This technique will be examined and analysed in chapter 5, 'Thematic Anticipation'.

praecedentia: it involves understanding what comes first from what comes after.

3. *The Objective Correlative*

So far the function of the problematic passage in *Odes* 1.28 has only been considered in its relation to the immediate context. How does it function in the poem as a whole? Here, and in many similar passages in Roman poetry, the distinction made by T. S. Eliot in his famous essay of 1919 on *Hamlet* offers a useful tool of analysis. He observes there:

The only way of expressing emotion in the form of art is by finding an 'objective correlative'; in other words, a set of objects, a situation, a chain of events which shall be the formula of that *particular* emotion; such that when the external facts, which must terminate in sensory experience, are given, the emotion is immediately evoked. If you examine any of Shakespeare's more successful tragedies, you will find this exact equivalence; you will find that the state of mind of Lady Macbeth walking in her sleep has been communicated to you by a skilful accumulation of imagined sensory impressions; the words of Macbeth on hearing of his wife's death strike us as if, given the sequence of events, these words were automatically released by the last event in the series. The artistic 'inevitability' lies in this complete adequacy of the external to the emotion.... [Eliot (1951) p. 145]

One might feel qualms about the sweeping 'The only way of expressing emotion...', and Eliot was talking specifically of drama. The point he makes, however, corresponds to some extent with the distinction in narrative between 'telling' and 'showing':[13] there can be no omniscient narrator in drama. Nor can there be in lyric poetry. A narrative or expository movement of ideas creates its own momentum, but the 'showing' of emotion, especially in a tiny genre like lyric poetry, needs a dramatic situation as a framework, and the expression of emotion then flows from the interaction of character and situation.

How does this work in *Odes* 1.28? The emotion is generated by the confrontation of an unnamed dead man (who therefore knows the facts of death) with the grave of the world-famous Archytas: the dead man knows that Archytas was wrong in the one respect

---

13. On this see, for example, Wayne Booth (1961), pp. 3–20.

that most mattered to him (and to most men), yet, for all the dead man's now superior knowledge, the one thing he craves is the final act of symbolic burial—which Archytas has received. The 'objective correlative' of that emotion is the *consolatio*, listing great men who have died, together with the dramatic situation in which it is set. For the dead man's triumph over Archytas is hollow, and it dooms all men; the only alleviation lies in the traditional ritual in which men, even at the expense of immediate profit (35–36), express regard for those who have been imprisoned in the common human condition. The effectiveness of the apparent *consolatio* as an objective correlative depends on its capacity to keep postponing full understanding. This is particularly achieved by the choice of such phrases to express the concept of 'death' as suit the immediate context without pre-empting revelation of the surprising sense which the speaker attaches to that concept; that does not become clear before lines 15–16, and that statement does not become authoritative till the speaker is revealed to be dead, too, in lines 21–22. Thus (7) *occidit* can be given a traditional sense by the reader that is conceivably acceptable for Tantalus and Minos but not for the intervening Tithonus. Again, (9–10) *habentque Tartara* can be understood as a denial of the kind of life after death that Pythagoras claimed, expressed in terms that conform at least minimally to a conventional view. That is, at this point a reader need see this as no more than an assertion that Pythagoras is not back in the world of the living. But why is he not back? The answer comes with devastating force in lines 15–16, where a view of death as nothingness is enforced; and, so that (16) *via leti* may not be misunderstood as arousing the traditional picture of a descent to a conventional under-world, the speaker goes on (17–19) to define that phrase as the sum of a series of different times and ways to die. Then total denial of traditional views of death is expressed by taking the conventional concept of Proserpina's cutting off a lock from the head of the dying and converting it into a bitter irony by collocating the adjective *saeva* with the astonishing verb *fugit*.

That irony, however, is converted into pathos by a contradiction: the dead man still craves the traditional rite of symbolic burial. The moral imperative to burial is expressed by (23) *ne parce malignus*: to refuse the most superficial act of burial is evidence of a meanness of spirit that should involve its author in loss of what human beings normally regard as requisite for happiness—worldly goods. The dead man, however, puts that positively in wishing wealth for the man who will not be mean enough to deny him burial. But that is mere wishful thinking. He only knows for certain about death. About life he can only, on the one hand, express a wish, with a reliance on conventional gods that sounds hollow (28–29); or, on the other, threaten by appeal to mere superstition (30–34). He ends with a pathetic appeal to the superficial materialistic values of the living (35–36). But why bother about burial? The poem does not say: it only suggests that in some undefined way men owe it to one another, and that, morally, that duty takes precedence over the trivial values which the living normally hold dear.

The power of this poem can be gauged to some extent by realising that its intellectual background was widespread philosophical discussion, in the late Republic, on the question of the existence of a life after death and the general assumption that such a life was incomparably superior to the life of this world of flux and becoming. It is to be seen in much of Cicero's writing, especially the *Tusculans*, as well as in the sustained ferocity of Lucretius' attack on the concept. This ode of Horace simply and flatly contradicts all that speculation and asserts a system of values that is based on life in this world and on man's respect for fellow human beings. The poem is moving because it does not say these things explicitly: it uses *ironia* and synecdoche to lure the reader into apprehension.

This is the function of the 'objective correlative': to enable emotion to be 'shown' rather than 'told'. The problem of how to show emotion was at its most acute for Roman love-poets. For this reason, and because personal love-elegy (apart from some remote precedents in Greek lyric poetry of the seventh century B.C.) was a Roman invention, the origins of techniques which employ mythical and other material in ways that have only remote precedents in Greek poetry (again lyric poetry) are probably to be sought in the earliest Roman love-poets, notably Catullus. For how does one express the emotions of love? The brevity of epigram disposes of this as a problem, and so there is little or no connexion in this respect between the Hellenistic epigrammatists in their amatory epigrams and Roman elegiac love-poetry. But when the scale of composition was extended the problem became acute. When the lover has squealed or shrieked with emotion or described (like Sappho) his physiological symptoms, how can he then proceed? This dilemma, which may be seen as consequent on the attempt to elevate epigram into a major poetic form (an attempt by no means confined to love-poetry, from Catullus onwards),[14] caused Roman poets to collect and organise, as it were, what may sweepingly be called a vast mass of referential or analogical material (it has been estimated that mythical exempla are three times as frequent in Roman poetry as in Greek).[15] The various ways in which this material could be related to, or substituted for, the contextual ideas were derived from the tropes described above.

4. *Primary and Secondary Language*

A distinction which is sometimes useful in analysis is one that may be made between primary and secondary language. Primary language may be defined as the immediate expression of experience or emotion in literal terms, and secondary language as the use of material that is, from the writer's point of view, objective, external, and involving characters other than his own or that of his subject. An example of this use of secondary language to substitute for primary statement has already been examined in the ending to Horace's ode 1.14, where, paradoxically, the language of erotic emotion is used to avoid explicit statement of political belief and feeling. But Roman love-poets used the technique most extensively. It is possible to speak of Roman love-poets using secondary language to alternate with primary language in an expansive or illustrative way or actually substituting it for the primary language that would have been strained to express the inter-action between their feelings and their situations. The latter possi-bility is, of course, the more interesting and gave greatest scope for invention and originality. The various modes of this substitution were derived from the tropes discussed above. A particularly difficult poem of Propertius may serve as an example.

The first poem of Propertius[16] purports in some degree to be programmatic and to convey the immediate sense of a painful personal situation. Yet it is composed almost entirely in secondary language, and such primary statements as it appears to contain are bafflingly obscure. The opening is deceptively simple (1–8):

14. On this, see Williams (1968), Index s.v. 'Epigram, elevated into major poetic form'.

15. Canter (1933), p. 220.

16. On this poem, see especially Steele Commager (1974), pp. 21–36.

Cynthia prima suis miserum me cepit ocellis,
    contactum nullis ante cupidinibus.
tum mihi constantis deiecit lumina fastus
    et caput impositis pressit Amor pedibus
donec me docuit castas odisse puellas   5
    improbus, et nullo vivere consilio.
et mihi iam toto furor hic non deficit anno,
    cum tamen adversos cogor habere deos.

'Cynthia was the first to make me captive with her eyes—pity me, I who had been touched with no desires before that. Then Love cast down upon me eyes of unrelenting contempt and, setting his feet on my head, pinned me to the ground, till he went so far as to teach me to dislike chaste girls (5) and live a life of total recklessness. And I find this madness now after a whole year not letting up, though, in spite of that, I am constrained to experience hostility from the gods.'

The prevailing metaphors are of war and slavery: Cynthia was the first to capture (and so enslave) him. It was a terrible experience (*miserum*), and the poet had no previous similar experience to help him (2). A transfer into secondary language follows this autobiographical statement. The god Cupid (*Amor*) used his eyes as weapons (3, *deicit*). This seems a more likely and relevant meaning than the usually accepted one that regards the eyes as the poet's; for the theme of contempt shown to the lover will be taken up by (10) *saevitiam durae . . . Iasidos*, and *Amor* is here almost a figure for Cynthia. (Further, the emphatic word-order *constantis . . . lumina fastus* would pointlessly stress the relentlessness of the poet's earlier arrogance, but not that of the Love-God.)[17] *Amor* treated the poet as an arrogant Eastern con-

---

17. It is a characteristic of Propertius to defeat linguistic expectation by using compound verbs in an unusual sense. A good example is 1.3.3, where *accubuit* is used of sleeping but the normal sense of the compound is 'to recline at table' or 'to lie (erotically) beside': see Camps (1961–67), ad loc. for further examples. The verb *deicere* is idiomatic with *oculos* in the sense 'to lower one's gaze (in shame or modesty)'; but, in my interpretation, the poet is using it in the literal sense 'to hurl down from a height'. The difference between this passage and 2.30.9–10 (*excubat ille acer custos et tollere numquam / te patietur humo lumina capta semel*) is that in the later scene *Amor* is guarding a prisoner; but in the earlier, the victim is lying on the ground, held down by the god's foot. The dative *mihi* expresses, as often especially in poetry, the force of *in* or *ad* with the accusative.

queror treated a captive enemy, setting his foot on his prostrate neck and glaring at him with contempt. Finally, the poet learned the needed lessons: the most hateful thing a girl can do is to say no, and a lover cannot live an orgaiused life. The couplet 5–6 seems to be primary in language, but what does it say? Apparently that the poet learned to despise the prized virtues of chastity and careful living. The poet's submission, then, ought to have entailed the god's favour; but, though the madness (described in 5–6) persists after a whole year, the gods are against the poet. Here he has lapsed again into remote secondary language so that 'the gods' (not just *Amor*) are against him. Why? There is no answer till lines 33–34, and then it is only the partial one that this deity is capricious and one needs experience to deal with him. The poet has here succeeded in conveying almost no information, simply the apprehension of a desperate situation. An exemplum now follows (9–18):

> Milanion nullos fugiendo, Tulle, labores
>   saevitiam durae contudit Iasidos.   10
> nam modo Partheniis amens errabat in antris,
>   ibat et hirsutas ille videre feras;
> ille etiam Hylaei percussus vulnere rami
>   saucius Arcadiis rupibus ingemuit.
> ergo velocem potuit domuisse puellam: 15
>   tantum in amore preces et benefacta valent.
> in me tardus Amor non ullas cogitat artis
>   nec meminit notas, ut prius, ire vias.

'Milanion, by avoiding no hardships, Tullus, crushed the cruel spirit of the hard-hearted daughter of Iasos [Atalanta] (10). For at one time he used to wander out of his mind in Parthenian valleys, and dared to come face to face with shaggy wild-beasts; he was even smitten by a blow from the club of Hylaeus, and, wounded by it, moaned among Arcadian rocks. For that reason he was able to dominate the swift girl (15): so great in love is the power of entreaties and services. In my case Love thinks up no wiles and does not even remember how to proceed as before on the well-known paths.'

The importance of the exemplum is underlined by setting the name of the poem's addressee in it, as though a crucial message were being conveyed at this point. The relevance of the exemplum, told in allusive language and with details altered by the poet to suit his pur-pose (for instance, the central theme of the myth—Atalanta's race—is

alluded to only in 15, *velocem*), does not become clear till lines 17–18—
and then it is clearly over-adequate[18] to its context (so that judgment
on it must be suspended till the whole poem has been read). It appears
to convey a situation the opposite of the poet's, since Milanion was
not only happy and fortunate in love but came to dominate the
girl (whereas the poet is a slave—lines 3–4). Yet that does not exhaust
the application of the myth, since there are also elements of similarity
with the poet's situation: first, Atalanta, designated as *dura* and characterised by *saevitia*, is like Cynthia (and *Amor*); secondly, Milanion's
sufferings are analogous to the poet's, but, unlike his, they came to an
end. They are also like the poet's in a way that is indeed relevant to
this poem but which also resonates through the whole collection: the
sufferings are somewhat ridiculous, unmanly, and ineffectual; Milanion cuts a sorry and undignified figure. So does Propertius in his
poetry. The myth, in fact, sets up a curious ideal: it is that a lover, after
a period of ordeal and suffering, crushes and dominates a girl who is
by nature cruel; and, paradoxically, this conquest, expressed in terms
of violence, is actually accomplished by the gentle means of *preces* and
benefacta. (This paradoxical nature of love is not otherwise stated in the
poem.) But the poet's situation is the opposite of Milanion's: lines
1–8 clearly outline an appropriate ordeal, lasting for a year, but no
progress has been made; Love does not help (cf. line 8), has 'forgotten'
his arts. The exemplum will also be seen to function as a thematic
anticipation (see chap. 5) of the happy lovers whom the poet will end
the poem by addressing (31–38). The poet does not explain the *paradeigma* by any return to primary language; instead he expresses his own
opposite situation in secondary Alexandrian language like that of lines
3–8, except that *Amor* here has a different meaning from that of the
earlier passage in which he was almost a figure for Cynthia. The secondary language continues (19–30):

> at vos, deductae quibus est fallacia lunae
>   et labor in magicis sacra piare focis,   20
> en agedum dominae mentem convertite nostrae
>   et facite illa meo palleat ore magis—

---

18. I use the word 'over-adequacy', here and elsewhere, to indicate a reader's
sense that an illustration or comparison goes beyond what the immediate context
needs or can absorb.

tunc ego crediderim vobis et sidera et amnis
    posse Cytaeines ducere carminibus.
et vos, qui sero lapsum revocatis, amici,   25
    quaerite non sani pectoris auxilia
(fortiter et ferrum saevos patiemur et ignis,
    sit modo libertas quae velit ira loqui);
ferte per extremas gentes et ferte per undas
    qua non ulla meum femina norit iter.   30

'But you who possess the trick of drawing down the moon and who toil
to perform rituals on magic hearths (20), come now, alter my mistress'
heart and cause her face to grow more pale than mine—in that case I should
credit your claim to have the power to attract stars and rivers by Medea's
spells. And you, my friends, who too late call back one who has fallen (25),
seek out remedies for a mind diseased (with fortitude shall I bear surgery
and cruel cautery, provided only there is freedom allowed me to express
what my anger dictates); take me away through the most distant races and
take me over the seas where no woman can know my path (30).'

The two addresses here to witches and to his friends are not appeals
for help. Both are secondary expressions of the poet's desperate situation, and arise by metonymy from it. For lovers could turn to witches
for magical help; or, on the other hand, love could be treated as a form
of insanity (that theme is prepared for by 7, *furor*) and cured by medical
and surgical means or by travel overseas.[19] The address to witches
reinforces the implied sense of the exemplum (9–16): 'I have done all
I can' (that is, by *preces* and *benefacta*), and adds to it the idea that nothing
can help him, by promising belief in a series of ἀδύνατα if witches can
change Cynthia's heart. Then the address to his friends adds two new
ideas: first, it is too late to help him; secondly, the poet's suffering is in
fact the source of his poetic inspiration, and this is so important to him
that his friends can subject him to any treatment, however painful,
provided he is allowed to write. This latter idea is clearly programmatic: love-elegy is created out of suffering. The final treatment
mentioned—physical removal overseas—is designed to provide the
possibility of a metonymic movement from his own situation to an
address to happy lovers (31–38):

19. Celsus 3.18.23: see Shackleton Bailey, (1956) p. 6.

THE
UNIVERSITY OF WINNIPEG
PORTAGE & BALMORAL
WINNIPEG, MAN. R3B 2E9
CANADA
Theoretical Considerations 39

vos remanete, quibus facili deus annuit aure,
    sitis et in tuto semper amore pares.
in me nostra Venus noctes exercet amaras
    et nullo vacuus tempore defit Amor.
hoc, moneo, vitate malum (sua quemque moretur   35
    cura, neque assueto mutet amore locum);
quod si quis monitis tardas adverterit auris,
    heu referet quanto verba dolore mea!

'But you stay at home to whom the god has assented with obliging ear, and be paired for ever in happy love. Against me our goddess Venus exerts nights of bitterness and at no time does Love depart or rest (34). This un-happiness—I warn you—avoid (may each of you be fully occupied by his beloved and may she not change place when love becomes settled); but if any one of you shall turn slow ears to my warnings, ah! with what pain shall he recall my words.'

The happy lovers are those to whom the capricious god is kind, and primary language momentarily describes what such happiness consists in (32). But to describe his own contrary situation the poet again lapses into secondary Alexandrian language in which Venus (like *Amor* in line 4) could almost be a figure for Cynthia, though (34) *Amor* cannot be (he is like *Amor* of line 17). The final warning contains a primary statement, in the form of a wish, of the ideal whereby men fall completely in love and women are faithful (*assueto ... amore* refers, as it were, to the ideal as it was expressed in the exemplum: it is the situation when the initial period of suffering and uncertainty has been resolved in the man's favour). The final reference to lateness (37, *tardas*) picks up the theme of line 25 that it is too late to do anything for the poet: his situation is hopeless, and so will be that of anyone who fails to heed his words in good time. If the poet had been less inexperienced (2), perhaps he too could have known what to do while there was still time.

    If it is at least part of the function of an introductory poem to catch a reader's attention and persuade him to read on, this poem succeeds admirably. A strange and dramatic situation between the poet and his beloved can be apprehended through forms of expression that are almost completely secondary; there is almost no direct statement that conveys objective information. Even the address to happy lovers at the end is secondary in the sense that it conceals two implications for the poet's own situation: first, that when the initial period of ordeal and suffering was over, Cynthia's love 'changed place'; secondly that now the poet knows from experience how to deal with such a situation, and this knowledge inspires and is the subject of his poetry. The first implication means that, contrary to the ideal expressed in the exemplum, the poet—not Cynthia—has become the slave. The second means that one of the advantages to be gained from reading the poetry of Propertius is to obtain important knowledge about love and how to handle a love-affair. It is no mere coincidence that no other poem of Propertius is so elusively secondary in its forms of expression until we reach the two final poems of Book 3, in which the poet purports to describe and celebrate his falling out of love and his final parting from Cynthia. Those two poems echo basic themes of this first poem, and this first poem may have been designed to serve the function not only of introducing the three books of Propertius' love-poetry and catching a reader's attention, but also of providing thematic material and a style of composition that would form a conspicuous ring-composition with the final poems.[20]

Here another poem is worth examining which demonstrates how a deliberated alternation of primary and secondary language can be used to distance the expression of emotion and yet make it more deeply communicable for that very reason. Horace's ode 1.24 seems to suffer from misjudgment because the skilful use of this technique has not been appreciated. The latest editors are dubious about the poem, saying 'the ode is perhaps too austere and formal for most modern taste', and quoting the derogatory comments which Landor put into the mouth of Boccaccio.[21] Another view can, however, be taken of the poem. Here it is:

> Quis desiderio sit pudor aut modus
> tam cari capitis? praecipe lugubris
> cantus, Melpomene, cui liquidam pater
>   vocem cum cithara dedit.
>
> ergo Quintilium perpetuus sopor   5

20. For the thesis that Propertius intended Books 1–3 to have a unity similar to that of Horace *Odes* 1–3, see Williams (1968), pp. 481 ff.

21. Nisbet and Hubbard (1970), p. 281.

urget? cui Pudor et Iustitiae soror,
incorrupta Fides, nudaque Veritas
    quando ullum inveniet parem?

multis ille bonis flebilis occidit,
nulli flebilior quam tibi, Vergili,   10
tu frustra pius, heu, non ita creditum
    poscis Quintilium deos.

quid? si Threicio blandius Orpheo
auditam moderere arboribus fidem,
num vanae redeat sanguis imagini   15
    quam virga semel horrida,

non lenis precibus fata recludere,
nigro compulerit Mercurius gregi?
durum: sed levius fit patientia
    quicquid corrigere est nefas.

'What restraint or limit can there be in feeling the loss of so dear a person? Teach me sad songs, Melpomene, whom your father endowed with a clear voice to be accompanied by the lyre (4).

So then! eternal sleep holds Quintilius down? When shall Modesty and incorruptible Honesty, sister of Justice, and naked Truth ever find his equal?

He died, to be wept by many—by none more than by you, Virgil (10). Vain alas! your piety: now you demand Quintilius back from the gods, deposited with them on no such terms.

Look: supposing you were to tune more sweetly than Thracian Orpheus the lyre to which trees gave ear, the blood would not return to the empty shade, would it (15)?—not once Mercury with his chilling rod has herded it in with the black flock, not a god to be softened by pleas to unlatch the gates of death. Hard: but what you cannot put right becomes lighter if you bear it.'

This poem is usually interpreted in terms of the traditional topics of *consolatio*. This causes the latest commentators to say of the opening question (1–2): 'Horace is defending the right to weep without restraint'.[22] But the parallels they quote all contain references to howling and weeping; this is because the traditional commonplace was designed to flatter the dead person (and so the living relatives) by asserting that unrestrained lamentation is the only possible response to the death.

22. Ibid., pp. 281–82.

Horace's opening can clearly be related to the topic, but just to do that is to miss the difference and the originality. What characterises his tone is the restrained emotion of the word *desiderium* and the intimate friendliness of the affectionate periphrasis *tam cari capitis*, together with the lively personal vigour of the question. But the poet then distances his own personality by a retreat into an appeal to the Muse for a particular type of inspiration. This takes the place of—or, rather, enacts—any *lugubres cantus* on the poet's part. This is shown by the notable fact that the appeal does not lead, as such appeals by Horace usually do, to the representation of an answer by the Muse.[23]

Instead, this figure of the traditional appeal to the Muse is used as a type of metonymy for the writing of a *lugubris cantus*, and the poet is freed to return to a highly personal reflection in an exclamation or, more probably, a question of astonishment, introduced by the very informal particle *ergo*: 'So: Is it really true that . . . ?' Once again the personal utterance is followed by another retreat into distancing formality: *Pudor*, *Fides*, and *Veritas* are represented as unable ever to find an equal to Quintilius. The figure of personification was, with some justification, treated by Quintilian as a type of metaphor (8.6.11). Here the effect of the personification of the virtues of Quintilius is to objectify and formalise the *laudatio* of the dead man, and so to relieve the poet from the embarrassment, as it were, of writing a personal testimonial for Quintilius. The personifications are the objective correlative of the poet's sense of loss: the reader is left to apprehend the depth of emotion.

The central stanza is, as often, pivotal (see chap. 1, n. 2). The poet's thoughts turn to an even closer friend of the dead man: Virgil will feel more grief than anyone. The apostrophe again makes the statement highly personal and intimate, an effect underpinned by the simple directness of the language. Then, even more intimately, Virgil's shock is depicted in the homely metaphor of a man vainly trying to get a deposit back from a dishonest banker. The surprising proportionality between metaphor and context is left for the reader to work out: by one's prayers on his behalf (*pius*), one deposits a friend to the safe-keeping of the gods, and they are fraudulent if they allow him to die. It is the same metaphor that Horace used to express his own affection for Virgil, about to sail overseas, in *Odes* 1.3.1–8.

23. See Williams (1968), p. 64.

At this point there is another distancing retreat, but the informal apostrophe to Virgil is maintained, as it is for the rest of the poem. This time the retreat is into myth, and into a myth peculiarly relevant to Virgil, who memorably treated the story of Orpheus and Eurydice at the end of *Georgics* 4 (see p. 260 ff.). The latest commentators say of this: 'Horace seems to be hinting at, and implicitly contradicting, the story of the recovery of Eurydice, which Virgil had told in the *Georgics*. His view of the power of poetry is more commonsensical than his friend's.'[24] This cannot be right. It is true that the interpretation of the myth is left to the reader, but it must be interpreted in terms of the contextual requirement. The use of the second-person address to the poet Virgil casts him as the poet-singer Orpheus. But Orpheus did not succeed in bringing back Eurydice: she remained an insubstantial shade. As she dissolved like smoke into the empty breezes (*Georg.* 4.499–500), she said farewell to Orpheus (497–98) *feror ingenti circumdata nocte | invalidasque tibi tendens, heu non tua, palmas* ('I am being swept away, sunk in the depths of darkness and, alas! yours no more, stretching out feeble arms towards you'). Just as Orpheus' grief is that of Virgil, so, in the unsubstantial shade, the reader sees not Eurydice but Quintilius. In this way the myth functions analogically in the mode of metaphor. But it has also, at the same time, another function which is in the mode of metonymy; for the myth is substituted for a contextual statement that the grief which Virgil and the poet feel is powerless to help the dead man (another commonplace topic of *consolatio*).

The poem ends with another statement which is highly personal both in its directness and in the informality of its syntax; it functions also as a type of ring-composition with the opening personal question, to which it is, as it were, an answer in terms of philosophical resignation.

The alternation of primary and secondary language is used here to produce a poem on one of the most commonplace topics that is yet fresh and original. It is particularly interesting in that, in each case, the retreat into secondary language is not made to expand or illustrate the primary statements, but, as in the first poem of Propertius, to substitute for primary statements that are not made. The movement is interesting too, for the address to Virgil in the second half of the poem is not an example of postponed address (which is quite frequent in the *Odes*). Here the poem starts with introverted personal reflection

24. Nisbet and Hubbard (1970), p. 287.

and then moves out to include Virgil and even draw him into a dialogue (since the recounting of the myth is syntactically organised to anticipate Virgil's answers).

The technique here used by Horace had a predecessor in poem 65 of Catullus, and in fact many of the techniques discussed theoretically in this chapter and analysed in poems of Horace and Propertius can be traced back to the original genius of Catullus, as will appear from the next chapter.

CHAPTER III

CATULLUS

The range and depth of the influence that Catullus exercised on later poets, particularly of the early Augustan Age, are hard to overestimate. In material and ideas, but especially in style and poetic technique, he was an innovator whose importance in the development of Roman poetry comes near to being comparable to Ennius'. It seems likely that with poem 68 he virtually invented the new literary genre of love-elegy, and the techniques of composition to be seen in that extraordinary poem will be the main focus of attention in this chapter. First, however, some unusual and effective ways of using figures—particularly the figure of simile—will be examined as a preliminary to consideration of poem 68.

1. *Some Techniques in Using Simile*

In poem 11, after the mock-solemn address to Furius and Aurelius (4 stanzas), the poet sends an obscene message by them to Lesbia, cursing her in crude terms (1 stanza). The poem then ends with a single stanza:

> nec meum respectet, ut ante, amorem,
> qui illius culpa cecidit velut prati
> ultimi flos, praetereunte postquam
>   tactus aratro est.

'And let her not look, as of old, to my love, which, through her fault, has fallen like a flower at the very edge of a field after it has been touched by the passing plough.'

The previous stanza was in the starkest and most brutal primary language, but here the simile is substituted for a description by the poet of the ending of his love for Lesbia; and the simile also enacts the nature and history of that love: its survival of all hazards and happenings, its longevity, its characteristic of being overlooked and ignored, the careless, unthinking act by which it was ended, the finality of the end, and so on. A special feature of the way the idea is expressed in the simile comes out by comparison with a simile of Virgil's, in which the later poet was certainly recalling that of Catullus. Virgil describes the death of Euryalus as seen by Nisus (*Aeneid* 9.433–37):

> volvitur Euryalus leto, pulchrosque per artus
> it cruor inque umeros cervix conlapsa recumbit:
> purpureus veluti cum flos succisus aratro
> languescit moriens, lassove papavera collo
> demisere caput pluvia cum forte gravantur.

'Euryalus collapsed in death: over his beautiful limbs the blood courses, and his neck droops to hang limply over his shoulder; just as when a bright-red flower, cut by the plough, droops in death, or the necks of poppies tire and droop their heads when once weighed down by rain.'

Virgil uses language to draw the images into the closest proximity to the human situation; the words are chosen because their primary reference is to mankind. Virgil, that is, has closed the gap between the simile and the contextual idea; the scene is apprehended, with utmost pathos and subjectivity, through the eyes of Nisus in words that are also anthropomorphic. But Catullus has done precisely the opposite. He has deliberately sited, as it were, the language of the simile in its own field, holding it as remote as possible from the human sphere to which it refers. Such distancing and objectivity leave the greatest scope for the reader's co-operative imagination. It has another effect too; for the reader is not only required to gather the obvious historical facts from the simile; the simile also enacts the poet's emotions of pain, neglect, humiliation, bitterness, and so on, which he does not attempt to express otherwise, but which form the essential basis and motivation for the preceding stanza—just as the historical facts provide the dramatic situation. The deliberate objectivity of the viewpoint and language of the simile entails the exclusion of emotion, and is paradoxically the most effective vehicle of the poet's complex feelings. The secondary language here functions poetically like the secondary language in Horace *Odes* 1.24: it provides a sensitive and appropriate objective correlative for the poet's emotion, and consequently relieves the poet from any need to attempt a more concrete description.

Another highly original manipulation of primary and secondary language can be seen in poem 65. Ostensibly the poem is an apology to the great orator, Q. Hortensius Hortalus, a slightly elder contemporary of Cicero. Catullus can only send him a translation of Callimachus' *Lock of Berenice* instead of an original poem. He explains that grief for his brother's death has prevented an original composition (*nec potis est dulcis Musarum expromere fetus*); here poetic activity is figured in secondary language as intercourse with the Muses, but his grief is expressed in stark primary simplicity (*me adsiduo confectum . . . dolore*). He then turns aside to speak of his brother's death, but in the secondary language of the mythic underworld (5–8). The next line is missing, but it was part of an emotional apostrophe to his brother (10–14):

> numquam ego te, vita frater amabilior,
> aspiciam posthac? at certe semper amabo,
> semper maesta tua carmina morte canam,
> qualia sub densis ramorum concinit umbris
> Daulias, absumpti fata gemens Ityli.

'Shall I never see you again, brother dearer to me than life? Yet certainly I shall always love you, and the songs I sing shall be saddened by your death, such songs as the Daulian bird sings beneath the dense shadows of the foliage, as it grieves over the fate of Itylus stolen from it.'

Here the excursion into primary language is motivated by the apostrophe, but it is, with perfect timing, cut short by the brief simile (here used illustratively, with several points of contact with the contextual ideas). Then the poet turns back in apologetic address to Hortensius (15–24):

> sed tamen in tantis maeroribus, Ortale, mitto
> haec expressa tibi carmina Battiadae,
> ne tua dicta vagis nequiquam credita ventis
> effluxisse meo forte putes animo,
> ut missum sponsi furtivo munere malum
> procurrit casto virginis e gremio,
> quod miserae oblitae molli sub veste locatum,

> dum adventu matris prosilit, excutitur,
> atque illud prono praeceps agitur decursu,
> huic manat tristi conscius ore rubor.

'But even in such depths of bereavement I send you, Hortalus, this translation of a poem of Callimachus, to prevent your thinking that your words, vainly entrusted to the unstable breezes, slipped right out of my mind, as an apple, sent as a furtive gift from her betrothed, jumps out of the virgin bosom of a girl; tucked away in her soft clothing and—poor girl!—forgotten, it is spilled out as she leaps up at her mother's coming, and it falls down and down irretrievably, while a blush of guilt spreads over her woebegone face.'

Here the simile, taking off from the idea of forgetting, not only has many points of contact with the contextual ideas, especially in the language, but is also substituted for a primary statement by the poet of the shame he would feel if he allowed his friend to suspect forgetfulness. The simile has another function; for it not only takes on an independent life of its own as the details build up a perfect genre-scene, but it also has a tone of its own: its mock-heroic splendour, increased by the grandeur of the structure and the domination of the syntactical units by the metrical divisions, is humorous, not only deflating any solemn pomposity the poet might otherwise have displayed, but also changing the tone from the deep grief of the self-centred beginning to a mood that comes close to self-mockery.

In this poem the alternation of primary and secondary language (similar to that of Horace *Odes* 1.24) permits the linking of two totally disparate subjects: the deeply felt grief at his brother's death and the apology for an inadequate poem. The continuous movement between the two levels leaves the poet totally in control and, paradoxically, creates the sense of an intensely personal form of expression that flows forth as an impromptu performance.[1]

The technique of using similes seems to have particularly interested Catullus. In the highly experimental poem 64 there are two similes which evade, with conspicuous success, the formulaic pattern of simile as it had been established by Homer. The fight between Theseus and the Minotaur is not described; instead there is this simile (105–11):

---

1. On this effect in Catullus, see Williams (1968), pp. 40, 699–716.

nam velut in summo quatientem bracchia Tauro
quercum aut conigeram sudanti cortice pinum
indomitus turbo contorquens flamine robur
eruit (illa procul radicitus exturbata
prona cadit, late quaevis cumque obvia frangens),
sic domito saevum prostravit corpore Theseus
nequiquam vanis iactantem cornua ventis.

'For as an oak that shakes its branches on the top of the Taurus mountains or a cone-bearing pine with sweating bark is uprooted by an overwhelming whirlwind that twists its trunk by its blast (it, torn high up from its roots, falls flat, shattering everything in its path far and wide), so did Theseus, overwhelming its body, lay flat the savage creature as it tossed its horns at the empty breezes.'

The simile bursts suddenly into a text that has been describing Ariadne's fears and prayers, and it is hard to convey in English translation the surprising effect of the opening, with the distant trees appearing in the accusative case and the poet's leisured description of two types of tree; the tornado finally comes as the climax and subject of the sentence. Then the simile changes direction to centre attention on the tree's fall and its inert destructiveness. The return to context concentrates on the monster, with contrast of *indomitus* and *domito* and a careful ring-composition between the oak waving its branches and the monster tossing its horns. Thus the simile enacts the epic struggle, relieving the poet of any need to describe it, and, as often, by its very obliquity suggests more than a primary statement could convey with conviction.

Another deliberately innovating technique is used to describe how Theseus forgot the sign agreed to with his father (238–40):

haec mandata prius constanti mente tenentem
Thesea ceu pulsae ventorum flamine nubes
aereum nivei montis liquere cacumen.

'Though Theseus previously kept these instructions steadfastly in his mind, ⟨they deserted him⟩, as often clouds, hit by blasting winds, desert the airy top of a snow-clad mountain.'

There is certainly imitation of Greek here—most notably in the Latin present participle used as if it were equivalent to a Greek aorist —but syncopated similes in Hellenistic poets simply use ellipse of the verb. Here *mandata* is accusative case in relation to *tenentem*, but must also function as the subject of the verb in ellipse. One commentator makes an incredible remark on this simile: 'Der Vergleich ist nicht glücklich, da der Wind lange wehen muss, ehe er die Wolken von einem Berge entfernt, während die Wirkung des Fluches auf Theseus eine plötzliche ist'.[2] In fact, all is haste and suddenness here; even the syncopation helps to enact the sudden, inexplicable blank in Theseus' mind—which is blank (*aereum*—the vacant mind) like a peak deserted by clouds, and it is also a snow-white peak. Simile and syntax enact what need not be described.

2. *Poem 68*

Poem 68 of Catullus is like poem 64 in the experimental novelty of every aspect of its composition. Structurally, as a central poem (41–148) surrounded by a dedicatory poem in an epistolary style (1–40 and 149– 60),[3] it supplied a model for one of Virgil's most original *Eclogues*, the tenth; and Propertius borrowed a device from Catullus 68 to unify the first elegy of his fourth book. But the main interest must lie in the variety of techniques used in the central poem to the Muses, and, in particular, in the lengthy treatment of the myth. For more than half of the central poem (72–130) is taken up by the myth of Laudamia and Protesilaus.

The myth is introduced by an assertion of similarity (73–74):

> coniugis ut quondam flagrans advenit amore
> Protesilaeam Laudamia domum . . .

'just as once, burning with love for her husband, Laudamia came to the house of Protesilaus'.

2. Kroll (1929), ad loc.

3. Nothing that I have read on the structure and interpretation of Catullus 68 persuades me to abandon the view, expressed in Williams (1968), pp. 229–39, that the poem is a unity of this type. In particular, no critic has taken into consideration its relationship to Virgil *Eclogue* 10 and Propertius 4.1.

The similarity purports to equate the coming of Lesbia to the house of Allius (to meet Catullus) with Laudamia's coming to the house of her husband. The poet leaves the myth to return to Lesbia's coming to him, with another—this time qualified—assertion of similarity (131–32):

> aut nihil aut paulo cui tum concedere digna
> lux mea se nostrum contulit in gremium.

'So, worthy in no respect, or else only to a small extent, to take second place to her [Laudamia] , my darling brought herself into my arms.'

Here *tum* marks the resumption of a theme from which a digression has been made (so, in 105, *tum* takes up the theme of Laudamia after the digression on the death of the poet's brother). The similarity now asserted is between the degree and range of love felt by Laudamia on the one hand, and by Lesbia on the other; but the poet qualifies that assertion by saying that Lesbia's love was equal to Laudamia's, or inferior only by a small margin. In spite of an occasional tendency on the part of Greek and Roman poets to qualify emotional assertions, there is no parallel to the cool and objective way it is done here, and the qualification must be disturbing.

There is an important feature in the way in which Catullus introduces the myth here, and this feature will turn out to be significant for later poets. I shall refer to it as an 'arbitrary assertion of similarity'. Its arbitrary nature can be identified by its lack of immediate legitimacy. In decorative mythological allusions there is clear to the reader an obvious explanation for the poet's choice of the myth and for the treatment that he gives it. But in an arbitrary assertion of similarity there is no obvious reason either for the choice or for the way in which the poet handles the myth. Such a use is often marked also by an obvious excess of adequacy to what seems to be the immediate purpose.[4] Sometimes, of course, the arbitrary nature of the assertion will reside in the fact that the myth precedes the context in which it will find its legitimation: that is the case with the myths in the three Horatian odes, 1.2, 16, and 28, and to some extent with the myth in the first poem of

4. See chapter 2, note 28.

Propertius. The important fact is that in every such case the identification of the assertion as arbitrary is a signal to the reader to suspend judgment and read on with his mind open for a meaning that he cannot yet grasp.

In poem 68 Catullus precedes the myth with a lengthy description of his own feelings (51–66), followed by a strikingly objective and yet impressionistic description of Lesbia's coming to meet him which focusses on the sound made by her feet. He abandons the myth at line 131 to commence a tense and disturbed reflection on the attitude that he should adopt towards Lesbia's unfaithfulness, which is resolved by an apparent decision to be content with at least occupying the first place in her love (131–148). Given this organisation of the poem, there is no possibility that the reader can begin to understand the meaning of the myth till the whole poem has been read; judgment must be suspended, and the use of the myth here is an outstanding example of synecdoche *e sequentibus praecedentia*. Thus the myth functions paradigmatically in relation to the contextual ideas, but structurally it functions as a type of synecdoche.

The poet's description of his own feelings of love, with which the poem to the Muses begins, has the ostensible purpose of demonstrating the value of Allius' kindness. A central element in this description is a remarkable pair of similes. Double similes of this extent and concentration are without precedent in poetry before Catullus, either Greek or Roman.[5] The similes themselves display an obvious excess of adequacy to the immediate context and consequently carry a signal to the reader to suspend judgment and to look beyond any obvious immediate reason for their legitimation. The first statement of the poet's love (51–56) distinguishes two elements in it: (*a*) *cura*, and (*b*) the burning flame; each is then developed in a couplet in the order (*b*) 53–54, (*a*) 55–56. Two features are notable in these six lines: first, the typically Hellenistic *doctrina* (*duplex Amathusia* for Venus; *Trinacria rupes* for Aetna; and the geographical details in *lymphaque in Oetaeis Malia Thermopylis*): secondly, the highly conventional and stereotyped nature of the expressions of emotion (*torrere, ardere, tabescere lumina fletu, imbre madere genae*). This is conventional Hellenistic composition; or, to put it another way, this purports to be primary statement, but the terms in which the statement is made are drawn completely from

5. See Williams (1968), pp. 709 ff., 751 ff.

secondary language—only in form is the statement primary (in this it is like the first poem of Propertius). The similes, however, which are on the face of it secondary, are highly original both in their linking and in their detailed working out (57–66):

> qualis in aerii perlucens vertice montis
>   rivus muscoso prosilit e lapide,
> qui cum de prona praeceps est valle volutus,
>   per medium densi transit iter populi,
> dulce viatori lasso in sudore levamen
>   cum gravis exustos aestus hiulcat agros;
> ac velut in nigro iactatis turbine nautis
>   lenius aspirans aura secunda venit
> iam prece Pollucis, iam Castoris implorata,
>   tale fuit nobis Allius auxilium.

'As, on the top of a sky-high mountain, a shining stream leaps forth from moss-covered rocks, which, after falling sheer from a steep valley, cuts right through a highway of crowded people, a sweet refreshment to a weary, sweating traveller when oppressive heat fissures the scorched fields; and as the gentle breath of a favouring breeze comes to sailors storm-tossed in a black hurricane, an answer to prayer made now to Pollux, now to Castor, such assistance was Allius to me.'

The two similes ostensibly illustrate the value of Allius' help; and that is their prime function. But their other function is less obvious and more important. The secondary language in which the poet made what purported to be primary statements about the nature of his love (51–56) relieved the poet from any need for concrete detail. The similes have the additional function of providing an indirect means of expressing the poet's emotion and suffering in such a way that the first simile expresses aspect (*b*), the second aspect (*a*). The first simile conveys burning desire and frustrated passion; the second the storms and troubles of love. Consequently, in the whole passage, which purports to be about his love, the poet distances himself from immediate description of his emotions, first by stylistic means (51–56), and then by similes apparently directed to quite another end (that is, by an analogy whose full meaning the reader can only grasp after realising the gross disproportion between the supposed terms). What emerges is the sense of a love-affair as troubled as it is hot.

The poet maintains his distance in the objective description of Lesbia's coming (70–72), but there is one detail here that will be found to resonate throughout the poem: (71–72) 'she placed (*constituit*) her shining foot on the shining threshold'. The detail seems at the moment simply ornamental and impressionistic; but marriage will play an important role in the themes of the poem, and the one thing a Roman bride carefully avoided doing was to place her foot on the threshold.[6] This detail anticipates the construction of a thematic field of marriage and non-marriage, and may be regarded as the first step towards constructing that field.

Now (73) the myth of Laudamia begins. In structure it is a ring-composition that ends with the theme of passion from which it began (73, *flagrans amore*; 129 *furores*). The theme of marriage is introduced with the first word (73) *coniugis*, and this field is surprisingly expanded by an aspect of the myth, unknown elsewhere and probably invented by Catullus for his special purpose here: the marriage of Laudamia and Protesilaus was flawed, because, in their haste (Protesilaus was going off to Troy), they did not wait for the marriage-sacrifice and so the gods (here called *eri* by the poet, viewing them as if from a slave's status vis-à-vis his owner) were angry.[7] The detail is striking, and the poet underlines it by entering his own narrative with a prayer (77–78) to Nemesis that nothing may ever seem so desirable to him as to cause him to begin it against the will of the gods. This prayer quite deliberately links the poet to this particular detail in the myth in a way that is at the moment incalculable, other than as suggesting apprehension on the part of the poet: he uses the same word (*eri*) of the gods in his prayer as in his narrative, suggesting a slave's fearful submission to the arbitrary whim of his master.

The detail is picked up and carried on by the poet (79–80): Laudamia was taught the importance of the flaw in her marriage when she lost her husband. Then the themes of marriage and passion and unsatisfied lust are brought to a climax in the idea (81–84) that the

6. See Williams (1958), pp. 16–18.

7. The motif is reminiscent of a post-Euripidean elaboration of the Alcestis legend: Admetus omitted the customary sacrifice to Artemis in the wedding ceremony and found the bridal-chamber filled with snakes (Apollodorus *Bibliotheca* 1.9.15); the motif may have had the purpose of explaining why Admetus had to die. Propertius makes Arethusa speculate (4.3.13–16) that a flaw in her wedding ceremony accounts for the prolonged absence abroad of her husband.

long nights of one or two winters could have satisfied her passion and enabled Laudamia to go on living after the destruction of her marriage (84, *abrupto . . . coniugio*). The poet never mentions Laudamia's suicide, only hinting at it in (84) *posset ut . . . vivere*. Troy is named at the end of this passage (86), as the poet looks forward to the death of Protesilaus.

With the mention of Troy the subject changes to the siege of Troy. This is a long and complex passage (87–104), clearly marked by ring-composition, on the theme of Helen and her adultery with Paris, which the Greeks had to punish by destroying Troy. Here is the theme of adultery, the opposite of marriage, its pleasures and its violent end (103–04):

> ne Paris abducta gavisus libera moecha
> otia pacato degeret in thalamo.

'to prevent Paris, taking his pleasure with the abducted whore, from spending all the time he pleased in the peaceful bedroom.'

The language suggests the poet's disgust at arrogant self-indulgence and blindness to the consequences. This adultery caused Troy to become the common grave of Asia and of Europe (89). At this point, by a most surprising metonymic leap from Troy as the object of Greek vengeance to Troy as it figured in his own personal life, the poet recalls that there too his brother died. The only direct primary expression of emotion in the poem follows (91–100) in the poet's distraught lamentation for his dead brother, stressing their mutual love (*amor*) which was once the basis of the poet's happiness: all has now perished.

At this point it becomes clear that the arbitrary assertion of similarity from which the myth started (73) has at least been modified, and that, if Laudamia is like Lesbia, she is no less like the poet, a similarity which, unlike that with Lesbia, has now been fully grounded by the context. This similarity is made even more pointed as the poet returns to Laudamia, after the ring-composition on Helen, Paris, and Troy is complete, with apostrophe (to mark the poet's sympathy with her): the same disaster (that is, Troy) violently robbed her of a marriage, sweeter to her than life or soul through a love (*amor*) that 'like a raging sea swept you in a great whirlpool down into a sheer abyss' (*barathrum*).

Here there is another digression, also marked by ring-composition (107–08 and 117). The poet again makes a most surprising metonymic leap from the metaphorical sense of *barathrum* (the 'abyss' of passion) to its literal sense of 'pit': he claims to illustrate the metaphorical *barathrum* of Laudamia's passion by describing the real *barathrum* dug by Hercules to drain off the flood waters of the Olbius. The style here becomes ornate and obscure and thoroughly Alexandrian. The poet's intention is clearly not to enforce his picture of Laudamia's love (for which the exemplum is grossly over-adequate), but to draw in the figure of Hercules. He is not so named, but only by the periphrasis *falsiparens Amphitryoniades*, a grandiose Alexandrianism in which both elements re-inforce the theme of adultery, of non-marriage, and look back to previous occurrences of the theme and forward to lines 138–40. By means of a reference to another feat of Hercules, the killing of the Stymphalian birds, the poet also draws in the theme of Hercules' true marriage (in heaven) that cut short Hebe's virginity. The virgin bride also belongs to the thematic field of marriage ideas.[8]

Ring-composition returns the poet again to Laudamia (117–18):

> sed tuus altus amor barathro fuit altior illo,
>   qui tamen indomitam ferre iugum docuit.

'But your deep love was deeper than that pit, and it brought you, though you were untamed, to bear the yoke.'

Here it is asserted that her love was deeper than the *barathrum* of Hercules; previously (109) only equivalence was asserted. The reference in the word 'untamed' is to virginity (the taming being thought of as done by a husband), and 'bear the yoke' is another clear allusion to Roman marriage ideals of obedience and faithfulness (in the wife).[9] The poetic strategy of this whole section is to use Laudamia's love (emphasising its strength and depth) to draw in Hercules as the vehicle for ideas of adultery on the one hand, and of happy marriage on the other: then to use Laudamia's love again (relying metonymically on *barathrum*) to identify ideals of marriage in the behaviour of this particular wife, and so to analyse the nature of Laudamia's love more directly.

8. See Williams (1958), p. 18 n.13, and pp. 23–25.

9. See Williams (1958), pp. 18, 24–25. This concept of 'taming' is what Propertius, in 1.1.10, *saevitiam durae contudit Iasidos*, enviously applies to Milanion: see p. 37 above.

This is done in a pair of comparisons (119–28) which are exactly parallel in structure and extent to the earlier pair of similes (57–66). The comparisons are (119–30):

> nam nec tam carum confecto aetate parenti
>   una caput seri nata nepotis alit,
> qui cum divitiis vix tandem inventus avitis
>   nomen testatas intulit in tabulas,
> impia derisi gentilis gaudia tollens,
>   suscitat a cano volturium capiti;
> nec tantum niveo gavisa est ulla columbo
>   compar, quae multo dicitur improbius
> oscula mordenti semper decerpere rostro,
>   quam quae praecipue multivola est mulier:
> sed tu horum magnos vicisti sola furores
>   ut semel es flavo conciliata viro.

'For neither so dear to a grandfather weak with age is the head of his late-born grandson which his only daughter nurses; for he, found at the last moment to inherit his grandfather's wealth, has seen his name entered on the authenticated will, and, annulling the disloyal gladness of a now derided kinsman, scares the vulture from the old grey head; nor so much in a snow-white dove does its female mate ever rejoice, who is said continuously to snatch kisses with her snapping beak far more shamelessly than a woman who is quite outstandingly lustful for many men: but you in your single self far outdid the passions of both of these, great as they are, when once you had been joined to your fair-haired husband.'

The first comparison enforces unselfish family love, or *pietas*, positively in the joy of the grandfather at the unexpected birth of a grandson as a direct heir, and negatively in the repulsion of the 'vulture', the kinsman, *impius* because he is interested only in the money. This is one aspect of Laudamia's love, but it is also parallel to Catullus' *amor* for his brother. The second comparison exemplifies physical passion in the figure of the female dove. But, once she was married (again the theme of marriage), Laudamia far outdid both types of love. Here the myth comes to an end by completing a picture of an ideal wife in a tragic marriage. But in the second comparison a note is struck by (128) *multivola*, which recalls the various allusions to adultery and unfaithfulness; that has, however, nothing to do with Laudamia (who was *univira*[10] not *multivola*), and it seems for the moment to be something that just naturally slipped off the poet's tongue.

The return is now made to the primary context at the point at which it was left in lines 70–71, Lesbia's visit to the poet at the house of Allius (131–32), with thematic echoes. But immediately the poet moves out into a baroque Alexandrian picture of Cupid circling round Lesbia as she enters the house. Most obviously this retreat into secondary language serves to relieve him from the need for any further factual detail; but it also injects a familiar theme into the context: Cupid is dressed as if Lesbia were coming as a bride to the home of her husband. But that theme of marriage is no sooner focussed than it appears that Lesbia is no *univira*, no ideal Roman bride. At this point the myth of Laudamia suddenly acquires new dimensions. Lesbia is not content with Catullus alone (unlike Laudamia with Protesilaus). But the poet excuses her with apologetic words (136); her *furta* are *rara*, she is *verecunda* (a surprising, even contradictory, and so wishful, word to use); but he also designates her as *era*, as if he were her slave (as Propertius pictures Cynthia in his first poem, and the opposite of Laudamia). A brief mythological excursion (138–40) pictures Juno as swallowing her anger at Juppiter's *plurima furta* (he is characterised as *omnivolens*, and the relevance of 128, *multivola*, becomes clear, as also the connexion with 112, *falsiparens*, where the god is the true father and adulterer). But the poet has used the word 'coniunx' of Juppiter and now pulls himself back: he should not compare gods and men (141), and anyway he and Lesbia observed no marriage rites (recalling the incomplete rites of Laudamia in 75–76); but she came to him in adultery, stolen from her husband's arms (recalling the adultery of Helen and Paris in 104–05). So the poet has to be content if Lesbia gives to him alone the day that she marks with whiter chalk.

What is remarkable here is the calm detachment, the absence of pain, the spare expression of highly complex emotions. All the pain and foreboding has been distilled into the objective correlative of the myth. That is introduced and abandoned with arbitrary assertions of similarity that compel the reader to recognise a metaphorical relationship between the myth and a context for which it has been substituted; that context must be reconstructed—*e sequentibus praecedentia*—by analogical analysis. In the case of so dense a treatment of a myth the

10. On *univira*, see Williams (1958), pp. 18 ff.

problem of knowing how far to go, or, rather, where to stop in analysis is acute. What follows is an attempt to keep within what seem to be relevant limits.

The arbitrary nature of the assertions of similarity by which the poet leads into and abandons the myth soon becomes clear, but there is nothing arbitrary in the connexion thereby established between the myth and the poet's relationship with Lesbia: the myth in some way expresses his view of that relationship. Within the myth there are two further movements of arbitrary association which draw in what seem to be extraneous ideas. The first relies on the accidental association, private to the poet, of Troy as the scene both of the death of Protesilaus and of Catullus' brother (91–100). The other depends on a sort of pun between the metaphorical and literal meanings of *barathrum* (109–16). To put it differently, in each case there are two fields of ideas which the poet has chosen to treat as contiguous by making them intersect at an arbitrarily selected point which he uses as a bridge to move from the one to the other. The deliberation of the arbitrary element in both cases compels the reader to reconstruct the wider pattern of internal connexions between both sets of paired fields.

In the case of the first, it instantly becomes clear that Laudamia is more truly a figure for Catullus than for Lesbia, and that Catullus' relationship with his brother was in some ways analogous to Laudamia's with Protesilaus. This is mirrored in the love-language the poet uses to describe his affection for his brother, though the full meaning of this cannot be grasped before lines 119–28, where two types of love are distinguished, and this aspect of Laudamia's love is expressed in the simile of family love, or *pietas* (119–24). The two types of love are also Catullus': the one felt towards his brother, the other more characteristic of his feeling for Lesbia—though it seems to be intended that he feels both types towards Lesbia (as in poem 72 he asserts not just physical passion for her, but also a father's love for his family). The agony of the poet over his brother's death is certainly self-contained and needs no external justification. Nevertheless, it seems to have a resonance which extends beyond itself, for the simple reason that, as Laudamia figures Catullus, so Protesilaus is a figure not only for the poet's brother but also for Lesbia. Hence the agony over his brother's death seems to foreshadow the loss (in a sense analogous to, but not necessarily identical with death) of Lesbia. The poet's extremity of desperation in these lines, the only direct expression of emotion in the poem, seems to move in the direction of Laudamia's suicide (84: she could not go on living after the destruction of her marriage), as if he were foreshadowing his own death also.

The second arbitrary movement of ideas (109–16) anticipates the later portrait of Juppiter and Juno (138–40) by means of Hercules, who, through no act of his own but only through Juppiter's adultery, was pursued by the wrath of Juno and compelled to undergo servitude to a master who was his inferior (114) *imperio deterioris eri*. The bliss he attained—an ideal marriage to the virgin Hebe—he attained only after death. The theme of the ideal marriage is then connected with Laudamia through the ideal of the virgin bride (118). How far is Hercules a figure for Catullus? There are possibilities: the servitude could be related to Catullus' servitude to Lesbia (136), the ideal marriage achieved after death, the trials—all have possible relevance, none necessary. Only one connexion is necessary: the theme of a flawed, or non-existent, marriage appears in the treatment of the myth in the error which was fatal to Laudamia's marriage; in the adultery of Paris with the whore Helen, fatal to Troy and many Greeks as well as to Paris; and in the adultery which led to Hercules' birth and subsequently to his torments. The theme anticipates the poet's later description of Lesbia's non-marriage with him (143–44). Catullus' inclination to view his relationship with Lesbia as either *amicitia* or as marriage provides the link.[11] Of those who stand in either relationship with someone, obligations and standards of conduct, sanctioned by custom, can be demanded—even if unsuccessfully. In other poems Catullus makes such demands of Lesbia.[12] But in this poem he recognises that the fact that it is not marriage is a fatal flaw in their relationship, which requires desperate (and perhaps impossible) adjustments on his part, for Lesbia does to Catullus what she (and he) did to her husband (146).

The love of Laudamia, figured in the double similes (119–28), is also Catullus' love for Lesbia—a balanced combination of sexual passion and *pietas*, or, to put it differently, of marriage and *amicitia*. Laudamia's relationship with Protesilaus not only figures Catullus' ideal view of his relationship with Lesbia, but also *e contrario*, Lesbia's view of her relationship with the poet. It is he who is her slave; she is neither obedient nor faithful, nor was she a virgin. The oblique reference to

11. On this theme, see further p. 217 below.
12. See Williams (1958), p. 25.

Laudamia's suicide and the agonizing over his brother's death point to ultimate despair and the tone of poem 76. In fact, it is noticeable that the themes of most of the subsequent epigrams that concern Lesbia appear variously in poem 68, which functions almost as programmatic to them.

3. *Conclusion*

The poems which have been examined show Catullus developing a technique for using figures in such a way that they do not expand or illustrate primary statements but take their place; the reader is consequently obliged to reconstruct the missing primary statements. In poem 68 the technique is at its most sophisticated. On a large scale, this concerns the way in which the extended treatment of the myth has been substituted for primary statements about his relationship with Lesbia. On a smaller scale, within the myth, the two double similes show the same technique as similes in poems 11, 64, and 65, but with the relationships of the similes to the contextual ideas much more complicated. Also notable and important is the twice-used technique, related to metonymy, of changing the direction of the movement of thought by arbitrary use of privately or randomly contiguous ideas. It is further important that in most instances the technique displays a characteristic of synecdoche: it involves understanding what precedes from what follows—*e sequentibus praecedentia*. The suspense of judgment thereby entailed on the reader throughout is crucial to the reading of this poetry.

CHAPTER IV

ARBITRARY ASSERTION
OF SIMILARITY

Later poets picked up from Catullus and developed the technique of
using similes or comparisons or *paradeigmata* not only to say more than
they were saying in primary language, but also to suggest more than
they actually expressed and to postpone full understanding. As a result,
readers of later poets, particularly of Propertius, are constantly required
to recognise an arbitrary element in assertions of similarity and to
suspend judgment till more, or all, of the poem has been read. The
technique has already been seen in the exemplum in the first poem of
Propertius, and it is more or less the same as that of Horace in *Odes* 1.16.
The assertion of similarity functions as a figure related to metaphor in
the larger context of the poem; but, in virtue of its inherent incom-
pleteness in its immediate context, it functions as a type of synecdoche.
Of course, all of these poets also used exempla in the traditional way
as an ornamental expansion or illustration, but such a use is notably
infrequent, not only in Catullus, but also in Propertius and Tibullus.
It returns as the major use of mythic material in the poetry of Ovid.

Extended similes of the type examined in Catullus are very rare
in Propertius and Tibullus. The figure of extended simile was too
heavy and ornate, too distracting, to be used in love-poetry that purported to be personal statement. In fact, there are only two extended
similes in Propertius,[1] and both function in the same way as those of
Catullus: that is, they provide a secondary language into which the
poet transfers and by means of which he expresses indirectly ideas
which are not expressed in primary language. One of them ends the

1. See Williams (1968), pp. 776–78.

poem 2.15 (as the simile ends poem 65 of Catullus):[2] that poem begins with cries of happiness as the poet recollects, on the morning after, the night (probably the first) spent with Cynthia. In the final simile the picture of withered petals floating in the wine-bowls creates a general sense of decay and loss which, in pathos, goes far beyond the poet's tentative apprehension that the lovers may die tomorrow. In poem 3.15 the simile depicts a storm passing out to sea; and its dying away is made precise in a detail of the sound of the shingle dying along the shore. This detail enacts the collapse of Antiope at the final act that breaks her—rejection by her sons. The collapse is not otherwise mentioned in the context, though it is understood.[3]

But, apart from similes, Propertius and the rest of these poets often use mythical exempla in a way that is analogous to the use of the myth of Laudamia by Catullus. Some of the most interesting of these will be examined in what follows, though some uses of the technique, which would be relevant here, will be considered in a following chapter on the use of thematic anticipation. The threefold classification used here is intended more to organise the material than to establish rigid categories, but there are three basic techniques which it is useful to distinguish at least in broad terms.

First there is the technique, derived from Catullus 68, of using a *paradeigma* to say much more in secondary language than is said in the primary context, or even to substitute completely for the primary context. Secondly, there is a technique of using elements, often unspoken, in the *paradeigmata* to anticipate and legitimate themes which arise later in the poem. Thirdly, there is a technique of making use of elements in the *paradeigmata*, which may be explicit or unspoken, to alter the movement of ideas: the poet can use the *paradeigma* ostensibly to expand or illustrate something just said, but then move out from the *paradeigma* in an entirely new direction, using some apparently accidental element in the *paradeigma* to legitimate the new theme. All of these techniques are clearly closely related, in that all of them depend on the fact that more is said in the *paradeigma* than is otherwise said in the context or exhausted in the immediate context (so that there is an excess of adequacy); furthermore, in each type the reader

2. On poem 2.15, see further pp. 163 ff. below.
3. On poem 3.15, see further pp. 68 ff. below.

needs to infer or reconstruct *e sequentibus praecedentia* the things that have not been said.

1. ∼ *to Substitute in Part or in Whole for a Primary Context*

Except for the first three poems, which may consequently be the latest compositions, the first book of Propertius' elegies shows little other than a fairly traditional paradigmatic use of myth. But one of these poems is worth noticing.[4]

The elegy 1.15 begins with the poet's anger at Cynthia's *perfidia*: he is in danger (2), he is frightened (3), and she is slow to visit him, spending time instead on her toilette. He suspects (8) that she is making herself up for a new lover. But, a reader may ask, what is the betrayal? What is the danger? There is no answer; instead the poet rehearses a series of mythical exempla (9–22):

at non sic Ithaci digressu mota Calypso	
desertis olim fleverat aequoribus:	10
multos illa dies incomptis maesta capillis	
sederat, iniusto multa locuta salo,	
et quamvis numquam post haec visura, dolebat	
illa tamen, longae conscia laetitiae.	14
nec sic Aesoniden rapientibus anxia ventis	17
Hypsipyle vacuo constitit in thalamo:	18
Hypsipyle nullos post illos sensit amores,	19
ut semel Haemonio tabuit hospitio.	20
Alphesiboea suos ulta est pro coniuge fratres,	15
sanguinis et cari vincula rupit amor.	16
coniugis Evadne miseros elata per ignis	21
occidit, Argivae fama pudicitiae.	

'But Calypso was different when, stricken by the departure of the Ithacan, she wept long ago by the deserted ocean: for many days, sad, her hair dishevelled, she sat there, speaking often to the cruel sea, and, though she was destined never again to see him, yet she grieved, remembering their long happiness (14). Different too was Hypsipyle as, distraught when the winds carried off the son of Aeson [Jason], she stood in the empty bedroom: Hypsipyle knew no love

---

4. Steele Commager (1974), pp. 12–16, discusses poem 1.13 and makes a convincing case for reading more into the mythical references than is made explicit by the poet.

again once she pined away after entertaining the Thessalian (20). Alphesiboea exacted vengeance, on behalf of her husband, from her own brothers, and love broke the chains of kindred blood (16).[5] Evadne, glory of Argive chastity, perished, finding her own funeral on the sad pyre of her husband (22).'

The myth of Calypso already suggests an unmentioned feature of the situation in the one word (9) *digressu* ('departure'): Calypso grieved over a departure. So did Hypsipyle; but a point is here added which takes up the 'new lover' of line 4: she never made love again. Alphesiboea actually killed her brothers because they had killed her husband. Finally, Evadne committed suicide on her husband's pyre. The myths reach a crescendo of devotion, and in the last two the husband dies. By this climax the myths enforce what is never said: the poet is seriously ill and (in his own estimation) likely to die. But that assumption is left to the reader. The only conclusion the poet draws is that Cynthia has not been inspired by the examples of these women (23–24). The poem is a dramatic monologue,[6] for there is a pause here (after line 24) during which the reader must suppose that Cynthia protests and swears her loyalty. The poet rejects her protests (25 ff.). Then she grows pale and weeps between lines 38 and 39. The poet is overcome (41, *quis ego nunc pereo*) and gives in—ending the poem by implicitly retracting his accusations.

Here the assertions of (dis-) similarity in the series of myths are arbitrary in the sense that the myths are over-adequate and not legitimated by the context until the reader has read beyond them. Then they surrender their information, *e sequentibus praecedentia*.

In poem 2.13 (a complex poem which will be discussed as a whole later) (pp. 125 ff.), a myth is used in Catullan fashion to take the place of a primary statement. The poet gives detailed instructions for his funeral (18–42). Then suddenly he wishes that he were dead and wonders why his life is prolonged (45–52):

> nam quo tam dubiae servetur spiritus horae?
> Nestoris est visus post tria saecla cinis:

5. This couplet (15–16) has clearly been displaced in the MSS, and this simple transposition (required to avoid separating the connexion of 9, *non sic*, and 17, *nec sic*) is universally accepted.

6. On the technique of dramatic monologue, see chapter 7, section 1.

> cui si longaevae minuisset fata senectae
>   Gallicus Iliacis miles in aggeribus,
> non ille Antilochi vidisset corpus humari,
>   diceret aut 'O mors, cur mihi sera venis?'   50
> tu tamen amisso non numquam flebis amico:
>   fas est praeteritos semper amare viros.

'Why should the breath of this fleeting life be preserved? Only after three generations were Nestor's ashes seen, but if a Phrygian soldier on the ramparts of Troy had lessened the doom of his long-drawn old age, he would not have seen the corpse of Antilochus being buried or said "O death, why come to me so late?" (50) But you shall sometimes weep for your friend when you have lost him: eternal love is the due of dead husbands.'

Here Nestor is a figure for the poet's unhappiness, which is not mentioned in this poem—its basis is to be inferred from four preceding poems (8–11).[7] This is a characteristically Catullan technique for avoiding a theme which, if treated in primary statement, would need concrete explanation and would disrupt the structure of the complex whole. The reader is left to infer the omitted theme for himself. But the myth here is also used in the third way defined above: to make a transition of thought (see sec. 3 below). For the mention of Antilochus' death and Nestor's grief legitimates the movement to Cynthia's grief —with the implication that she will know her true feelings too late.

In poem 2.16 the myths are more complex. Cynthia has deserted the poet for a *praetor* back from Illyria: she loves gifts[8] and through them he has bought her. The poet warns her (29–42):

> aspice quid donis Eriphyla invenit amaris,
>   arserit et quantis nupta Creusa malis.   30
> nullane sedabit nostros iniuria fletus?
>   an dolor hic vitiis nescit abesse tuis?
> tot iam abiere dies, cum me nec cura theatri
>   nec tetigit Campi, nec mea mensa iuvat.
> at pudeat certe, pudeat!—nisi forte, quod aiunt,   35
>   turpis amor surdis auribus esse solet.
> cerne ducem, modo qui fremitu complevit inani
>   Actia damnatis aequora militibus:

---

7. On this type of connexion in Book 2 of Propertius, see p. 129 below.
8. The theme of *munera* goes right through the poem and unifies it.

> hunc infamis amor versis dare terga carinis
>> iussit et extremo quaerere in orbe fugam.   40
> Caesaris haec virtus et gloria Caesaris haec est:
>> illa, qua vicit, condidit arma manu.

'See what Eriphyle got from gifts that turned bitter, and with what agony the bride Creusa burned (30). Shall no outrage done to me quiet my weeping? Is this pain incapable of dissociating itself from your sins? So many days have now passed, and no interest in theatre or Campus has roused me, nor does food please me. But certainly she should feel shame, she should feel shame—unless, as they say (35), shameful love has deaf ears. See the commander, who recently filled the waters of Actium with vain cries as his soldiers were doomed: infamous love made him turn his ships and flee and seek refuge at the ends of the earth (40). This is the greatness of Caesar and this his glory: with that same hand by which he conquered he put away the sword.'

The poem ends with the poet cursing the praetor's gifts and warning Cynthia that Juppiter will sooner or later punish perjury (43–56). The couplet on Augustus (41–42) is usually condemned as irrelevant flattery. If so, that is not at all in the manner of Propertius. But the difficulty goes back to the earlier *paradeigmata*. It is true that Eriphyle (who sent her husband to his death for a necklace) was killed by one of her sons. But what she really earned was not so much death as eternal infamy: her name became synonymous with greed and shame. On the other hand, Creusa was innocent of anything other than stealing Jason from Medea; here, therefore, the poet is, as it were, Medea, and this is a threat to Cynthia. Then for two couplets the poet indulges self-pity (31–34). The following couplet (35–36) seems nowadays to be normally understood as self-address: the poet should be ashamed; his is a *turpis amor*. If so, then in the exemplum, Antony is the poet and Cleopatra is Cynthia—and Augustus is, indeed, irrelevant. But if lines 35–36 are treated as angry in tone (which the words most naturally suggest), then the shame arises out of the first myth of Eriphyle, and the *turpis amor* is Cynthia's with the praetor. In that case, Antony is Cynthia and Augustus is the poet—so to speak. This interpretation produces coherence. For in the second myth the poet threatens Cynthia; but, as he reflects on *turpis amor*, he praises Augustus for *clementia*, and this theme leads him to end the poem by resolving not to exact vengeance on Cynthia himself (this is unsaid) but to turn her over to Juppiter for punishment. The transitions in thought are unspoken: they are inherent, first in the two myths which introduce the themes of shame and vengeance, and then in the exempla of Antony and Augustus, which alter the direction of those two themes by an easy metonymic movement from Antony as the shameless lover to Antony as responsible for civil war (Augustus is then praised as the man who brought civil war to an end). Thus, from the myths the reader must infer themes that are not made explicit; and from the exempla of Antony and Augustus, not only must the transition of thought be recognised in the crucial figure of Augustus, but, the unspoken resolve of the poet to be clement must be reconstructed from it also.

Poem 2.20 opens with a question: why is Cynthia weeping more bitterly than Briseis parted from Achilles or Andromache taken into slavery? Then a couplet makes the question specific (3–4): why does she think the poet is unfaithful? She is weeping more than Philomela (5–6) or Niobe (7–8). The poet swears that he has been, is, and will be faithful; and, if he should forget Cynthia's kindness, may the Furies torture, and Aeacus condemn him; and may he suffer the penalties of Tityos and Sisyphus (29–32). It is not at all reassuring here that the poet thinks of Tityos and Sisyphus, both associated with rape and seduction. At least at that point, if not before, the four arbitrary assertions of similarity, with which the poem opens, have a meaning additional to their function as ornamental illustrations of bitter grief. Not only did every one of the women the poet mentions have something real and serious to lament, but of the first two women whose names occur to the poet one had lost a lover, the other a husband. It does not help either that, immediately after mentioning Niobe, the poet, to illustrate how much he desires Cynthia, figures her as Danae in a brass tower; for then the assertion that he would break into the tower casts him as the adulterous Juppiter. In fact, the myths that occur to the poet in this poem have an obvious primary meaning in the poet's protestations of innocence; but their further meaning, noticed only when the arbitrary nature of the assertions of similarity is given weight, speaks against the poet and betrays him out of his own mouth. And, indeed, in the next three poems the poet will be found to be unfaithful.[9]

In poem 3.15 the poet speaks of a very early affair with Lycinna, who seems to be Cynthia's maid. The poem opens with an ominous hope that there will be no rift between Cynthia and the poet. Then (3–

9. See note 8 above.

10) he tells how, when he first came of age, Lycinna instructed him in the art of love. It is now three years since then and he cannot remember ten words spoken between them—love of Cynthia has blotted out every other interest. Then, with the words (11) *testis erit Dirce*, comes the story of Antiope told in thirty-two lines. When it ends (42) with the killing of Dirce, a couplet (43–44) warns Cynthia not to harm Lycinna, and a final couplet (45–46) asserts the poet's love of Cynthia even beyond death.

Editors try three ways of settling the problem that *testis erit Dirce* does not illustrate anything which has been said in the poem so far (1–10). They suppose a lacuna before line 11; or they variously transpose the ending of the poem to this point; or they search for some psychological explanation. But this is a very clear example of the technique of using a *paradeigma* to substitute for a statement in primary language that has to be reconstructed from the whole context by the reader. It is the technique of Catullus in using the legend of Laudamia in poem 68. Here the legend takes the place of a moral disquisition by the poet against jealousy, and a stern warning of punishment if Cynthia harms Lycinna. It is exactly the technique, too, by which Horace substituted Thyestes for Atreus in *Odes* 1.16: the unexpected opening with Dirce, instead of Antiope, concentrates on the threat directed at Cynthia, for Cynthia is figured as Dirce (while Lycinna is Antiope). In this poem the poet is concerned to give artistic treatment to the legend: so it is told in significant detail, in the best Hellenistic style, with lively entrances by the poet into his own story, as if the events were happening at the very moment when he recounts them. These details are clearly significant only for the story and not for the context; here there is no temptation, let alone compulsion, as there is with the Laudamia-legend in Catullus 68, to reconstruct an elaborate pattern of correspondences with the larger context. The closest parallel with the myth in this poem is the exemplum of Cleopatra in 3.11, where the exemplum is legitimated by the context but is then treated for its own sake.[10] What the poem 3.15 does most successfully is to allow the immediate crisis between the poet and Cynthia to emerge gradually and indirectly by the technique of dramatic monologue. The relationship of the myth to the general context is both paradigmatic and also synecdochic (*e sequentibus praecedentia*).

10. The same technique can be seen to be used by Horace in *Odes* 3.11 and 27.

Examples of this technique in Horace's *Odes* are generally simple, if subtle, and this is certainly due in part to the brevity constrained on the poet by the demands of the small, highly wrought poetic form. For instance, in *Odes* 3.7 the go-between tells the faithful Gyges the myths of Sthenoboea and Hippolyte (13–18); these myths are not only designed to convey a warning to Gyges, but they also make clear to the reader what is not otherwise mentioned in the text: Chloe, the woman in the case, is married. The technique is more difficult and more imaginative in *Odes* 1.34. The ode begins with the poet confessing error in being an adherent of an 'insane philosophy' and in failing to worship the gods. The explanation follows with an impressive (5) *namque*: he saw lightning and heard thunder from a cloudless sky. A grandiose stanza (9–12) extends the echoes of the thunder from one side of the world to the other. The poem then ends thus (12–16):

> valet ima summis
>
> mutare et insignem attenuat deus,
> obscura promens: hinc apicem rapax
> fortuna cum stridore acuto
> sustulit, hic posuisse gaudet.

'God has the power to interchange the lowest with the highest, and he makes less the splendid as he promotes the obscure: from this ⟨man⟩ grasping Fortune has, with shrill scream, removed the mitre, on this ⟨man⟩ she rejoices to have set it.'

The final idea depends upon the famous story of Tarquinius Priscus, who was persuaded by his ambitious wife, Tanaquil, to leave Tarquinii and try his luck in Rome; as they came by the Janiculum an eagle swooped down, took the mitred cap (*apex*) from his head, and then, flying down again, replaced it on his head. His wife recognised the omen: Juppiter intended him to be king of Rome.[11] The poet has converted this story into a statement that Fortune crowns and uncrowns kings; the myth is left to be understood from *rapax* (the bird of prey) and *stridore acuto* (the familiar scream of air through wings as a large bird swoops). Thus, with great deftness, exemplum and primary statement are combined to gener-

---

11. Cicero *de legibus* 1.4 and Livy 1.34.8. The allusive brevity of Cicero shows this to have been a commonplace story.

alise the power of God as widely as possible in an assertion that relies upon, or is constructed from, a famous single instance. There is another point that emerges from this interpretation of the exemplum. It is often stated that Horace here identifies *deus* and *Fortuna*.[12] Not so. The antique (5) *Diespiter* is not an ornamental archaism: it marks the tone of (mock-) heroic religiosity.[13] But this is a poem that moves from humour to seriousness at the end. So when this mock-heroic word is taken up by the simple *deus*, the tone becomes solemn. That *Fortuna* is not identical with *deus*, but is rather his agent or messenger, is to be deduced both from the myth and from the wording by which *Fortuna* is cast as the eagle, recognised by Tanaquil as the messenger of Juppiter. Important ideas, therefore, are to be extracted from the actual allusion to the myth that are not expressed in the rest of the poem; this is done with the utmost brevity and artistry at the same time as a convincing closure to the poem is achieved.

More difficult again is *Odes* 1.7, where the concluding myth of Teucer is substituted for a primary context that would explain what is meant by Plancus' (18) *tristitiam vitaeque labores*. That is the kind of riddling allusion designed to alert a reader to a theme that is inadequately worked out in its immediate context. It is only by assimilating the situation of Teucer (which is not mentioned, let alone explained) to that of Plancus that the meaning becomes clear: the poet is making oblique allusion to Plancus' loss of a brother under tragic circumstances in the proscriptions of 42 B.C.[14]

2. ~ *to Legitimate Later Thematic Material*

Propertius occasionally uses a technique of drawing, as it were, at a later stage in a poem on accumulated, but undeclared, reserves in mythic deposits made at an earlier stage of the same poem. This is a conspicuous technique in poem 1.3. There the poet arrives very late and drunk to find Cynthia asleep. The poem opens with a grand assertion of similarity (1–8):

> Qualis Thesea iacuit cedente carina
>   languida desertis Cnosia litoribus;

12. Nisbet and Hubbard (1970), pp. 377, 385.
13. Cf. *Odes* 3.2.29 (p. 187 below).
14. See Williams (1968), pp. 83–86.

> qualis et accubuit primo Cepheia somno
>   libera iam duris cotibus Andromede;
> nec minus assiduis Edonis fessa choreis
>   qualis in herboso concidit Apidano:
> talis visa mihi mollem spirare quietem
>   Cynthia non certis nixa caput manibus . . .

'Like the Cretan woman when she lay swooning on the deserted shores as
Theseus fled in his ship; and like Andromeda as she slept her first sleep, freed
now from the hard[15] rocks; and like the Bacchante as she collapsed by the
grassy Apidanus, no less wearied by her continuous dancing—so Cynthia met
my eyes as she breathed in gentle sleep, propping her head on unstable
hands . . .'

The exempla clearly go far beyond the needs of the immediate context. But already, in the conclusion drawn by the poet, an anticipated
theme appears (which has sometimes even been emended away). Cynthia's hands are an unstable prop; yet hands are not unstable for people
who have laid themselves down properly to sleep. The poem ends (41–
46) with Cynthia's description of her trying every way to keep awake
and finally simply falling unconscious—another link with the women in
the exempla, all of whom suffered physically and emotionally before
collapsing. The poet's observation of the detail about her hands anticipates her own account at the end.

The poet is then tempted to make love to her (11–18), and this episode, too, is anticipated in the exemplum of Ariadne, with whom Bacchus
fell in love when he found her asleep and deserted by Theseus. But the
poet is afraid of her (18) *saevitia*, and does not dare. In these words he portrays her as something of a Bacchante, easily aroused to frenzy. When
Cynthia is finally awoken by the moon shining on her eyes (33), she displays just that quality of frenzy in her furious address to the poet. At that
point another connexion with the exempla appears; for Cynthia knows
quite well that the poet has been unfaithful to her, and she describes herself as having felt deserted (43, *mecum deserta querebar*): that connects
directly with the opening *paradeigma*, that of Ariadne.

There is another minor mythic anticipation. When the poet feared to
disturb Cynthia, he watched her instead (19–20) 'with eyes as intently
fixed on her as Argus on the strange horns of the daughter of Inachus'.

---

15. That is, normally impossible to sleep on.

The reference to Io and the jealousy of Juno is exploited ten lines later, because the jealous poet imagines Cynthia dreaming of being made love to by someone else (30).

Of the three major exempla with which the poem opens, Andromeda works least for her place: she figures the sleep of Cynthia, and, in the verb (3) *accubuit*, which normally has erotic connotations, suggestively anticipates the poet's erotic temptation. All of them figure her beauty, and the Bacchante her swiftness to fury; but Ariadne, placed first, plays the most important part. None of this can be known to the reader till the whole poem has been read, but the arbitrary nature of the opening assertions of similarity enjoins suspension of judgment and reconstruction *e sequentibus praecedentia.*

The appearance of a rival opens the poem 2.9, and the poet is expansively indignant (1–46):

> Iste quod est, ego saepe fui; sed fors et in hora
>   hoc ipso eiecto carior alter erit.
> Penelope poterat bis denos salva per annos
>   vivere, tam multis femina digna procis;
> coniugium falsa poterat differre Minerva,   5
>   nocturno solvens texta diurna dolo;
> visura et quamvis numquam speraret Ulixem,
>   illum expectando facta remansit anus.
> nec non exanimem amplectens Briseis Achillem
>   candida vesana verberat ora manu;   10
> et dominum lavit maerens captiva cruentum,
>   propositum flavis in Simoente vadis,
> foedavitque comas, et tanti corpus Achilli
>   maximaque in parva sustulit ossa manu;
> cum tibi nec Peleus aderat nec caerula mater,   15
>   Scyria nec viduo Deidamia toro.
> tunc igitur veris gaudebat Graecia nuptis,
>   tunc etiam felix inter et arma pudor.
> at tu non una potuisti nocte vacare,
>   impia, non unum sola manere diem!   20
> quin etiam multo duxistis pocula risu;
>   forsitan et de me verba fuere mala.
> hic etiam petitur, qui te prius ipse reliquit:
>   di faciant isto capta fruare viro!
> haec mihi vota tuam propter suscepta salutem,   25
>   cum capite hoc Stygiae iam poterentur aquae,

et lectum flentes circum staremus amici?
  hic ubi tum, pro di, perfida, quisve fuit?
quis si longinquos retinerer miles ad Indos,
  aut mea si staret navis in Oceano?   30
sed vobis facile est verba et componere fraudes:
  hoc unum didicit femina semper opus.
non sic incerto mutantur flamine Syrtes,
  nec folia hiberno tam tremefacta Noto,
quam cito feminea non constat foedus in ira,   35
  sive ea causa gravis sive ea causa levis.
nunc, quoniam ista tibi placuit sententia, cedam:
  tela, precor, pueri, promite acuta magis,
figite certantes atque hanc mihi solvite vitam:
  sanguis erit vobis maxima palma meus.   40
sidera sunt testes et matutina pruina
  et furtim misero ianua aperta mihi,
te nihil in vita nobis acceptius umquam:
  nunc quoque erit, quamvis sis inimica, nihil.
nec domina ulla meo ponet vestigia lecto: 45
  solus ero, quoniam non licet esse tuum.

'I have often been what that man is; yet even within the hour this very man
may be ejected and another held dearer. Penelope was able to live true for
twenty years, a woman attractive to so many suitors; she was able to fend off
marriage with pretended weaving (5), unravelling in nightly deceit the cloth
woven by day; and, although she never expected to see Ulysses again, she stayed there and became an old woman waiting for him. And, again, Briseis, em-
bracing the dead Achilles, beat her fair face with frenzied hand (10), and, a captive mourning over her blood-stained master, she laid him out and washed him
in the yellow waters of Simois, and filthied her hair, and held in that small hand
the body of the huge Achilles and his enormous bones—when there was no
Peleus and no sea-blue mother to help you [Achilles] (15) and no Deidamia of
Scyros from her widowed bed. So at that time Greece rejoiced in true wives,
at that time even at war chastity flourished. But you could not be without a
man for one night, disloyal woman, nor alone for a single day (20). You both
laughed long as you drank, and probably even spoke ill of me. You even went
and begged this fellow, though he took the initiative in leaving you before:
heaven grant you enjoy being subjected to such a man! What about the vows
I undertook for your recovery (25) when the Stygian waters were alredy closing over your head, and we, your friends, stood weeping about your bed?
Where was this fellow then, damn it!, traitress, and who was he ⟨to you⟩?
What if I were to be detained on military service against distant Indians, or

if my ship were becalmed on Ocean (30)? But it is easy for you women to invent words and deceits: in this one occupation woman has always been specially skilled. Not so quickly is Syrtes changed by the shifting blast, nor so swiftly are the leaves shaken by the winter southwind, as a solemn pledge is broken when a woman is angry (35), whether the reason for it be weighty or whether the reason for it be light. As it is, since that is the decision you have made, I shall give up: bring out yet sharper arrows, Cupids; vie in piercing me and free me from this life—my blood shall be your finest trophy (40). The stars are my witnesses and the frosts at dawn and the door stealthily opened in pity to let me in, that nothing in life has ever been dearer to me than you: even now there will be nothing, however hostile you are to me. No mistress shall leave her tracks on my bed (45): I shall live alone since I cannot be yours.'

The first couplet makes one think that the poem will be about the rival, so that the *paradeigmata* seem at first sight to be without connexion. In fact the first couplet has two functions: one is to legitimate the ending of the poem (47–52), which will be discussed in a later chapter (see p. 166); the other is to set up the theme of fickleness. But the reader cannot realise the real import of the couplet till he has read lines 19 ff. This is, therefore, another example of anticipated theme. The exempla are both unexplained in their context and display an obvious excess of adequacy. Penelope and Briseis are figures to contrast with Cynthia— especially the twenty years of waiting with the failure to wait a single day; that is obvious. But both women are identified as married (17, *nuptis* is a certain correction for MSS *natis*, since 'children' have no point in the context).[16] The relevance of that theme only becomes clear at line 35, *foedus*: here Cynthia is, as often, being treated as if she were married to the poet. So Briseis and Penelope are approximated as closely as possible to her, in all respects except the vital one of the faithfulness they display and she does not.

The poet, however, is the opposite: like Briseis, he did all he could when Cynthia was dying (25–27), and like Penelope, he will spend his

---

16. MSS *natis* with *veris* could give the sense of 'legitimate children'; but this is not the test of faithfulness that the poet has in mind. The emendation *nuptis* (Baehrens) gives the sense of 'real wives', i.e. wives who stuck steadfastly by their husbands. The immediate force of the poet's treatment of Briseis as a wife is weakened by the fact that at this stage the reader can imagine that line 17 refers to Penelope and line 18 to Briseis; the emptiness of that distinction only becomes clear at line 35.

whole life alone (44–46). These themes are inherent in the myths. But that is not all. The poet uses the myths further, for Ulysses and Achilles also are figures for himself. So he imagines himself, like Ulysses, detained far overseas (29–30), and he prays to be dead like Achilles (38–40)—though he uses two Hellenistic erotic epigrams to implore the sort of death appropriate for a lover (see p. 168) rather than a Homeric warrior. In these ways the *paradeigmata* are used as sources of thematic material to anticipate later stages of the poem.

Poem 2.14 opens excitedly with arbitrary assertion of four successive similarities: Agamemnon's joy at his triumph over Troy, Ulysses' at his return to Ithaca, Electra's at recognising Orestes, and Ariadne's at seeing Theseus emerging from the labyrinth (1–8): those joys were less than the poet's the previous night. The elegy is the poet's triumph-song at being admitted to Cynthia's bed. Here the first exemplum is a synecdoche of the whole poem. But it also has a special point, for the poet has achieved this success by behaving like an arrogant conqueror, quite unlike his former role of captive in a triumph (11), and he takes up the triumph-motif specifically in lines 23–28: his victory is finer than a Parthian triumph to him and he will set up a *tropaeum*. Each of the myths has an echo later in the poem: Ulysses in lines 29–32 where the poet's ship is almost in port; Electra in lines 15 ff., in the length of time his suit has taken and the lateness of the recognition, so that the poet feels almost in his grave; and Ariadne, with forebodings for the future, in Cynthia's repulse of the poet's rivals in lines 21–22.

Here the myths anticipate and legitimate the later themes in such a way that their implications are not fully exhausted until the last couplet of the poem. A final example of the technique from Propertius is simpler, though it has caused trouble to commentators.

Poem 2.27 starts from mankind's complaints about the uncertainty of death's coming. Then the poet asserts (11–16):

> solus amans novit quando periturus et a qua
>   morte, neque hic Boreae flabra neque arma timet.
> iam licet et Stygia sedeat sub harundine remex
>   cernat et infernae tristia vela ratis,
> si modo clamantis revocaverit aura puellae,
>   concessum nulla lege redibit iter.

'Only the lover knows when he will perish and by what death: so he fears neither blasts of the northwind nor swords. In fact, though he should be seated at the oar among the reeds of Styx and be gazing at the dismal sails of the underworld ship, if only the faintest breath of his girl's shouting shall recall him, he will make the return journey that no law permits.'

This is an ellipse such that the nature of the lover's death and his certainty about it must be inferred—*e sequentibus praecedentia*—from the image of the underworld and the summons to return. Death comes to the lover when his girl leaves or rejects him. Only the converse of that is stated in the image: even when he is dead, his girl can call him back to life. Here the mythic exemplum of Charon's boat is transformed into primary statement by a technique similar to that of Horace in *Odes* 1.34 (see p. 71) to create an image of special power. It is a total reversal of the Virgilian account of Orpheus and Eurydice.

Horace, though less complex than Propertius, often uses this technique effectively. For instance, in *Odes* 2.4, he addresses a man called Xanthias from Phocis, telling him not to feel shame at being in love with a slave-girl. There follow three mythic examples to reinforce the exhortation: the insolent Achilles was moved by his slave Briseis (2–4); the beauty of the captive Tecmessa moved Ajax (5–6); and Agamemnon, in the midst of his triumph over Troy, was set on fire by the virgin (Cassandra) he carried off (7–12). The argument then goes on: 'You could not tell whether her parents are a credit to you; she certainly laments [the loss of] a royal family and unfair household gods' (13–16). The climactic example of Cassandra, treated at length and from the conqueror's point of view, unobtrusively prepares the ironic theme 'your slave-girl was probably a princess'. The three examples are chosen to legitimate this thematic movement: Briseis is not known to have been a princess (Homer *Iliad* 19.291–94); Tecmessa was a princess, but the poet treats her as a precise parallel to Briseis; it is only with Cassandra that the manner and scale of treatment are altered in such a way that the reader perceives an excess of adequacy to the context which is only satisfied by the new movement of ideas. The use of the figure is characteristically neat and small-scale.

Even more so is that in *Odes* 2.20.13–20:

> iam Daedaleo notior Icaro
> visam gementis litora Bosphori
> Syrtisque Gaetulas canorus
> ales Hyperboreosque campos.

> me Colchus et qui dissimulat metum
> Marsae cohortis Dacus et ultimi
> noscent Geloni, me peritus
> discet Hiber Rhodanique potor.

'Soon, better known than Icarus son of Daedalus, I shall visit the shores of lamenting Bosphorus and the Gaetulian Syrtes and the plains of the Hyperboreans, a tuneful bird. The Colchian and the Dacian who conceals his fear of Italian troops shall know of me; the Spaniard and he who drinks the Rhone shall
expertly learn me by heart.'

Here (13) *notior* has frequently been emended to produce the idea of
safety rather than fame, since Icarus' fame was posthumous—a theme
echoed by the adjective (14) *gementis* applied to the Bosphorus. But not
only is it true that the poet's fame will be posthumus like that of Icarus,
it will also be far more extensive—as witnessed by the list of names that
cover the whole Roman empire (whereas Icarus' memory is confined to
the Bosphorus). This theme is taken up not only by the wide-spreading
names, but also by the echoing verb *noscent*. Thus the anticipatory
adjective (13) *notior*, over-adequate to its immediate context to such
an extent that it can even appear (paradoxically) senseless, enforces a
suspension of judgment throughout the two stanzas it introduces.

Odes 4.4 opens with a grand double simile like those in Catullus
68.[17] Three stanzas picture a young eagle ready to make his first attack
(1–12); then the simpler and briefer picture of a young lion about to kill
a newly weaned kid (13–16) leads straight into the major context of
Drusus' attack on the Vindelici. The insistent over-adequacy of the
eagle-simile, however, is not satisfied till lines 25–36 (which signal the
connexion by the thematic echo 32, *aquilae*), where the essential ideas of
training and inheritance are explored by the poet in the relationship of
Augustus to his adoptive sons, Drusus and Tiberius. Only in this wider
context can not only the whole simile but even the details of (1) *minis-
trum fulminis* and (2) *rex deorum* and (3) *expertus fidelem* be seen to work
to the full. The signal for a suspension of judgment here is the way in
which the extensive simile comes to an end and is then replaced without
a pause by a briefer, more conventional simile that is fully exhausted
within its own immediate context.

17. See Williams (1968), pp. 750–53.

Odes 4.12 opens with a detailed picture of the delights of spring (1–12). This happy scene is oddly broken by what should have been the charming detail of the nesting swallow; this, however, is not described factually, but is allusively treated by means of the sinister legend of Procne and Philomela, and the poet's tone becomes solemn and doom-laden. This curious tonal change between two stanzas filled with the pleasures of spring remains unsatisfied until the final stanza of the poem, where the poet's thoughts turn to life's end and the black flames of the funeral pyre (26), though this tone is itself momentarily anticipated in the function, attributed to wine, of washing away (19–20) *amara curarum*, 'the bitterness of anxiety'. The mythic anticipation of that theme strikingly mediates what is otherwise a surprising juxtaposition of tones in this short poem ranging from broad humour to morbid fear of death.

3. ～ *to Alter the Movement of Thought*

Poem 1.2 of Propertius begins with what seems to be a conventional lecture to Cynthia against using make-up: (4) why does she need to sell herself with gifts (*muneribus*) from abroad, and (5) ruin the beauty of nature with bought (*mercato*) make-up? Examples follow to show that the earth, plants, water, shores, and birds use no artifice. Then, with *non sic* picking up line 6, the poet asserts (15–32):

> non sic Leucippis succendit Castora Phoebe,
>   Pollucem cultu non Hilaira soror;
> non, Idae et cupido quondam discordia Phoebo,
>   Eveni patriis filia litoribus;
> nec Phrygium falso traxit candore maritum
>   avecta externis Hippodamia rotis: 20
> sed facies aderat nullis obnoxia gemmis,
>   qualis Apelleis est color in tabulis.
> non illis studium vulgo conquirere amantis:
>   illis ampla satis forma pudicitia.
> non ego nunc vereor ne sim tibi vilior istis: 25
>   uni si qua placet, culta puella sat est;
> cum tibi praesertim Phoebus sua carmina donet
>   Aoniamque libens Calliopea lyram,
> unica nec desit iucundis gratia verbis,
>   omnia quaeque Venus, quaeque Minerva probat.   30

> his tu semper eris nostrae gratissima vitae,
> taedia dum miserae sint tibi luxuriae.

'Not like that, with make-up, did Phoebe, daughter of Leucippus, set Castor aflame, nor Hilaira, her sister, Pollux; nor did the daughter of Evenus, once by her father's banks a cause of war between Idas and Phoebus; nor with counterfeit beauty did Hippodamia attract a Phrygian husband as she rode away on foreign wheels (20). But their beauty was indebted to no jewels; it was like the colour you find in paintings of Apelles. They had no wish to hunt for lovers in public: they considered chastity beauty enough. In saying all this, I am not worried that you will consider me more worthless than you-know-who (25): if a girl finds favour with one man, she is sufficiently made-up—especially since in your case Phoebus has endowed you with his poetry and Calliopea has been gracious to give you her Aonian lyre; and a unique grace adorns your charming voice; and ⟨you have⟩ everything that Venus, everything that Minerva values (30). With those endowments you will always find most favour with me as long as I live—provided you despise wretched fripperies.'

The myths in lines 15–20 clearly go far beyond what the context warrants. Further, they introduce a surprising element, made explicit by the word (17) *discordia*. The two daughters of Leucippus did not simply attract Castor and Pollux; they were already betrothed to Idas and Lynceus. In the ensuing battle, Castor, Idas, and Lynceus were all killed. The same Idas (at an earlier time, of course) had fought with Apollo over Marpessa, daughter of Evenus. Hippodamia certainly attracted Pelops; but she had also (in one version of the legend) attracted her own father, and she only rode off with Pelops at the cost of her father's death. So the myths start with the idea that unadorned beauty is enough, but, as it were, get out of hand and end up demonstrating that a beauty such as Cynthia's, even unadorned, is enough to cause murderous jealousy. They are arranged in ascending order of horror: in the first, two men and a hero die; in the second, a god and a man figure, fighting; in the third, a father is killed by treachery.

The poet clearly intended this movement of thought, because he leads out of the myths (23–24) with a new and surprising assertion: these mythical girls had no wish to procure lots of lovers for themselves (the word *vulgo* comes close to implying prostitution, certainly wantonness). The assertion could be based on the unexpected implication of the myths: 'if they caused jealousy, at least they did so unintentionally'. But, in fact, the assertion takes up and gives point to disturbing words in the poem's opening lines: (4) *muneribus* and (5) *mercato*. The poet, it now appears, was not just lecturing Cynthia on make-up for her own good; what concerned him was the reason for her making-up—her wish to be unfaithful to him. So he now (24) asserts that chastity was beauty enough for the mythical girls. Thus one thing the myths have done has been to enable him to substitute the concept of unchastity for 'make-up' in his argument. But they have also supplied the theme of jealousy: so the poet now denies that he feels any—here (25) *istis* 'you-know-who' is to be defined out of (23) *vulgo conquirere amantes*. It hardly needs saying that the reader does not need to believe the poet: jealousy is exactly what he does feel and is the originating motive of the poem. After this claim, making use of the now established equivalence of 'lack of make-up' and 'chastity', he asserts (26) 'if a girl finds favour with one man, she is made-up enough'. This does not mean 'when there happens to be one man who approves a girl', but 'the girl who finds favour with no more than one man' (that is, a girl who does not look to attract others—*vulgo conquirere amantes*).

What is notable here is that unstated features in the *paradeigmata* legitimate a totally new movement of ideas; and this picks up an idea that lurked in the opening of the poem: make-up is evidence of unfaithfulness. The myths supply the motivation of the poet: he is jealous. The myths also have another function which should be classified with the preceding category: they look towards and anticipate the end of the poem. A minor aspect of this is the anticipation of the entrance of Apollo (27) by his appearance in the myths. More important is the ending of the poem. What motivates the final declaration of lifelong devotion, linked to the chastity (lack of make-up) of Cynthia? Cynthia might well reply to the poet's lecture: 'Fine: but how can I be sure of you?' That theme, too, is anticipated in the myths; for, in the contest between Idas and Phoebus, Marpessa chose Idas in preference to Phoebus, fearing that the god would desert her when she grew old. There is no reason to deny that that aspect of the myth influenced the poet's choice and should be recognised by the reader. This is another example of thematic anticipation: a hint that occurs at an earlier stage of a poem is exploited later on. As in line 23 the poet anticipates an unspoken objection raised by his mythic *paradeigmata*, so in the final couplet he answers an unspoken query by Cynthia, using a theme that was implicit in one of the myths. But that theme has in fact already begun to be raised in the poet's listing of Cynthia's particular qualities that he admires (27–30)—all are unharmed by the ageing process. On analysis, then, the myths begin by seeming to bear an obvious metaphoric relationship to the context but end up displaying metonymic (that is, synecdochic) relations to a wider context of the poem.

But the most complex examples of this technique are in the second book of Propertius. The poem 2.6, like 1.3, opens with a series of three comparisons (1–8):

> Non ita complebant Ephyraeae Laidos aedis,
>   ad cuius iacuit Graecia tota fores;
> turba Menandreae fuerat nec Thaidos olim
>   tanta, in qua populus lusit Ericthonius;
> nec quae deletas potuit componere Thebas,   5
>   Phryne tam multis facta beata viris.
> quin etiam falsos fingis tibi saepe propinquos,
>   oscula nec desunt qui tibi iure ferant.

'Not in such numbers did they fill the house of Lais at Corinth, before whose doors all Greece lay prostrate; nor did Menandrian Thais, in whom the people of Athens took its pleasure, have so great a crowd of admirers long ago; nor was Phryne, who could have rebuilt ruined Thebes(5), enriched by so many men. Why, you even invent crowds of false relatives and you are never short of those who have a right to kiss you.'

The surprise opening is not explained; the reader is left to infer its meaning from the final couplet quoted above. Cynthia's house has been crowded with admirers. The poet then explains, in apology, that he is jealous—even of the kisses of a mother or a sister (9–14). His words serve to lighten the weight of any accusation on Cynthia, for the reader would certainly understand that the famous Greek courtesans, Lais, Thais, and Phryne, are simply figures for Cynthia. In that case, the poet would be accusing Cynthia of being unfaithful. But the poem now takes an unexpected turn (15–18):

> his olim, ut fama est, vitiis ad proelia ventum est,
>   his Troiana vides funera principiis;
> aspera Centauros eadem dementia iussit
>   frangere in adversum pocula Pirithoum.

'Through these vices in earlier times, so the story goes, men went to war, you can see these as the origins of the deaths at Troy; the same insanity bade the Centaurs break embossed cups on Pirithous, now their enemy.'

The unexpected reference to 'vices' is seen, on reflection, to be legitimated by the opening comparisons. The arbitrary assertions of similarity there seemed at first to lay weight on Lais, Thais, and Phryne; but they merely concealed another element in the assertion of similarity that is only implicit—their customers. The apology (9–14) shifts blame away from Cynthia and consequently the women in the comparisons. Then the words *his vitiis* identifies their customers as the culprits; man's sexual lust is at fault. The myths in lines 15–18 complete the change of direction: in the myth of Troy both Paris and Helen were guilty (perhaps Helen less so), but Hippodamia was totally innocent and the crime was male. The poet then continues (19–42):

> cur exempla petam Graium? tu criminis auctor,
>> nutritus duro, Romule, lacte lupae: 20
> tu rapere intactas docuisti impune Sabinas;
>> per te nunc Romae quidlibet audet Amor.
> felix Admeti coniunx et lectus Ulixis,
>> et quaecumque viri femina limen amat!
> templa Pudicitiae quid opus statuisse puellis   25
>> si cuivis nuptae quidlibet esse licet?
> quae manus obscenas depinxit prima tabellas
>> et posuit casta turpia visa domo,
> illa puellarum ingenuos corrupit ocellos
>> nequitiaeque suae noluit esse rudis.   30
> a gemat, in terris ista qui protulit arte
>> turpia sub tacita condita laetitia!
> non istis olim variabant tecta figuris:
>> tum paries nullo crimine pictus erat.
> sed non immerito velavit aranea fanum   35
>> et mala desertos occupat herba deos.
> quos igitur tibi custodes, quae limina ponam,
>> quae numquam supra pes inimicus eat?
> nam nihil invitae tristis custodia prodest:
>> quam peccare pudet, Cynthia, tuta sat est.   40
> nos uxor numquam, numquam seducet amica:
>> semper amica mihi, semper et uxor eris.

'But why should I seek examples from Greeks? You, Romulus, nurtured on a she-wolf's harsh milk (20), instigated the crime: you showed them how to rape the virgin Sabine girls and get away with it; because of you there is nothing that Love does not now dare in Rome. Lucky the wife of Admetus and the bed of Ulysses, and any woman who loves her husband's threshold!

What good is it for women to have built a temple to Chastity (25), if a married woman is allowed to behave as she likes? The hand that first painted obscene pictures and set up disgraceful objects in a chaste house, that hand corrupted the pure eyes of girls and wanted them versed in its own wickedness (30). May he rue it who by that kind of art brought out into the world lewdnesses that used to be concealed in a pleasure that did not speak! In olden times they used not to decorate houses with such figures: then no wall was painted with a crime. But not without good reason has the spider veiled the temple (35), and weeds overgrow the abandoned gods. So what guards, what doorway can I appoint for you that an enemy foot will not pass? For a stern guard is useless when a girl does not want that: if a girl is ashamed to sin, Cynthia, she is safe enough (40). As for me, never shall a wife, never shall a girl-friend seduce me: you shall for ever be my girl-friend, and for ever my wife.'

The movement of thought is confirmed by the shift to Rome: women are basically innocent but corrupted by men—a theme that can be extracted from the opening comparisons (though only *e sequentibus praecedentia*). Wives who are content with their husbands are happy (the examples are Alcestis and Penelope). The theme of marriage is now maintained: a temple of Chastity is useless if wives are not subject to law. This is another way of expressing the idea that men corrupt women, by asserting, as it were, the corollary of that idea: men have a responsibility to institute laws to control women's behaviour. The idea of corruption by art follows (27–34) and by neglect of religion (35–36). In that case, the poet asks, how can he guard Cynthia against such widespread male corruption (taking the marriage-theme of *limen* from line 24)? She herself does not want to be guarded (that is, she too is infected by the general corruption). The poet ends with a declaration of eternal faithfulness and figures Cynthia as his wife, which takes up and completes the theme of marriage, surprisingly introduced in lines 23–26. This is another good example of anticipating a theme that is only later satisfied, and the poet's own declaration of eternal faithfulness is itself an echo of Roman marital idealism (though normally only expected of the female partner).[18]

Here, then, the arbitrary assertions of similarity, with which the poem opens, conceal another implicit assertion of similarity which only emerges in the course of the whole poem. Also, in lines 15–18, two

18. See Williams (1958), pp. 23–29.

myths are used to produce a change in the movement of ideas that is merely inherent in the myths and not otherwise made explicit.

There is a particularly surprising example of the technique in Propertius 2.8. The poet has had his girl taken from him and justifies his weeping over the loss. He then (11 ff.) thinks of all that he has given to, and done for, Cynthia, and turns to anger mixed with pathos and self-pity (17–40):

> sic igitur prima moriere aetate, Properti?
>> sed morere: interitu gaudeat illa tuo;
> exagitet nostros Manis, sectetur et umbras,
>> insultetque rogis, calcet et ossa mea.   20
> quid? non Antigonae tumulo Boeotius Haemon
>> corruit ipse suo saucius ense latus,
> et sua cum miserae permiscuit ossa puellae
>> qua sine Thebanam noluit ire domum?
> sed non effugies: mecum moriaris oportet;   25
>> hoc eodem ferro stillet uterque cruor.
> quamvis ista mihi mors est inhonesta futura:
>> mors inhonesta quidem, tu moriere tamen.
> ille etiam abrepta desertus coniuge Achilles
>> cessare in tectis pertulit arma sua.   30
> viderat ille fuga stratos in litore Achivos,
>> fervere et Hectorea Dorica castra face;
> viderat informen multa Patroclon harena
>> porrectum et sparsas caede iacere comas,
> omnia formosam propter Briseida passus: 35
>> tantus in erepto saevit amore dolor.
> at postquam sera captiva est reddita poena,
>> fortem illum Haemoniis Hectora traxit equis.
> inferior multo cum sim vel matre vel armis,
>> mirum si de me iure triumphat Amor?

'So then shall you die in your prime of life, Propertius? Yes, die, and let her take pleasure in your death. Let her vex my shades, and harry my ghost, and dance on my pyre, and trample on my bones (20). But then did not Boeotian Haemon collapse on the tomb of Antigone, stabbing his side with his own sword, and mingle his bones with those of the pitiable girl—without whom he had no desire to go to his home in Thebes? But you shall not escape: you must die with me (25); let the blood of both of us drip from the same sword. Though, that sort of death is bound to be dishonorable for me: a dishonorable death indeed, yet die you shall. Even the great Achilles, deserted when his wife was stolen, put up with seeing his weapons idle in his tent (30). He had watched the Greeks strewn in flight over the shore, and the Doric camp blaze under Hector's torch; he had watched Patroclus as he was laid low, filthied with sand, his hair straggling with clotted blood—all of that he endured for lovely Briseis (35): so fiercely does grief rage over a stolen love. But when in tardy restitution the captive girl was returned to him, he dragged the brave Hector behind his Thracian steeds. Is it any wonder, then, that over me, who am much inferior to him both in mother and in weapons, Love exercises a rightful triumph?'

Here the idea of an early death (to the applause of Cynthia) moves into the idea of suicide—not stated, except in the myth of Haemon. But, as the poet recalls the myth, he realises that Antigone was dead when Haemon killed himself. So he adjusts his own situation to complete the similarity by resolving to murder Cynthia first. That process of thought has to be extrapolated from the myth. The myth then serves a final turn (27–28): Haemon was famed for his loving devotion exemplified in the suicide (unsaid), but the poet's death by suicide after murdering his girl will be disgraceful. Yet he will stick by his resolve. Now, to justify himself, he thinks of the disgrace of Achilles, sulking in his tent and allowing the Greeks and his friend to be killed. Why? Because grief over a stolen love produces rage. Here the surprising verb (36) *saevit* is carefully chosen to enable the poet to share the explanation with Achilles. But it is, of course, better designed to express the motivation of the poet's proposed murder than of Achilles' sulks. At that point the argument is complete, but the poet goes on to Achilles' recovery (37–38). This is an analogue to the unstated idea that the poet would recover if he had Cynthia back. He then ties the analogue and his own situation together by an assertion which is equivalent to saying that, since he is not famous and important to others as Achilles was, he has no chance of having his girl returned to him. So (the implication is left to the reader) the poet will be left, unlike Achilles, in the condition of (36) *saevit* in which murder and suicide and disgrace provide the only solution.

Here the myth of Haemon is used to construct a most unexpected shift of thought. The myth of Achilles, however, is used by the first technique in the classification above to say much that is not said in primary language. Incidentally, by the end of the poem (if not before) the reader realises that the tears with which the poem began (2) were tears of anger as much as grief: the poet is despairing but enraged.

In 2.25, the second poem of what looks like a new series, Cynthia is addressed as the unique and most beautiful cause of torment to the poet (2) 'since my lot often excludes ⟨the word⟩ "come"', but he promises fame to her beauty. Then he asserts (5–15):

> miles depositis annosus secubat armis   5
> grandaevique negant ducere aratra boves,
> putris et in vacua requiescit navis harena,
> et vetus in templo bellica parma vacat:
> at me ab amore tuo deducet nulla senectus,
> sive ego Tithonus sive ego Nestor ero.
> nonne fuit satius duro servire tyranno
> et gemere in tauro, saeve Perille, tuo?
> Gorgonis et satius fuit obdurescere vultu,
> Caucasias etiam si pateremur avis.
> sed tamen obsistam.   15

'The superannuated soldier rests in retirement (5), his weapons put aside, and aged oxen refuse to draw the plough, and the rotting ship is at peace on the empty beach, and the old war-shield hangs peacefully in the temple: but old age will never free me from love of you, whether I shall be a Tithonus or a Nestor (10). Would it not have been better to be a slave to the harsh tyrant and bellow, cruel Perillus, in your bull? And better to be turned to stone by the Gorgon's head? And better even if I were to be tortured by Caucasian birds? Nevertheless I shall persist (15).'

Here the series of four comparisons in lines 5–9 seems at first only to prepare the idea of retirement. But the transition from line 10 to the following argument becomes clear only if the unspoken idea is extracted from the comparisons that all were engaged in hard, and most also in dangerous, occupations before retirement. In this way the idea is expressed that the poet's life is made so arduous by Cynthia that being a slave to the tyrant Phalaris or having his liver eaten out by vultures would be an alleviation. That is, an unexpressed element in the *paradeigmata* is used to pick up the opening theme of the poem and take it in an entirely new direction. The process is synecdoche of the type *e sequentibus praecedentia*.

Poem 3.11 of Propertius begins with indignant address to an accuser (1–8):

Quid mirare meam si versat femina vitam
  et trahit addictum sub sua iura virum,
criminaque ignavi capitis mihi turpia fingis
  quod nequeam fracto rumpere vincla iugo?
venturam melius praesagit navita mortem,   5
  vulneribus didicit miles habere metum.
ista ego praeterita iactavi verba iuventa:
  tu nunc exemplo disce timere meo.

'Why are you astonished that a woman controls my life and draws a man to be
a bondservant under her dominium? And why do you invent shameful charges
of spinelessness against me because I am unable to shatter the yoke and burst my
bonds? A sailor is better at foretelling the death that will come to him (5); a
soldier always learns fear through wounds. I uttered confident words like yours
in my past youth: take a lesson from me now and learn fear.'

Here line 5 is often emended on the ground that something characteristic of a sailor's experience ought to be said. This is only true, however, if the poet is to be judged by the standards of the most literal prose.
The structure in lines 5 and 6 is that of an elegant double synecdoche:
'sailors know better how they will die [because they learn fear from the
sea]; soldiers learn fear from wounds [and know better how they will
die]'. The figure is equivalent to the figure of ἀπὸ κοινοῦ in word-
order. But the *paradeigmata* are also substituted for a statement in
primary language of the way the poet learnt to be afraid. He learnt
it, clearly, in learning the power of a woman, and so joined sailors
and soldiers in being more accurate than ordinary men in foreseeing
his own end. This formulation underlines a further element that is
enforced by the synecdochic form of the *paradeigmata*; this is that,
like sailors and soldiers, the poet's fear is of death—a woman's power
is deadly. This will be important later in the structure of the poem.
    There follow immediately four elaborate mythic *paradeigmata*
(9–32):

Colchis flagrantis adamantina sub iuga tauros
  egit et armigera proelia sevit humo,   10
custodisque feros clausit serpentis hiatus
  iret ut Aesonias aurea lana domos.
ausa ferox ab equo quondam oppugnare sagittis

Maeotis Danaum Penthesilea ratis;
aurea cui postquam nudavit cassida frontem,   15
    vicit victorem candida forma virum.
Omphale in tantum formae processit honorem,
    Lydia Gygaeo tincta puella lacu,
ut, qui pacato statuisset in orbe columnas,
    tam dura traheret mollia pensa manu.   20
Persarum statuit Babylona Semiramis urbem
    ut solidum cocto tolleret aggere opus
et duo in adversum mitti per moenia currus
    nec possent tacto stringere ab axe latus;
duxit et Euphraten medium, quam condidit, arcis,   25
    iussit et imperio subdere Bactra caput.
nam quid ego heroas, quid raptem in crimina divos?
    Iuppiter infamat seque suamque domum.
quid, modo quae nostris opprobria vexerit armis,
    et famulos inter femina trita suos?   30
coniugii obsceni pretium Romana poposcit
    moenia et addictos in sua regna Patres.

'The Colchian girl drove the fiery bulls under adamantine yokes and sowed war in the arms-producing earth (10), and closed the ferocious jaws of the guardian snake so that the golden fleece might reach the halls of Aeson. Penthesilea of old, from lake Maeotis, had the courage fighting on horseback to attack with her arrows the ships of the Greeks, and, when her golden helmet laid bare her face (15), her shining beauty conquered the man who conquered her. Omphale, the girl from Lydia who bathed in Gyges' lake, attained such renown for her beauty that he, who erected pillars over a world he had pacified, worked soft wool with his hard hand (20). Semiramis built Babylon, city of the Persians, erecting a solid work of brick so that two chariots could be driven from opposite directions and not graze sides with touching axles; and she directed the Euphrates through the middle of the citadel which she founded (25), and ordered Bactria to submit its neck to her command.

I need not indict a series of heroes, or a series of gods—Juppiter defames both himself and his house. What of her who brought disgrace on our armies, a woman who was used even among her own slaves (30)? She demanded the walls of Rome as the price of her obscene marriage and the senators as bondsmen under her dominium. . . .'

The rest of the poem concerns Cleopatra and the gratitude of Romans to Augustus for freeing them of the danger from her (33–72).

Thus Cleopatra's place in the structure of the poem is as an example of a woman who not only brought death to her lover but actually threatened Rome with destruction. She is drawn into the situation by various verbal echoes, most notably the use of (32) *addictos* (cf. 2 *addictum*).

It is obvious enough that the women in the *paradeigmata* are figures for Cynthia. So in the first (9–12) Medea holds the limelight and Jason is not even mentioned. The second (13–16), however, not only figures Penthesilea as Cynthia, but also Achilles (falling in love as she dies) as the poet: this is the beauty that reverses the position of victor and victim at the moment of death. The third (17–20) has been altered by the poet to give the impression that Hercules deliberately chose his servitude to Omphale because of her beauty. Here Hercules is used to figure the poet as a slave, and the domination is that brought about by sexual attraction. The argument in the second and third examples is, as far as the figure of the poet is concerned, a fortiori. The fourth and most detailed (21–26), like the first, mentions no man: the domination here is of Bactria by the imperial power of Semiramis (illustrated by her building of Babylon). The reason for this is that the argument is being warped in such a way that the poet can move from Semiramis to her evil modern counterpart, Cleopatra. But, since the women are all figures for Cynthia, he feels obliged to insulate his girl, as it were, from being cast as the unspeakably wicked Cleopatra, enemy of Rome. That is the function of lines 27–28: the poet re-interprets his activity so far, as if he had really been assigning blame to the men involved in each of the myths; he does so by a rhetorical device (*occupatio*) which supposes a question from an imaginary interlocutor. Here the inter-locutor is supposed to have asked: 'Why not list heroes and gods?' And the poet answers (with *nam* to indicate an ellipse that contained this question): 'There is no need: Juppiter is example of infamy enough.' This serves, both to go back over the myths to the addressee's supposed accusations at the beginning of the poem, and also to introduce the theme of blame and infamy which has not been relevant to any of the characters so far. The blame here attaches to the male. But that is sufficient to allow the poet to proceed to a *paradeigma* in which the blame attaches not only to the male but, far more notoriously, to the female.

This, then, is a highly complex example of the technique by which *paradeigmata* are used to alter the movement of ideas, connecting with what precedes while they also prepare for what follows. The mention of death in the exemplum of the sailor (5) is clearly influenced by the poet's plans for the poem's structure: the theme of death anticipates the *paradeigma* of Cleopatra; or, rather, by suggesting clearly the deadly element in a woman's power and by implicitly assigning the same fear of a fore-ordained death also to the poet-lover, the poet has made it legitimate for him, without absurd hyperbole, to treat the *paradeigma* of Cleopatra as the last and most extreme of the series. The importance of the sailor in the poet's design is shown by ring-composition: the poem ends (71–72) with advice to a sailor in danger-ous waters always to remember Caesar (who saved Rome from the destruction threatened by Cleopatra).

There is only one extended mythic exemplum of the Propertian type in Tibullus, and, characteristic of this deft composer, it is made to work in all three of the ways that have been analysed above. In poem 2.3 Nemesis has gone off to the country and, the poet declares, only a man of iron could stay in the city (1–2). If only he could see her, he would be prepared to undertake all the heavy work of the farm (3–10). Already the tone is puzzling for the reader who knows other poems of Tibullus and thinks the poet to be—as he has hitherto represented himself—a lover of the country above the city and happy to be at work there. There follows the myth of Apollo and Admetus, treated at length (11–32). The myth works first as a substitute for a primary context; for not only is the information that Nemesis has in fact gone off with another man postponed to lines 33 ff. and (more explicitly) 59 ff., but, more important, the myth enacts the poet's feeling of hope-lessness which is not otherwise expressed: Apollo's love for Admetus was hopeless; so too—it is implied—is the poet's for Nemesis. The very next poem is concentrated on this feeling of hopelessness and the frustration of being in love with a girl whose only interest is in money.

Secondly, however, the myth works also to anticipate and legit-imate later thematic material. It ends with the poet's reflection that Apollo's behaviour made him an object of scandal (*fabula*), but better that than to be without love. The poem itself ends with an intensification of the opening theme: (79–80) the poet will be a mere working slave on the farm, subject to fetters and punishment. Nothing could con-ceivably be more scandalous for a freeborn man. This theme of the poet's physical slavery ironically echoes the alleged origin of the poet's successful rival—(59–60) he was frequently sold as a slave (that is, even as a slave he was not highly regarded).

Thirdly, the myth works to modify the movement of ideas. The opening of the poem (3–10) and even its ending (79–80) could sound happy if they were not viewed through the lens of the myth: they could suggest the happiness the lover finds in hard labour for his beloved in ideal surroundings. But what emerges from the myth is a picture of Apollo as a total misfit in his new surroundings: all his accustomed arts and graces are either absent or without function. Similarly, the poet will be as great a misfit in the country, and that is because the menial tasks imposed on Apollo, and imagined as imposed on the poet also, are a function of lack of success in love: the tasks are degrading in these circumstances because they are symbols of unrequited love. What is learnt only at a late stage in the poem (59 ff.) is that the successful rival is a wealthy ex-slave who is rich in landed estates. Consequently, the proprieties have to be reversed and the poet must speak as if he were by preference (if love of Nemesis did not compel him otherwise) a city man: for instance, he laments (78) *heu miserum laxam quid iuvat esse togam?* 'Alas for my pitiful state, what pleasure can I feel in an elegantly loose [city] toga?' For this poet, who loves the country, that very country has become the domain of a successful rival and is as alien to the poet as the farm of Admetus was to Apollo. But these ideas are never given explicit expression: they only emerge from the interaction of the myth with the context of the poem as a whole.

There are two briefer and simpler examples of Tibullus' technique in using myth to alter the movement of ideas. In poem 1.3 the poet is ill and has been left by Messalla in Corcyra. The entire poem is composed of the poet's fevered thoughts of love and death. He foresees his death (53 ff.) and then by metonymic association pictures the criminals in the underworld—Ixion and Tityos and Tantalus (73–78); the vision then continues (79–84):

> et Danai proles, Veneris quod numina laesit,
>   in cava Lethaeas dolia portat aquas.   80
> illic sit quicumque meos violavit amores,
>   optavit lentas et mihi militias.
> at tu casta precor maneas, sanctique pudoris
>   adsideat custos sedula semper anus.

'And the children of Danaus, because they sinned against the godhead of Venus, pour waters of Lethe into bottomless casks (80). May he find himself there who has violated my love and has wished on me a long-drawn military service. But I pray that you [Delia] remain chaste, and that a conscientious old woman sit always by you to guard you and keep sacred your chastity.'

Here the series of criminals of passion is broken by the figure of Tantalus but taken up again in a different form by the daughters of Danaus, whose crime (of murdering their husbands on their wedding-night) was an affront to Venus. This is an unexpected series of metonymic connexions, depending on association by means of the underworld existence of criminals in general and those whose crimes were of passion. The crime of the daughters of Danaus was not one of passion in the normal sense, but its mention permits the introduction of Venus. Here the violation of Venus, or, rather, of her ordinances, is metonymically associated with the imagined violation of the poet's girl by a rival. That association carries the implication that a violation of the poet's girl is also a violation of Venus' ordinances and so punishable by tortures in the underworld. That unexpected connexion of ideas is then converted (by another metonymic movement) into a prayer that Delia remain faithful to the poet, and so avert any possible violation of her chastity. The myth of tortures in the underworld is used to achieve these various changes in the direction of thought.

In poem 1.5 the poet and Delia have been parted for a long time. He is miserable and has tried every remedy, including other girls, but the thought of Delia made him impotent (39–48):

> saepe aliam tenui, sed iam cum gaudia adirem,
>   admonuit dominae deseruitque Venus. 40
> tunc me discedens devotum femina dixit—
>   a pudet!—et narrat scire nefanda meam.
> non facit hoc verbis, facie tenerisque lacertis
>   devovet et flavis nostra puella comis
> (talis ad Haemonium Nereis Pelea quondam 45
>   vecta est frenato caerula pisce Thetis).
> haec nocuere mihi—quod adest huic dives amator,
>   venit in exitium callida lena meum.

'Often I embraced another girl, but, when I was on the point of consummating my pleasure, Venus warned me of my mistress and abandoned me. Then the woman as she left me said I was bewitched—ah the shame!—and told me that my girl was possessed of unspeakable skills. She does not accomplish this by spells; with her beauty and her soft arms and her blonde hair my girl bewitches me (like her was the Nereid Thetis when once she rode to Thessalian Peleus, sea-blue upon a bridled fish). These are the things that worked my harm—the presence of a wealthy lover at her side ⟨shows that⟩ a scheming *lena* has arrived for my destruction.'

The continuing theme throughout this passage is that of witch-craft, and it is sustained by a series of metonymic and metaphoric movements. The girl attributes the poet's impotence to Delia's skill in witchcraft (42, *scire nefanda*). The poet then uses the same verb (*devovere*) metaphorically to assert that her beauty has bewitched him, and saying this, slides obliquely into a mythic comparison of what appears at first to be a conventional and ornamental type between Delia and Thetis. But the form of the legend that emerges is that in which Peleus had to use spells to capture Thetis, and these arcane skills are underlined by the apparently ornamental adjective (45) *Haemonium*, for Thessaly was famous for its skill in witchcraft. Thus the myth does not fit the poet's situation. If Thetis is Delia, Peleus should be the poet; but in fact Thetis is more like the poet as he has represented himself, since it was on Thetis that the spells were used. A suspension of judgment is needed till it becomes clear that the myth looks as much forward as backward, and that it serves to create in the poet's mind a picture of Delia trapped by a cunning *lena* (a conventional character who combined the arts of procuress and witch). Here (47) *haec* also looks backward as well as forward. This transitional function is supported by *nocuere*, a verb that continues the association of witchcraft. But it is a harsh verb to apply to Delia's beauty, and its associative power really carries over from (41) *devotum*, through the myth to the real injury that has been done to the poet by the kind of witch that (like Peleus) has special skills in luring pretty girls but (unlike him) to the financially attractive kind of lover. The apparent discontinuity of thought, expressive of the poet's agitation, is skilfully held together by associative movements that also modulate emotional changes from self-pity to anger. The function of the myth is crucial to these movements.

CHAPTER V

THEMATIC ANTICIPATION

In poem 2.9 of Propertius, examined above (p. 75), the theme of fickleness implicit in the first couplet does not become properly evident until lines 19 ff., and, in the same poem, the surprising appearance of the word *nuptae* (17) does not find its explanatory context until the theme of marriage appears in line 35. In a more simple way, in poem 1.2, the mention of Phoebus in line 17 is picked up when the god appears in line 27. A little more complex is the poet's choice of Thebes and Troy to illustrate the fall of kings and tyrants in 2.8.10; at a later stage in that poem (21 ff.) the story of Antigone appears, and at 29 ff. that of Achilles (see pp. 85 ff.). There is a satisfying link established by such echoes. Much more complex is the way it was suggested above (p. 81) that Propertius used the unnamed figure of Marpessa (1.2.17–18), and then, at the end of the poem, introduced a theme suggested by the criterion which she applied to make her choice between Idas and Phoebus as a husband.

In some of the simplest cases there is little difference between thematic anticipation and thematic repetition, except in the degree of deliberation among alternatives exercised by the poet in shaping the prior occurrence of the theme. For instance, when Catullus in poem 68 refers to the gods as *eri* and actually so addresses them in prayer, that is surprising and suggests the poet's sense of total subjection to arbitrary powers (76 and 78). But not only does he use the same word of the tyrant Eurystheus to whom, an inferior, Hercules was forced to be subject (114); that is also the word he uses of Lesbia as he tries to excuse her betrayals (136). The significance of the theme builds as the poem goes on (see pp. 54 ff.). In some other cases the thematic echo is used to form a ring-composition. In the most interesting cases, however, thematic anticipation comes close to arbitrary assertion of similarity: a new, often surprising, field is opened up very briefly, which extends beyond, and is not satisfied by, the immediate context so that a suspension of judgment is entailed and an expectation of completion. An example of this is the theme of *ultio* in Horace *Odes* 1.2, where the first occurrence of the theme (18) cannot be understood and points the reader forward (see pp. 10 f.). It is like the arbitrary assertion of similarity in being a device particularly suited to creating coherence and sustaining the energy of a poem without submitting the movement of ideas to a prosaic system of logic. It is also a device which can be used to hold complex structures together, and so permits a wide range of experimentation. These more complex techniques of thematic anticipation normally display the feature *e sequentibus praecedentia*. Ancient rhetorical theorists seem to have been aware of this figure, but, since they regarded it as part of a system that was concerned with *viva voce* address to an audience, they confined their analysis to situations where a speaker mentions a theme to arouse the expectation of an audience in order to keep them in suspense for some time before giving satisfaction.[1] Quintilian calls the figure *sustentatio* (9.2.22–24).[2]

1. *Simple Thematic Anticipation and Ring-Composition*

A simple form of thematic anticipation may be used merely to organise material, as in Propertius 4.2. The poem opens with an invitation to a reader, who is amazed at the various forms adopted by Vertumnus, to hear about the god's origin (1–2), treated in lines 3–8. Then come three explanations of his name (9–10, 11–18, and 19 ff.). But the third explanation turns into an account of his various forms. Similar types of anticipation, where a subject is announced but its treatment only

---

1. The technique is often used with great artistry by Cicero. For instance, in the opening of the *Brutus* the theme *opinione omnium maiorem cepi dolorem*, which is just mentioned in the first sentence, is not exploited until the end of paragraph 2; and the theme (4) *lugere facilius rem publicam* is only taken up in paragraphs 6 ff.

2. Quintilian's remarks in 10.1.20–21 are relevant: 'The whole work must be read and read through again, especially if it is a speech, since its merits are frequently concealed, even deliberately. For often an orator anticipates, dissembles, or sets a trap, and says things at the beginning that will only have force at the end. So what he says has less effect at that time, since the motive is unknown to us and the whole will have to be re-read after its drift has been grasped.'

follows after intervening material, can be seen in the didactic poetry of Lucretius and Virgil and in the *Ars poetica* of Horace: in such long serial poems the device was useful for achieving movement and coherence.[3]

Similar is the technique in Propertius 3.21: the poet has decided that his only way of escape from a tormenting love is a journey abroad, and he adds (9–10):

> unum erit auxilium: mutatis Cynthia terris
> quantum oculis, animo tam procul ibit amor.

'There will be one remedy: with a change of territory, love will depart as far from my mind as Cynthia from my eyes.'

The playfully pedantic distinction, more characteristic of Ovid than of Propertius, between *oculi* and *animus* finds its point later in the poem:[4] in Athens the poet will improve (25–28) his *animus* by study of Plato, Epicurus, Demosthenes, and Menander; his eyes (29–30, *mea lumina*) will be occupied with works of art.

Slightly different is Propertius 3.13. There a question is supposed as to why women are greedy and love costs so much money (1–2). The answer starts from the import of luxury goods from the East (3–8), with the comment (9–10):

> haec etiam clausas expugnant arma pudicas,
> quaeque gerunt fastus, Icarioti, tuos.

'These weapons storm even closely guarded chaste women, and such as display your kind of puritanical pride, daughter of Icarius.'

A few examples of stormed chastity follow (11–14); then the poet launches into a portrait of the admirable custom of the East—suttee (15–22), followed by the comment (23–24):

> hoc genus infidum nuptarum, hic nulla puella
> nec fida Evadne nec pia Penelope.

3. See Williams (1968), pp. 352–53, 355–56, 720–21, 731–32.
4. See Camps (1961–67), ad loc.

'Here married women are typically unfaithful; here no girl is either a faithful Evadne or a loyal Penelope.'

The daughter of Icarius was Penelope, and the connexion is underlined by putting the patronymic first: Evadne, who committed suttee, is relevant to the immediate theme, but Penelope is the contrast-figure for the whole context. The poem, after line 24, swerves away into a picture of rural bliss in the Golden Age; thus the echo created by using two different types of name for the same person has something of the force of ring-composition in closing a section of the poem.

Ring-composition was frequently used by Roman poets of the late Republic and of the Augustan Age to effect poetic closure.[5] Propertius often uses it in this way, while at the same time also effecting an important connexion of ideas. For instance, in poem 3.21 just examined, the opening couplet is (1–2):

> Magnum iter ad doctas proficisci cogor Athenas
>   ut me longa gravi solvat amore via.

'I am constrained to set off on a grand tour to learned Athens so that the long journey may relieve me from a burdensome love.'

The poem ends (31–34):

> aut spatia annorum aut longa intervalla profundi
>   lenibunt tacito vulnera nostra sinu:
> seu moriar, fato, non turpi fractus amore;
>   atque erit illa mihi mortis honesta dies.

'Either length of years or the wide spaces of the sea will heal my wounds silently within my heart: or, if I shall die, it will be by fate and not broken by a disgraceful love; and so that day of my death will be honourable.'

Here the ring-composition expands to bring in the theme, not otherwise mentioned in the poem, of the poet's death.

There is a similarly pregnant ring-composition in Propertius 2.3. The poem opens with an imagined attack on the poet for inconsistency: he boasted that no woman could harm him, but now (3–4) 'you can

5. See, for instance, Williams (1968), Index s.v.

hardly be quiet a month but there will be another disgraceful book about you'. Nothing in the poem explains or answers the idea of 'disgraceful' until the ending is reached (45–54):

> his saltem ut tenear finibus, aut, mihi si quis   45
>   acrior, ut moriar, venerit alter amor!
> ac veluti primo taurus detractat aratra,
>   post venit assueto mollis ad arva iugo,
> sic primo iuvenes trepidant in amore feroces,
>   dehinc domiti post haec aequa et iniqua ferunt.   50
> turpia perpessus vates est vincla Melampus,
>   cognitus Iphicli surrupuisse boves;
> quem non lucra, magis Pero formosa coegit,
>   mox Amythaonia nupta futura domo.

'I hope I may now be confined within these limits, or that I may die if a second sharper love shall come to me. And, just as at first the bull balks at the plough, but later, accustomed to the yoke, comes docilely to the fields, so at first young men fret and rage in love, but thereafter tamed, put up then with good and bad alike (50). The seer Melampus put up with disgraceful fetters when discovered to have stolen the cattle of Iphicles; no profit drove him to it, but rather the beauty of Pero, soon to be a bride in the house of Amythaon.'

It is clear that Melampus, a *vates* like the poet (though in a different sense), is a figure for the poet, and that the exemplum does not illustrate the immediate context but the whole poem: a love that compels a man to undergo disgraceful sufferings (the point of the immediate context is that submission is best). But the element of disgrace appears only in the opening accusation by an interlocutor and in the final *paradeigma*; the poet thus avoids expressing it in primary language or giving any account of his own situation. This structural detail alone should be sufficient proof against attempts to mark a new elegy at line 45: the reality at which the poet hints, but which he does not express in primary language, is that in his desperate situation submission is the only solution, disgraceful though it may appear. He just hopes never to experience a more piercing love—death would be preferable.

There is a further internal ring-composition in this poem, of a type that is quite frequent. The poet praises Cynthia's beauty and talents, and declares that they are not human but the gifts of the gods (25–28); in fact, Cynthia will become the mistress of Juppiter (29–44):

gloria Romanis una es tu nata puellis:
    Romana accumbes prima puella Iovi,   30
nec semper nobiscum humana cubilia vises;
    post Helenam haec terris forma secunda redit.
hac ego nunc mirer si flagret nostra iuventus?
    pulchrius hac fuerat, Troia, perire tibi.
olim mirabar quod tanti ad Pergama belli   35
    Europae atque Asiae causa puella fuit:
nunc, Pari, tu sapiens, et tu, Menelae, fuisti,
    tu quia poscebas, tu quia lentus eras.
digna quidem facies pro qua vel obiret Achilles;
    vel Priamo belli causa probanda fuit.   40
si quis vult fama tabulas anteire vetustas,
    hic dominam exemplo ponat in arte meam:
sive illam Hesperiis, sive illam ostendet Eois,
    uret et Eoos, uret et Hesperios.

'You were born to be the unique glory of Roman girls: you will be the first Roman girl to sleep with Juppiter (30), and you will not always visit human beds here among us; after Helen this beauty appears again on earth for the second time. Am I now to be astonished if our youth is set on fire by it? More honourable, O Troy, had it been for you to be destroyed for this. I used to be amazed that the cause of such a war at Troy (35), on the part of Europe and of Asia, was a girl: but now I see, Paris, that you were wise, and you too, Menelaus—you [Menelaus] for demanding, you [Paris] for being slow to respond. Cynthia's beauty would have been a cause worthy of Achilles' death; even Priam would have approved it as a cause of war (40). Whoever is ambitious to outdo ancient paintings, let him set my mistress as a model for his skill: whether he shall show her to men of the West, or to men of the East, he will set on fire men of the East, and he will set on fire men of the West.'

There is a clear ring-composition between (36) Europe and Asia, and (43–44) men of the West and of the East. The passage is important in the structure of the poem. Nothing is said against Cynthia, nothing that might account for (4) *turpis* or for the apparent anguish of the poet—except the bare suggestion of faithlessness in these lines. The theme of adultery enters with Helen, is widened to include the poet's Rome (33) for a moment (in an apologetic way that is reminiscent of Catullus 68.135 ff.), before being dissipated into the Trojan War (with Cynthia now as the cause of it). The passage is, as it were, a self-contained digression, and in its technique is closely reminiscent of the two digressions within the Laudamia legend in Catullus 68. There, too, ring-composition was used to incorporate the digressions. The technique is similar to that of Plautus when he introduces a section of his own material into a passage where he is basically using a Greek model: he breaks the Greek text to introduce his own ideas and then, to provide a coherent connexion of ideas, he repeats, after his insertion, the same theme that he had already used from the Greek text at the point where he momentarily abandoned using it as a model; the effect of the repetition of the same theme before and after the characteristically Roman passage is like that of ring-composition. The technique serves to incorporate digressive ideas into what may be regarded as a basically coherent movement of thought. Here the adultery theme, which connects with (4) *turpis* and (51) *turpia*, could disrupt the poet's ecstatic praise of his mistress if it were not handled with such insulating artistry.

A recognition of this type of ring-composition can sometimes save lines from editorial transposition. In Propertius 3.19, a poem on the theme that women's passions are far more uncontrollable than men's, the poet follows the assertion (1–4) with a series of four comparisons drawn from nature (5–10); then a series of six mythical *paradeigmata* end the poem (11–28)—Pasiphae, Tyro, Myrrha, Medea, Clytaemnestra, and finally (21–28):

> tuque, o Minoa venumdata Scylla figura,
>   tondes purpurea regna paterna coma.
> hanc igitur dotem virgo desponderat hosti:
>   Nise, tuas portas fraude reclusit amor.
> at (vos, innuptae, felicius urite taedas)   25
>   pendet Cretaea tracta puella rate.
> non tamen immerito Minos sedet arbiter Orci:
>   victor erat quamvis, aequus in hoste fuit.

'And you, O Scylla, sold for the beauty of Minos, are shearing the kingdom of your father by means of his crimson lock. So this was the dowry the maiden had pledged as a marriage-gift to the enemy: Nisus, love has opened your gates by deceit. But (maidens, light your marriage-torches more happily— 25) the girl dangles, dragged behind the Cretan ship. Nevertheless, it is right that Minos sits as judge in the underworld: though he was the conqueror, he was fair towards his enemy.'

The examples are in ascending order of moral turpitude: three sexual deviants, a murderess of her own children, a murderess of her husband, and a betrayer of her father to an enemy. However, in the last example, editors sometimes transpose lines 27–28 to precede 25–26, following the lead of Housman: '. . . it is with the punishment of the sinner, the woman whom lust led to treason and parricide, that the poem should end rather than with the praise of Minos for his justice to the victim of her treachery.'[6] But, in that case, the praise of Minos has no relevance, and the ring-composition on his name is destroyed—quite apart from the satisfying gnomic closure that line 28 provides. And there is a still more important point that is missed if the traditional order is disrupted. The poem has been about the force of passion in women, and the poet has concentrated on sexual passion. The poem ends neatly with a man who, having resisted and punished female temptation and deceit, showed restraint under conditions generally recognised in the ancient world to excuse all kinds of excess; the poet praises his *aequitas*, obliquely asserting the point he has been aiming at in the whole poem—that men are capable of self-control.

Recognition of a simpler form of this technique of ring-composition should also protect Propertius 4.10.23–26 from disruption. The section 23–38 tells the story of Cossus' winning of the *spolia opima* by killing Tolumnius in single combat. With the traditional order of lines, the first couplet (23–24) mentions the slaughter of Tolumnius, and then that theme is taken up again in the final couplet (37–38) of the section, with varied detail. The couplet 25–26, which is sometimes transposed to precede 23–24 in order to produce what seems a more logical (and prosaic) progression, simply makes the statement that Rome's wars so far had not gone beyond the Tiber; it is an aside in parentheses, following the first mention of Veii (23–24), a town by the standards of that time distant from Rome. Here the ring-composition serves to insert a little story, skilfully designed with telling detail, into the aetiological exposition.

2. *Anticipation by Synecdoche* e sequentibus praecedentia

The mark of this more sophisticated form of thematic anticipation is that not only is the theme not satisfied within the context of its first

6. Butler and Barber (1933), ad loc.

occurrence, but that full understanding can only come after later occurrences. In some cases this means that the various occurrences of the theme taken together yield a sense that was absent from the first occurrence. For instance, in Propertius 3.16, a soliloquy, the poet has been summoned urgently to his mistress at Tibur by night. He hesitates, but fears to disobey (9–10):

> peccaram semel, et totum sum pulsus in annum:
> in me mansuetas non habet illa manus.

'I had sinned just once, and I have been exiled for a whole year: against me her hands are not merciful.'

The meaning here is ambiguous in Latin, and could be: 'I had sinned just once and was exiled for a whole year'. If the meaning is the latter, then it is only one example of her harshness from the past. But the poet goes on to reflect that lovers are safe, even at night (11–20). It was apparently a commonplace topic that Venus watches over lovers, and the poet ends with the assertion (20) *exclusis fit comes ipsa Venus*, 'Venus in person stands as protectress with lovers who are shut out'. Here *exclusis* has often been emended or explained away. For instance: 'the poet is not *exclusus* (forbidden access to his mistress) in the situation that gives rise to this elegy; and the lover has been described in 11–18 as enjoying immunity simply as a lover, whether *exclusus* or not. But in line 19 the lover's immunity has begun to be attributed to his pathetic condition; and "exclusion" and "immunity" are juxtaposed in Tibullus 1.2.7 ff. and 25–28, passages which Propertius had somewhere in his mind when writing this elegy.'[7] But all this difficulty vanishes when *exclusis* is recognised as an expansion of the theme *totum sum pulsus in annum*: the poet has been *exclusus* for a whole year, and this summons promises to break the period of rejection. This idea better motivates both the poet's anxiety at having to undertake the dangerous journey and the following reflection (21–30) that, even if he is murdered, Cynthia will give him tender burial.

In poem 2.24B, which seems to be the beginning of a new sequence of elegies, the poet is angry at Cynthia for her unfaithfulness (17–22);

---

7. Camps (1961–67), ad loc.

then he compares a rival with himself (23–32: the subject of the verbs is dramatically postponed to line 30). The poet asserts his eternal faithfulness (33–34) and imagines Cynthia's words when he is dead (35–38):

> tu mea compones et dices 'ossa, Properti,
> 　haec tua sunt? eheu tu mihi certus eras,
> certus eras eheu, quamvis nec sanguine avito
> 　nobilis et quamvis non ita dives eras'.

'You will lay out my bones and say "Are these your bones, Propertius? Alas! you were dependable to me: you were dependable, alas! Though you were neither noble by your ancestors' blood nor were you at all rich".'

The meaning of the strange qualifications does not become clear till the end of the poem (47–52):

> dura est quae multis simulatum fingit amorem,
> 　et se plus uni si qua parare potest.
> noli nobilibus, noli conferre beatis:
> 　vix venit extremo qui legat ossa die.　　　　　　50
> hi tibi nos erimus: sed tu potius precor ut me
> 　demissis plangas pectora nuda comis.

'She is cruel who makes up a simulated love for many men, and who is ready to give herself to more than one. Do not measure me against the nobly born, do not measure me against the wealthy: it is hard to find a man to collect your bones on the last day (50). That I shall do for you: but my prayer is rather that you may let down your hair and beat your bare breast over me.'

It now becomes clear that Cynthia's unfaithfulness was not with the one rival described earlier, but that he was simply representative of many, and that her criteria for selecting lovers were birth and wealth. Hence the condescending qualifications that the poet put into her mouth earlier.

In a number of cases the first occurrence of the anticipated theme is used to legitimate the second. This was noticed in Propertius 2.6 (see p. 84), where the narrowing of the focus to married women (26) is surprising, in spite of the preceding myths of Alcestis and Penelope, and only makes full sense when the poet represents Cynthia as his wife at the end of the poem (41–42). These figures are very infrequent in

Book 1 of Propertius, but (apart from 1.2) there is an example of this type of anticipation in 1.17. The poet has fled from Cynthia and imagines himself caught in a storm at sea. He anticipates death, asks for mercy (9–10), and then says (11–12):

> an poteris siccis mea fata reposcere ocellis,
> ossaque nulla tuo nostra tenere sinu?

'Will you be able with dry eyes to enquire about my death, and to hold no bones of mine in your bosom?'

This theme prepares for the lengthy regrets (19–24) of the poet as he imagines the way Cynthia would have made sure that he had a proper funeral if only he had stayed at home.

In poem 2.15 the poet ecstatically recalls the previous night spent making love with Cynthia. The poem ends with the impressive simile (examined above, p. 63) and apprehension of the death that will end their love. That theme appeared only fleetingly earlier, and in connexion with a lengthy disquisition (11–22) on how important it is to see when making love (23–24):

> dum nos fata sinunt oculos satiemus amore:
> nox tibi longa venit nec reditura dies.

'While fate allows, let us satiate our eyes with love: a long night is coming to you and a day that will not return.'

The first line connects with what precedes; the second with what follows (25–26):

> atque utinam haerentis sic nos vincire catena
> velles ut numquam solveret ulla dies.

'And would that as we clung together like that you had wanted to bind us with a chain so that no day could part us.'

The theme of death is no sooner raised than it is immediately extinguished by the context. It only finds full satisfaction in lines 49–54.

Similarly, in poem 4.3 Arethusa writes a letter to her young husband who is abroad with the Roman army fighting against the Parthians.

She recalls his long service in many lands and their brief marriage; she is now weaving a fourth cloak for him (18) and curses whoever invented war (19–22). Then she says (23–30):

> dic mihi, num teneros urit lorica lacertos?
> num gravis imbellis atterit hasta manus?
> haec noceant potius quam dentibus ulla puella   25
> det mihi plorandas per tua colla notas.
> diceris et macie vultum tenuasse: sed opto
> e desiderio sit color iste meo.
> at mihi cum noctes induxit vesper amaras,
> si qua relicta iacent, osculor arma tua.   30

'Tell me, I hope the breastplate does not gall your soft arms, or the weight of a spear harden your hands not meant for war? But I should rather these hurt you than that some girl put marks with her teeth on your neck that would certainly make me cry. And they say your face is drawn and thin: but I hope that pallor comes from longing for me. But when evenings have brought on nights of bitterness for me, I kiss whatever weapons of yours there are lying about.'

The theme of jealousy is both briefly and surprisingly inserted, and it is done with an Ovidian lightness of touch and authorial irony. But converted into the theme of marital faithfulness, it is seriously treated at the end of the poem (67–72):

> sed (tua sic domitis Parthae telluris alumnis
> pura triumphantis hasta sequatur equos)
> incorrupta mei conserva foedera lecti:
> hac ego te sola lege redisse velim;   70
> armaque cum tulero portae votiva Capenae,
> subscribam SALVO GRATA PUELLA VIRO.

'But preserve untainted the vows that you made to my bed (in return I wish that, when the nurslings of the land of Parthia have been subdued, an unpointed spear[8] may follow your triumphing horses): on that condition alone should I want to see you come back (70). Then, when I shall take your armour as a votive offering to the Porta Capena, I shall inscribe beneath it: "From a grateful girl ⟨in thanks for⟩ her husband's safety."'

8. A mark of honour for distinguished service.

This is the genuine spirit of Augustan marriage-legislation, as Propertius expressed it also in the elegy of Cornelia (4.11).[9] The theme of chastity, humorously handled in the first passage, is taken up and completed in the second, and the ideals of patriotism are fused with the Augustan ideals of marriage. This would be unbearably pompous without the earlier occurrence of the theme. The two treatments mutually support and qualify one another.

The most interesting form of this type of thematic anticipation is that in which the first occurrence of the theme is not complete or not fully intelligible without the later. This form is sometimes marked by the fact that the first occurrence is introduced into its context as if it were an aside or a momentary digression. For instance, in Propertius 2.10 the poet declares that it is time for a different type of poetry on Roman wars rather than love (1–4). Then, before describing how this is to come about and how the new poetry relates to the old, he says (5–6):

> quod si deficiant vires, audacia certe
> laus erit: in magnis et voluisse sat est.

'But if my powers should be deficient, the will to dare will be my claim to fame: in great affairs just to have wanted is sufficient.'

This statement only achieves its explanation at the end of the poem:

> haec ego castra sequar; vates tua castra canendo
>   magnus ero: servent hunc mihi fata diem!   20
> at caput in magnis ubi non est tangere signis,
>   ponitur haec imos ante corona pedes;
> sic nos nunc, inopes laudis conscendere carmen,
>   pauperibus sacris vilia tura damus.
> nondum etiam Ascraeos norunt mea carmina fontis,   25
>   sed modo Permessi flumine lavit Amor.

'This is the camp I shall follow; by singing of your [Augustus'] camp I shall become a great poet: may fate preserve that day for me (20). But since it is not possible to reach the head of huge statues, this garland is being placed below at its feet. So, as things are, incapable of climbing into the poetic chariot of

9. See, for instance, Williams (1968), pp. 387–400.

fame, in a poor man's sacrifice I present cheap incense. Not yet does my poetry know the fountains of Ascra (25), but Love has only dipped it in the stream of Permessus.'

The poet here recognises that he has not the ability to carry out the project he announced; that would have required epic poetry (of the Hesiodic type approved by Alexandrians), whereas he is only capable of elegy (the poetry of love). Now the real meaning of the couplet 5–6 becomes clear: it anticipated[10] the poet's realisation that the new type of poetry was quite beyond his powers.

Similarly, poem 2.14 opens with a barrage of *paradeigmata* (1–8), already examined (p. 76), and the poet's feeling of immortality after the previous night with Cynthia. Then he asserts (11–14):

> at dum demissis supplex cervicibus ibam,
>   dicebar sicco vilior esse lacu.
> nec mihi iam fastus opponere quaerit iniquos,
>   nec mihi ploranti lenta sedere potest.

'But while I walked humbly with drooping neck, I used to be held more worthless than a dry cistern. And now she neither looks to meet me with cruel disdain, nor can she sit unmoved as I complain.'

These two couplets are sometimes reversed by editors because 'in the order given by the MSS . . . they make a *non sequitur*'.[11] But the lines 11–12 are explained at 19–20:

> hoc sensi prodesse magis: contemnite, amantes!
>   sic hodie veniet si qua negavit heri.

'This is what I discovered to be more help: despise them, lovers! In that way she will come to-day who said no yesterday.'

The poet has made a crucial discovery: treat women roughly and they will submit. The view is prefigured in the opening *paradeigma* of Agamemnon's violent triumph over Troy but is not explained until

---

10. A figure that might be treated under Quintilian's label of *praesumptio* (9.2.16).
11. Camps (1961–67), in his introductory remarks to 2.14 (p. 121).

now. What the couplet 11–12 achieves is a sudden and surprising picture from the past, the very opposite of the god the poet has felt himself becoming in the previous couplet. The poet then goes on to elaborate the present situation, postponing as long as possible the explanation of the riddling lines 11–12. The particle (11) *at* is needed to produce the contrast with the ecstasy of the previous night expressed in lines 9–10 and not with the conventional ideas of 13–14—in fact, the 'dry cistern' is a perfect example of the *fastus* which the poet is so pleased belongs to the past.

Propertius 2.16 has already been discussed for the way in which the *paradeigmata* are used (pp. 66 ff.). But it is a poem of shifting topics and there are also examples of thematic anticipation. The theme of 'gifts', *munera* or *dona*, goes right through the poem: (4) *dona*, (9) *munera*, (15) *muneribus*, (18) *dona*, (21) *munus*, (29) *donis*, (43 ff.) various gifts, (55) *Sidonia vestis*. Within this thematic framework, the poet in lines 17–18 specifies two gifts that he is particularly required to obtain for Cynthia: (17) *gemmas*, (18) *ex ipsa . . . dona Tyro*. Then, in the *paradeigmata* in lines 29–30, *gemmae* are relevant to Eriphyle and *ex ipsa . . . dona Tyro* to Creusa. This is merely the type of thematic anticipation that is close to being an echo. There is, however, an example of the more interesting type of thematic anticipation in lines 25–26. The poet wishes that no one was rich in Rome (19), for then girls would not sell themselves, and in particular (23–24) Cynthia would never have slept apart from him for seven nights, putting her arms round a man so foul; and he asserts (25–26):

> non quia peccarim (testor te), sed quia vulgo
> formosis levitas semper amica fuit.

'not because I have done anything wrong (I call on you to witness to that fact), but because in general pretty women always have a preference for fickleness.'

That seems a strange explanation of her behaviour, seeing that he has characterised her conduct as purely mercenary and goes on to describe her affair as 'disgraceful'. The theme is taken up, however, in lines 47–54, where *levitas* is converted into the less venial accusation of *periuria*, which the poet is convinced Juppiter will punish. The poet sees more evil in Cynthia than greed for money, but to express it gently as *levitas* and to generalise it as a characteristic of pretty women as such, creates that interesting sense of something that is not legitimated by its context but which goes beyond it. So *levitas* looks forward to its satisfaction in *periuria*: Cynthia really breaks her solemn word. That is her real crime against the poet, and it is the basic crime since it permits her greed for money to achieve satisfaction. Faithfulness would exclude the possibility of *munera*, which, apparently the major theme of the poem, is revealed really to be subordinate.

There is a complex movement of thought in poem 3.5 of Propertius, which opens thus (1–22):

> Pacis Amor deus est, pacem veneramur amantes:
>   stant mihi cum domina proelia dura mea.
> nec tamen inviso pectus mihi carpitur auro,
>   nec bibit e gemma divite nostra sitis,
> nec mihi mille iugis Campania pinguis aratur,   5
>   nec miser aera paro clade, Corinthe, tua.
> o prima infelix fingenti terra Prometheo:
>   ille parum cauti pectoris egit opus.
> corpora disponens mentem non vidit in arte:
>   recta animi primum debuit esse via.   10
> nunc maris in tantum vento iactamur, et hostem
>   quaerimus, atque armis nectimus arma nova.
> haud ullas portabis opes Acherontis ad undas:
>   nudus in inferna, stulte, vehere rate;
> victor cum victis pariter miscebitur umbris: 15
>   consule cum Mario, capte Iugurtha, sedes;
> Lydus Dulichio non distat Croesus ab Iro;
>   optima mors, Parcae quae venit acta die.
> me iuvat in prima coluisse Helicona iuventa
>   Musarumque choris implicuisse manus: 20
> me iuvat et multo mentem vincire Lyaeo,
>   et caput in verna semper habere rosa.
> atque ubi iam Venerem gravis interceperit aetas,
>   sparserit et nigras alba senecta comas,
> tum mihi naturae libeat perdiscere mores,   25
>   quis deus hanc mundi temperet arte domum . . .

'Love is the god of Peace, and we lovers worship Peace: my hard-fought battles are with my mistress. Yet, however, my heart is not eaten away with hateful gold, nor is my thirst quenched from a richly jewelled goblet, nor is rich Campanian land ploughed by a thousand yoke of oxen for me (5), nor am I so sick that I collect bronzes from your ruin, Corinth. O primal clay, unpropitious to Prometheus' moulding: his work on the heart was not careful enough. Organising the flesh, he did not pay attention to the mind in exercising his talent: the path of the intelligence should first have been set straight (10). Hence we are tossed over such reaches of the sea by winds, and we search for an enemy, and for ever we keep connecting wars to further wars. You will carry no wealth to the waters of Acheron: idiot creature, you will be carried naked in the boat of the underworld; the victor will mingle on equal terms with the shades of the vanquished (15): you are sitting beside the Roman consul Marius, captive Jugurtha; Croesus of Lydia is right beside Irus of Dulichium; the best death is that which comes appointed on the day of the Fate. My pleasure it has been in earliest youth to frequent Helicon and to join hands in the choruses of the Muses (20); and it is my pleasure to fetter my mind with much wine, and even to surround my head with spring roses. But when the weight of years shall have cut me off from Love and grey old age has sprinkled my black hair, then be it my pleasure to learn the ways of Nature (25), what god controls this home of the world by his skill . . .'

There is here a clear ring-composition between lines 1–2 and 19–20: the latter lines take up and develop what exactly the poet means by Peace. Then the next movement of the poem (into old age) is connected with what preceded by anticipating the absence of the one outstanding element of Peace, in the poet's view, an element otherwise omitted from the re-definition in lines 19–22 except in so far as it is represented by its symbols, wine and roses:[12] that element is Love.

The relationship between lines 2 and 3 is established by *nec tamen* 'yet however' (words sometimes emended) in a way that is not easily intelligible before the full meaning of lines 11–12 has been grasped. That explanation is deliberately postponed by the poet's turning aside (7–10) to reflect on the bad workmanship of Prometheus in moulding mankind from the primaeval clay. The connexion of thought implicit in (3) *nec tamen* is that the battles of lovers, unlike those of ordinary men, are not motivated by greed for wealth. The reader must realise from the poet's introspective musing that an idea in the poet's mind, not yet shared with the reader, explains the ellipse of thought implied by the combination of particles *nec tamen*. That idea begins to emerge in the mention of Corinth (6), but still ambiguously. Lines 11–12 then express the thesis that wars are motivated in the same way as sea-faring— by greed for profit.[13] There is another ring-composition in the section

---

12. See especially Propertius 2.15 (pp. 62 ff. above).
13. See, for instance, Kirby Smith (1913) on Tibullus 1.3.47–48; 10.7–8.

11–18: from line 12 on war is extracted the idea of death in general, not just a particular kind of death. But in line 18 the 'best death' is contrasted with death by violence, and that idea has been extracted from the theme of war in lines 11–12, rather than from the warriors chosen in lines 15–16 to illustrate the equality of death; for that list is not confined to soldiers but is casually expanded by the figures of Croesus and Irus. The death that obsesses the poet in 3.5, and with which the poem ends, is death in battle.

Poem 3.7 of Propertius has inspired to the most extreme surgery editors who have tried to produce orderly and logical exposition by wholesale transposition of lines. But if the MSS are heeded, there is here a particularly interesting example of thematic anticipation.[14] The poem is a lament for Paetus, lost at sea on a merchant trip to Alexandria. It opens with curses on the profit-motive (1–6); there follows a lament on his lack of burial (7–12). At this point the poet launches into reproaches of the wind and the sea-god (13–20):

> infelix Aquilo, raptae timor Orithyiae,
> quae spolia ex illo tanta fuere tibi?
> aut quidnam fracta gaudes, Neptune, carina?   15
> portabat sanctos alveus ille viros.
> Paete, quid aetatem numeras? quid cara natanti
> mater in ore tibi est? non habet unda deos.
> nam tibi nocturnis ad saxa ligata procellis
> omnia detrito vincula fune cadunt.   20

'Accursed North Wind, terror of raped Orithyia, what spoils from him were worth so much to you? Or why do you find joy in breaking the ship, Neptune (15)? That hull was carrying no sinners. Paetus, why do you enumerate your years? Why is your mother's name on your lips as you swim? The sea knows no gods. For in the night your cables, though all made fast to rocks, fell away as the strands were worn through by the storm.'

The objection of some editors that it is inconsistent for the poet to address the North Wind and Neptune and then deny that the sea has gods needs no comment: the rhetorical movement from the prayer to the assertion is clear enough. But this editorial comment needs consideration: 'It is strange that in 17–18 the poet should cry *Paete, quid...*, words which seem to allude to his actual speech in 57–64,

14. See especially Vahlen (1883).

forty-one lines before the speech occurs.'[15] Indeed, just before describing Paetus' final sinking beneath the waves, the poet records his hysterical prayer to the 'winds, gods of the sea . . .' (57–64), the two themes of which are his youthful years and his mother. This is a very clear example of a theme that calls attention to itself by its unexpected setting and by its lack of legitimation in the immediate context. Thereby the expectation of its fulfillment is created, and then satisfied forty-one lines later. The requirement to suspend judgment is part of the artistry, holding the poem together, and is not to be emended away.

In the second half of Propertius 4.1, an odd Egyptian astrologer called Horus speaks. He warns the poet against trying to write on Roman history (71–74). He assures the poet that his own credentials as a seer are the best (75–76); he gives an account of his ancestry (77–80); he regrets the commercialization of astrology (81–86), implying that he has no part in it. Then he says (87–92):

> dicam 'Troia cades et Troica Roma resurges',
>   et maris et terrae longa sepulcra canam.
> dixi ego, cum geminos produceret Arria natos
>   (illa dabat natis arma vetante deo),   90
> non posse ad patrios sua pila referre Penatis:
>   nempe meam firmant nunc duo busta fidem.

'I shall say "Troy, you shall fall, and, Trojan Rome, you shall rise again", and I shall foretell the catalogue of deaths by sea and by land. It was I who said, when Arria was giving birth to twin sons (she was for putting weapons in her sons' hands, though god forbade it—90), that they could not bring their spears back to their ancestral home: now, as you know, two tombs confirm my credibility.'

Most editors excise the first couplet, or transfer it elsewhere, as being entirely irrelevant to the context. But Horus goes on to tell of other predictions in what seems to be Propertius' family (93–102). He then explains that his accuracy in prophecy has nothing to do with traditional rites of divination, but (107–20):

> aspicienda via est caeli verusque per astra
>   trames, et ab zonis quinque petenda fides.
> exemplum grave erit Calchas: namque Aulide solvit

15. Butler and Barber (1933), p. 276.

ille bene haerentis ad pia saxa ratis;   110
idem Agamemnoniae ferrum cervice puellae
    tinxit, et Atrides vela cruenta dedit;
nec rediere tamen Danai: tu diruta fletum
    supprime et Euboicos respice, Troia, sinus!
Nauplius ultores sub noctem porrigit ignis,   115
et natat exuviis Graecia pressa suis.
victor Oiliade, rape nunc et dilige vatem
    quam vetat avelli veste Minerva sua!
hactenus historiae; nunc ad tua devehar astra;
    incipe tu lacrimis aequus adesse novis.   120

'The path of heaven must be observed and the track of truth through the stars, and credit must be sought from the five zones. A terrible example shall be Calchas: for he launched from Aulis ships that were wisely clinging to god-fearing rocks (110); he it was who stained the knife in the neck of Agamemon's daughter, and the son of Atreus set bloody sails; and yet the Greeks did not return: though destroyed, suppress your lamentation, Troy, and just look towards the gulf of Euboea! Nauplius is lifting up by night avenging fires (115), and Greece is in the water, sunk beneath her own spoils. Victorious son of Oileus, now rape and love the prophetess whom Minerva forbids should be dragged away from her robe. Thus far then the story of the past: now I shall embark on your stars; make ready to give fair hearing to new causes for weeping.'

The passage as a whole, from line 87 to 118, is a ring-composition. Horus begins the boastful rehearsal of his prophetic powers with a correct prophecy about Greece and Troy (it had already been reported by the poet as coming from the mouth of Cassandra, 53–54); the 'catalogue of deaths' has nothing to do with the voyage of Aeneas, but concerns the Greek homecoming. Having delivered himself of this properly puzzling example of the prophetic art, he turns aside to recent examples of his prowess, working round, in the end, to the assertion (by implication) that he is not a Calchas who got his prophecy about Greece and Troy quite wrong. Here Propertius has used the technique of thematic anticipation to dramatic effect in portraying the self-confident character of the odd Egyptian. For the initial assertion about the Trojan War (87–88) can be seen, after lines 107–20 have been read, to mean, in a riddling way, that if Horus should be in Calchas' position, he would give the Greeks a correct prophecy and so dissuade them from the sacrifice at Aulis and the whole Trojan adventure that was to result in the rise of Rome (see further p. 123). The anticipated theme has exactly the sense of being unfulfilled in its context which impelled editors to remove what they saw as a blemish and to ruin the poet's conception. The ring-composition marks the astrologer's proof of his powers in the field of *historiae*; in line 119 he turns to the poet's own life.

The great ode with which the second book of Horace's *Odes* opens contains a striking example of the type of thematic anticipation that is not understood till a later stage in the poem. The ode is addressed to Asinius Pollio, who is writing a history of the civil wars from the year 60 B.C. (1–8):

> Motum ex Metello consule civicum
> bellique causas et vitia et modos
> ludumque Fortunae gravisque
> principum amicitias et arma
>
> nondum expiatis uncta cruoribus,
> periculosae plenum opus aleae,
> tractas, et incedis per ignis
> suppositos cineri doloso.

'Of civic turmoil from the consulship of Metellus and the causes of the war and its crimes and stages and of the game of Fortune and the dangerous friendships of great men and of weapons smeared with blood that is not yet expiated—of all this you treat, a work full of perilous hazard, and you tread on flames that smoulder beneath treacherous ash.'

The work is dangerous because the fires lit by the civil wars are not yet dead. The poet's personal warning has been immediately preceded by an equally personal comment that appears to provide the ground for it. The killings of kith and kin that Pollio will describe in his history have not yet been expiated. It is a remarkable and sombre idea, and must arouse in the reader's mind the question: how, then, can such bloodshed be expiated? The poet does not answer. He turns aside for two stanzas (9–16) to hope that the interruption this will cause to Pollio's composition of tragedy will be brief, and he recalls Pollio's other distinctions as advocate and senator and triumphant general. Two stanzas then follow in which the poet imagines, with immediate excitement, the emotional impact that the reading of Pollio's history will have on him (17–24):

iam nunc minaci murmure cornuum
perstringis auris, iam litui strepunt,
   iam fulgor armorum fugaces
      terret equos equitumque vultus.

audire magnos iam videor duces
non indecoro pulvere sordidos,
   et cuncta terrarum subacta
      praeter atrocem animum Catonis.

'Already you assail my ears with the menacing roar of horns, already the trumpets blare, already the glitter of weapons terrifies the horses into flight and marks the faces of the cavalrymen. Already I fancy I hear of generals filthied with a dust that does them honour and of the whole world battered to subjection—except the fiercely independent spirit of Cato.'

The poet's vision of the war reaches a climax with the picture of Cato's suicide at Utica in 46 B.C. Cato, the champion against Caesar of Republican constitutionality, was analogous to Pollio himself, who stood out firmly against Augustus, an intransigent but inactive opponent; and the poet shows remarkable realism in foreseeing that Pollio's history will find its own climax in Cato, not Caesar. But that realism will in no way have offended Augustus, who professed a Catonian rather than a Caesarian attitude to Republican constitutionality (see p. 18). In fact, the reconciliation of Republicans was one of the major aims of Augustus, and the poet could not, in 28 or 27 B.C., foresee the implacable intransigence of Pollio throughout more than the following thirty years. Such realism, however, was not the only motive the poet had in making Cato the climax to his vision. The next stanza is (25–28):

Iuno et deorum quisquis amicior
Afris inulta cesserat impotens
   tellure victorum nepotes
      rettulit inferias Iugurthae.

'Juno and any other god who, more favourable to the African side, retreated from the land they were powerless to save, devoted the grandsons of the victors as a due tomb-sacrifice to Jugurtha.'

The mention of Cato in a phrase that points only to his suicide permits here a metonymic movement of ideas to the battle of Thapsus in 46 B.C. After that defeat Cato committed suicide rather than submit to Julius Caesar. The battle does not need to be mentioned specifically. Instead the poet regards all the dead in the battle, Caesarians as well as Republicans, grandsons of the very men who had conquered Jugurtha more than half a century earlier, as a human sacrifice to the shade of Jugurtha. It is a grim and foreboding idea in itself, but it has a further resonance: it is also an expiation exacted by Juno and associated deities on the Romans for their treatment of north Africa. The theme picks up (5) *nondum expiatis uncta cruoribus* and makes the transition to the two stanzas which virtually close the poem (in a final stanza the poet prays to his Muse to desist from so mournful a subject). The poet now deliberately turns away from Pollio to his own foreboding thoughts (29–36):

> quis non Latino sanguine pinguior
> campus sepulcris impia proelia
>   testatur auditumque Medis
>   Hesperiae sonitum ruinae?
>
> qui gurges aut quae flumina lugubris
> ignara belli? quod mare Dauniae
>   non decoloravere caedes?
>   quae caret ora cruore nostro?

'What plain, fertilized with Latin blood, does not bear witness by its graves to unholy battles and to the sound of Italy's fall, heard by the Parthians? What tide or what rivers are in ignorance of the mournful war? What sea have Italian murders not discoloured? What shore is unstained by our blood?'

The theme of (5) *nondum expiatis uncta cruoribus* is here fully taken up in a tone of unrelenting doom, and the question of expiation is answered by the unobtrusive, but strictly unnecessary, mention of the Parthians. Just as the deaths in Africa brought satisfaction to the shade of Jugurtha, so the noise of Rome's fall, destroyed by herself, reached the ears of the Parthians. Jugurtha had symbolically earned the expiation paid in Roman blood by his own death. The Parthian delight in Roman disaster is a synecdoche for Parthia's bloody triumph over Roman forces under Crassus in 53 B.C.; this suggests the idea, synecdochically related to the vision of Parthian delight, that Rome can only expiate the guilt of civil war by a victorious expedition against the Parthians. As it were, the Parthians are presented as ripe to provide

Rome with an expiation of their civil war parallel to the expiation which that civil war offered to the dead Jugurtha. Only with this idea is the theme of (5) *nondum expiatis* adequately fulfilled. The two ideas of civil war and an expedition against the Parthians stand in a metonymic relationship in the first three books of Horace's *Odes*, connected by the idea of expiation. In this poem that connexion is left to be inferred by the striking thematic anticipation where the idea, in its early occurrence, is over-adequate to its immediate context and looks forward to satisfaction later. The concept that expiation is necessary is carried by the one word (30) *impia*, and its significance is explained by the recurring adjectives that signify Italy: the civil war excited the hostility of the gods. The themes and tone are close to those of *Odes* 1.35, and the two poems are close in time also (see pp. 153 ff.). It is a remarkable idea that Actium ended, but did not expiate, the civil wars; that this was Augustus' view too, at least by the year 28 B.C., is shown by his abandonment of his vow to the gods to celebrate the vengeance exacted on the murderers of Julius Caesar with a temple to Mars Ultor (see p. 12).

Thematic anticipation of this sort should be recognised also in another difficult ode of Horace. Of *Odes* 1.18 the latest commentators say:[16] 'A poem of this sort makes little appeal to moderns. It depends for its effect on an intricate network of allusions, some of which are now obscure. Its subject veers disconcertingly, though not untypically of its author. It contains no sentiments to which every bosom returns an echo: dithyrambic exhortations to sobriety sound very odd unless one realises that Horace is playing a complicated literary game. In many other poems, of course, he is equally artificial; but where the commonplaces are less esoteric it is easier to persuade oneself that he is speaking from the heart. But though the ode lacks that reference to life which must be demanded from the greatest poetry, one should not underestimate its ingenuity.' Their interpretation certainly bears out this censorious summary, but more may be said about the poem. It is short and may be quoted in full:

> Nullam, Vare, sacra vite prius severis arborem
> circa mite solum Tiburis et moenia Catili.
> siccis omnia nam dura deus proposuit, neque
> mordaces aliter diffugiunt sollicitudines.

16. Nisbet and Hubbard (1970), p. 220.

quis post vina gravem militiam aut pauperiem crepat?   5
quis non te potius, Bacche pater, teque, decens Venus?
ac ne quis modici transiliat munera Liberi,
Centaurea monet cum Lapithis rixa super mero

debellata, monet Sithoniis non levis Euhius
cum fas atque nefas exiguo fine libidinum   10
discernunt avidi. non ego te, candide Bassareu,
invitum quatiam nec variis obsita frondibus

sub divum rapiam. saeva tene cum Berecyntio
cornu tympana, quae subsequitur caecus Amor sui
et tollens vacuum plus nimio Gloria verticem   15
arcanique Fides prodiga, perlucidior vitro.

'You must not plant any tree, Varus, in preference to the sacred vine in and around the mild soil of Tibur and the walls of Catilus.[17] For to teetotalers God has ordained that everything be hard to bear, and wine is the only means for dispelling gnawing anxieties. Who, after wine, chatters about the burdens of military service or of poverty (5)? Who does not talk rather of you, father Bacchus, and of you, pretty Venus? And against a man's overleaping the bounties of Liber [Bacchus] who observes moderation there is the warning of the Centaurs' quarrel in their cups with the Lapiths that was battled out to the end; there is the warning of Euhius' [Bacchus] harshness to the Sithonians when greedy men distinguish right and wrong by the tenuous limit of their lusts (11). I shall not shake you, handsome Bassareus [Bacchus], when it is not your will, nor expose your mystic emblems, veiled with variegated leaves, to the light of day. Restrain the wild drums and the Berecynthian horn that are closely accompanied by blind Self-Love and Conceit that raises her empty head far too high (15) and Faith that blabs out her secret, easier to see through than glass.'

The structure of the poem is clear: after the address to Varus (1–2), the poet begins with one extreme (total abstinence) and moves through moderation (7) to the opposite extreme (drunkenness). Whereas total abstinence offends against a law of the universe, drunkenness offends against the rules of Bacchus, and the movement towards excess is mirrored in the orgiastic titles attributed to Bacchus (Euhius and Bassareus). This unexpected aspect of theology is thematically anticipated in the adjective (1) *sacra*, which has no corresponding Greek word in the line

17. According to legend, the founder of Tibur.

of Alcaeus that Horace used allusively as an opening to the poem. It is no decorative epithet: it anticipates the way in which the poet is going to treat the theme of wine. The novel revelation of the poet is that the vine belongs to Bacchus and is under his control in such a way that drunkenness is the god's own punishment for excessive use of it. By what is almost an oxymoron, the god, under his title of Liber (suggesting freedom and liberality) is characterised as 'loving moderation' (7, *modici*). The meaning of 'rites' sometimes assigned to (7) *munera* here must be wrong. The sense must be the usual one of 'gifts'. The following objection has been made to this: 'But this sense seems impossible with *transiluisse*; one needs a word which refers to what the drinker does and not what Bacchus does.'[18] The emphasis, however, is not on the drinker but on the god's ordinance, and the metaphor in *transiliat* is expended on *modici*: the god gives generously, but sets limits which a man must not overleap.[19] The mythic examples which establish this piece of theology pick up the theme anticipated in (6) *quis non te potius, Bacche pater, teque, decens Venus?* and transform it into the types of excess represented by drunkenness and lust. (The unspoken element of lust needs to be supplied synecdochically to the myth of the Centaurs.) Just as in line 6 the poet relied on the metonymic association of wine and love-making, so in lines 8–11 he relies on the metonymic association of drunkenness and lust.

Why, when the poet addresses Bacchus (11), does he use the orgiastic title Bassareus? And what is he saying? The latest commentators say:[20] 'It does not seem to be understood that this is a deprecation, expressed paratactically; Horace says "I shall not offend you, so do not hurt me".... Müller is wrong in supposing that the *non ego* clause refers allegorically to drunkenness; there is no point in saying "I'll not get drunk, so don't make me drunk". Horace purports to be thinking of a real profanation of the Bacchic rites'. But in what possible sense could the poet commit such a 'real' profanation? In any case, while *nec variis obsita frondibus / sub divum rapiam* could certainly suggest profanation, the preceding and parallel act—*non ego te ... invitum quatiam*—suggests only choice of the wrong time. The reason why the poet addresses Bacchus as Bassareus can only be because the metonymic relationship of

18. Nisbet and Hubbard (1970), p. 232; they actually consider emending to *moenia*.

19. Cf. *Odes* 1.3.24.

20. Nisbet and Hubbard (1970), p. 234.

wine and lust is now being translated into another, closely associated, metonymic relationship of orgiastic rites with moral delinquency. The reason for making that translation is that the poet is shaping circumstances that will be relevant to his own situation. But he is assuredly not saying that he will never indulge in orgies; that, despite the apparent separateness of each ode, would be an odd thing for the poet to say who wrote (3.19.18–19) *insanire iuvat: cur Berecyntiae | cessant flamina tibiae?* ('It is my pleasure to go mad: why do the blasts of the Phrygian pipe hold back?'). What he is saying is that he will not engage in such an orgy when the god is unwilling nor will he expose the mysteries to daylight: that is, there is a right time for orgiastic celebration; and the phrase *sub divum rapiam* at least recalls the proverbial Roman prohibition on *de die potare* (drinking before sundown). What the poet is saying here is said very simply at *Odes* 4.12.28, *dulce est desipere in loco*. What the Centaurs and Sithonians did wrong was to ignore the appropriate limitations; the wrong that the poet will avoid is to ignore the appropriate time and occasion. The penalty for the mythical characters was fighting and bloodshed. For the transgressions that the poet hopes to avoid the penalties are the moral failings of self-love, conceit, and a loose tongue. The poet's prayer is that, since he will not commit the wrong, he may not suffer the penalty. But why say that since, without the wrong, there should naturally be no penalty? Commentators note that '[Horace] dedicates the poem to Varus by way of compliment, and then ignores him'.[21] But a different way of regarding the structure of the poem produces a more lively and responsive interaction of poet and addressee.

If the poem is interpreted, like many of Horace's *Odes*, as a dramatic monologue, then, with the word (3) *siccis*, the poet is to be imagined pouring wine for Varus.[22] Then the apostrophes to Bacchus and Venus (6) function as a sort of libation, and the prayer to Bacchus has something of the same purpose as the assurances to Maecenas in a similar dramatic monologue (*Odes* 3.8.15–16) that the party will be sober:[23] in both poems the poet can represent himself as responsible for the conduct of the party, since he is *magister bibendi*. Here the poet lectures Varus on wine as they drink. The two friends are to be imagined as drinking in daylight in the sort of circumstances described in *Odes* 2.3.5–14. The poet's as-

---

21. Ibid., p. 229.

22. For this type of setting in odes of Horace, cf. 1.9, 11, 20, 36; 3.8: see pp. 202 ff.

23. See Williams (1968), pp. 103–07, and (1969), pp. 72–74.

surance to the god in lines 11–13 is both general (a rule of the poet's life) and also particular to this special occasion. This is not a time to get drunk and go wild (Varus is being reassured). When it is the right time, such behaviour is perfectly acceptable; when it is not, men become self-indulgent, conceited blabbermouths. That is the god's punishment.

The ending of the poem, then, is not quite equivalent to saying 'I'll not get drunk, so don't make me drunk'; but it does recognise that the drinking man has a problem: he treads a narrow path between sobriety and drunkenness, with only his sense of propriety or of the god's regulations to guide him. The poet acknowledges that the present is an occasion when the god is unwilling; he declares his good intention to the god, but also prays that the god give him credit for it. Bacchus is a dangerous and unpredictable god (*Odes* 2.19—especially lines 5–8—and 3.25), with opposing characteristics: he is both peaceful and violent (these opposite aspects are the subject of *Odes* 2.19). The final prayer to Bacchus is nicely anticipated in the apostrophe (6) to Bacchus and Venus where the poet is still addressing Varus directly; here the apostrophe to the two deities, functioning as a sort of libation, is an appeal to the peace-loving aspect of Bacchus, while the final prayer is addressed to his other aspect. The opening motto from Alcaeus is made more understandable as advice to Varus if the particularising situation of a private and restrained symposium is understood. It is also made relevant to the whole poem by the thematic anticipation in *sacra*. The particular dramatic situation makes this (by a technique to be examined later, chap. 7, sec. 1) a more interesting poem than critics allow: it does not consist of 'dithyrambic exhortations to sobriety'; but the address to a friend, together with the Roman references (2), make a bridge from the private setting to a general view of life. The poem is also poignant if, as there seems no good reason to deny, Varus is Quintilius Varus whose death is mourned six poems later and of whom the poet gives a moving portrait towards the end of the *Ars poetica*.

3. *Structural Anticipation*

In a sense, most of the examples of thematic anticipation so far discussed can be regarded as structural. But the type to be examined now belongs to poems where the poet has almost deliberately created a divisive and potentially incoherent structure, and has sought to produce unity by a number of means but especially by thematic anticipation. I regard

Catullus 68 as the model for all such experiments, but on the hypothesis that it is one poem with an introductory and closing poetic epistle surrounding the central, highly wrought poem to the Muses.[24]

A start may be made with poem 4.1 of Propertius, which was discussed under the previous category; for, quite apart from the ring-composition with thematic anticipation in lines 87–118, the poem falls into two distinct halves to such an extent that many editors have divided it into two separate elegies. A recent editor says:[25] 'The relation between iA and iB is thus peculiar. They are neither (in the ordinary sense) a single elegy, nor two completely separate elegies, but a pair, related by a certain common function in their respective conclusions, and linked by a formal device at the point of transition.' But this may be put otherwise: in the first half of the poem Propertius makes a speech, setting out a programme of future works for himself; in the second half an Egyptian astrologer replies to the poet, warning him that his aims are unsuited to his talents, setting out the merits of his own claim to be heard with respect, and finally pointing the poet in a different direction. The poem, taken as a unit, is thus programmatic to Book 4, which combines both the types of poetry that Propertius proposed for himself and also the type that the astrologer enjoined. The poem also functions as a *recusatio*, in that Horus' reply in effect apologises for any shortcoming that the poet displays in the execution of his own ambitious programme. This potentially divisive structure the poet has carefully linked by a series of thematic anticipations.

The most obvious is that Horus picks up immediately the last topic raised by the poet, in order to rebuke him for it. A specifically thematic connexion is that, when the astrologer speaks the couplet 87–88, he echoes the words of Cassandra already quoted by the poet (53–54), and the two themes are closely related since thereby the astrologer shows himself—what he claims to be—a Cassandra and not a Calchas (as he goes on to demonstrate). Again, when the poet declares his future material to be the history of Rome, he himself has doubts, since he is an elegiac poet with a small voice (58–60); this anticipates, and creates the basis for, what will be the advice of Horus—to stick to elegiac (that is, love-) poetry (135–36). But by far the most important

24. Explained in Williams (1968), pp. 229–33. For the opposing view, see Wiseman (1974), pp. 77–103.

25. Camps (1962–67), in his introductory remarks to Propertius 4.1.

link is the word-for-word repetition in lines 121–26 of things the poet has already said about himself in lines 63–66. There is no parallel for such a procedure in Roman poetry outside of the repetition by Catullus in poem 68 of lines 19–24 in lines 91–96 on the theme of his brother's death. Repetition of this type would be inane if it were not intended to interlock the two sections of the poem. The other thematic antici-pations guarantee this to have been Propertius' intention here, and at least it can be said on that evidence that Propertius read poem 68 of Catullus in the same way.

There are pairs of elegies, marked as separate poems in the MSS tradition, where a good case can be made out for regarding them as intended by the poet to be single poems; and some editors have been persuaded. For example, Propertius 3.1 and 2. In 3.1 the poet talks of his poetic aims and his hopes for immortality; in 3.2 he talks of poetry's power to immortalize both poet and subject. But an important section of 3.1 (21–34) expresses the idea that the poet, in immortalizing his subject, also immortalizes himself (see pp. 172 ff.). This passage can be regarded as a clear thematic anticipation of the major theme of 3.2. If the two elegies are regarded as a unity, then the ending of 3.2 displays a major inclusive ring-composition with the opening of 3.1, bringing together the two themes of the poet's fame and the girl's fame (17–26). The ring-composition by which an allusion to Callimachus in 3.1.37–38 picks up the opening prayer to Callimachus (3.1.1) would be internal and an example of Propertius' frequent practice of completing a section of a poem by ring-composition. A thematic echo would then be discernible between the assurance of approval by 'the Lycian god' (3.1.38) and the assertion of the favour of Bacchus and Apollo (3.2.9). The fact that the first line of 3.2 has *interea* as its second word, in clear reference to the preceding poem, would then be able to be used as an argument for the unity of the two poems.

Similar arguments could be used to connect 3.4 and 3.5. In the former the poet praises Augustus' military venture against the Parthians, but, while doing that, maintains that his own way of life is so different as to exclude the possibility of participation other than as a spectator of the triumph. The poem, as it were, defines the poet's ideal of life negatively—in relation to something which he praises but refuses for himself. It opens with the words *arma deus Caesar*; here the deliberation with which Augustus is deified in his political self goes far beyond the claim of the dead Cornelia (4.11.60) that 'tears were seen on the god's face': the formulation here in 3.4 can only have been devised to balance and contrast with the opening of 3.5. The poem 3.5 defines the poet's ideal positively, and opens with the poet's interest in peace rather than war expressed in the assertion *pacis Amor deus*; the theme of war is here treated generally and condemned as the product of men's avarice. Against this the poet develops his own contrasting ideals both as a young man and in old age (23–46). But he ends the poem (47–48):

> exitus hic vitae superest mihi:vos, quibus arma
> grata magis, Crassi signa referte domum.

'Such is the final period of life that awaits me: you, whose pleasure is rather in arms, bring home the standards of Crassus.'

Here the theme of war is treated not in the terms in which it has been handled in this poem (as a product of avarice), but in the terms of Roman military glory and patriotism in which it was treated in 3.4. Consequently, lines 47–48 of this poem would better be regarded as a closing ring-composition which picks up the patriotic theme of 3.4.1–10.

Both of the structures just examined (3.1 with 3.2 and 3.4 with 3.5) could be regarded as models for the bolder 4.1. Everything guarantees the unity of 4.1 as intended by the poet. Of 3.1, 2 and 3.4, 5 it can be argued that not only does it make them more interesting intellectual and artistic structures to regard them as single poems, but that the degree of close reference between both pairs cannot be seen elsewhere between poems that are certainly separate. The MSS speak as unanimously against the unity of 3.1 and 2 and 3.4 and 5 as they speak for the unity of 4.1. But the value of their evidence for elegy-division in Propertius is dubious; the best to be said is that all the evidence must be weighed in each doubtful case, but that it would not be irresponsible to act against the evidence of the MSS. There are many doubtful cases, especially in Book 2, and some of these will now be examined, and the criterion of thematic anticipation will be applied.

The MSS are unanimous that Propertius 2.13 is a single poem, but most editors have divided it into two (1–16 and 17–58). The reason, as stated by one pair of editors, is this:[26] 'The inconsistency

26. Butler and Barber (1933), p. 212.

of tone which exists between them, the one full of thoughts of life, the other written in deep dejection and permeated with brooding anticipation of death, precludes their union, while the change from the third person of the first section to the second person (18) of the next is impossibly abrupt.' That last point, at least, will not stand a moment's scrutiny: abrupt changes of address are characteristic of Propertius' manner of composition, and here there is dramatic reason for it. But also the tone of lines 1–16 is missed if it is characterised as 'full of thoughts of life'. The poet is so badly wounded by *Amor* that he is compelled to revere the frail Muses and dwell in the Ascraean grove (like Hesiod), not to emulate Orpheus but simply to bewitch Cynthia. It is not her beauty nor her ancestry that captivates him (9–10), but, he says tentatively, 'it would be my pleasure to read in the arms of a poetic girl and have her approve my poems with her perfect ear'. He is not interested in the world's judgment (13–14). Then he says (15–16):

> quae si forte bonas ad pacem verterit auris,
>   possum inimicitias tunc ego ferre Iovis.

'It she will be kind and turn her ears in the direction of peace, then I can bear the hostility of Juppiter.'

It becomes clear that the tentative subjunctive (11) *iuvet* is due to the fact that the poet has no certainty of obtaining his desire; and that point is underlined by his hope for peace (15). His relationship with Cynthia is not happy. Is the 'hostility of Juppiter' just a conventional mythic metaphor? The next couplet, where a new elegy is usually started, is (17–18):

> quandocumque igitur nostros mors claudet ocellos,
>   accipe quae serves funeris acta mei.

'So then, hear the dispositions you are to observe for my funeral, whenever death shall close my eyes.'

The immediate connexion is that the hostility of Juppiter suggests, by metonymy, the poet's death. But *igitur* connects the centrality of his poetry in the poet's life with the instruction that follows to dispense with all funeral pomp except for the three books of his poetry (25–26).

A further aspect of this connexion is that the rejection of common opinion (9–14) anticipates the theme of rejecting the pompous and the grandiose (19–38), and both are Callimachean themes and related to the Callimachean ideals expressed in lines 3–7.[27] Then the theme of unhappiness between himself and Cynthia, which just appears in lines 11 and 15, is taken up, though still not explicitly, in his wondering why he did not die an infant (43–44), in the myth of Nestor (45–50), and in the idea that only after his death will he be appreciated by Cynthia and consequently mourned—too late (51–56). The poem ends (57–58):

> sed frustra mutos revocabis, Cynthia, Manis:
> nam mea quid poterunt ossa minuta loqui?

'But it will be useless for you to call back a shade—it is dumb: for what will my crumbled bones be able to say?'

This is another clear example of ring-composition. The ideas move from Cynthia's longing for the poet, now dead, to her longing for his poetry—but it will be too late. This takes up the theme with which the poem opened: the importance of his poetry to him and its indissoluble link with Cynthia. The shades of the dead, the poet emphasises, are dumb, not deaf: that is what matters to the poet and to Cynthia.

The poem is constructed from two elements: a short section (1–16) in which the poet is overheard speaking to himself, and a long section (17–58) in which the poet addresses Cynthia. The two sections are contrasted in many ways: the first is reflective, philosophical, detached without being unemotional; the second is fatalistic, unhappy, and concentrates on the poet's death, even wishing for it. The first is largely composed of primary statements about poetry and life and the rejection of common opinions; where the form of expression is secondary it is of a simple, easily and unambiguously penetrable type. The second section is almost completely in secondary language in that the surface meaning of what is said does not represent the real intention of the poet—that lies behind the symbols of the funeral and the myths of Nestor and Adonis. Thus the two sections are disparate in many ways —in length, tone, language, address—but the first supplies the base for the second, in that they both look at the same themes from different

---

27. See Wilkinson (1966), pp. 141 ff.

points of view (in this respect their relationship is very similar to that
of 3.1 with 3.2 or of 3.4 with 3.5). The poet's objective formulation
of his ideals (guaranteed as objective by the absence of addressee) is
followed by an appeal to Cynthia that is designed to help him achieve
some of them, but too late for the two lovers. These two sections the
poet has linked together in all the ways described above. It is an experimental poem in the sense that the poet deliberately confronted
himself with this particular difficulty of disparity and solved it.

There is a further point. He says in the first section (3–8):

> hic me tam gracilis vetuit contemnere Musas,
>   iussit et Ascraeum sic habitare nemus,
> non ut Pieriae quercus mea verba sequantur
>   aut possim Ismaria ducere valle feras,
> sed magis ut nostro stupefiat Cynthia versu:
>   tunc ego sim Inachio notior arte Lino.

'⟨Love⟩ forbade me to reject Muses so delicate and so bade me dwell in the
grove of Ascra, not to make Pierian oaks follow my words or to enable me
to lead wild beasts down the Ismarian vale, but rather so that Cynthia might
be thunderstruck by my poetry: then I should be a poet more famous for my
technique than Inachian Linus.'

The language is as Alexandrian as the ideas: avoidance of the
grand and epic, emphasis on technique, and the adoption of Hesiod as
a symbol. But the purpose is not Alexandrian: Cynthia is to be struck
dumb by his poetry; if he succeeds in that, he will be a more famous
poet than Linus. The claim is as large as the aim is strange. But another
aspect of the relationship between the two sections of the poem is
that the second executes in Alexandrian style this purpose stated in
the first. The relationship between the two sections mirrors that of
Catullus 68: the letter in primary language explaining a purpose, the
poem to the Muses executing that purpose in secondary language.
For the second section of Propertius 2.13 exercises on Cynthia—or
rather seeks to exercise—the type of influence that the poet claims
in the first section his poetry aims at: it serves a practical purpose in
his love-affair with Cynthia. Thus the poem can be read partly as,
in a sense, programmatic.

There are considerable differences between Books 1 and 2 of
Propertius. One is the small scale of the elegies in Book 1; another lies

in the way in which dramatic situations that involve externals—both people and surroundings—are constituted as the setting of elegies in Book 1; another can be seen in the way in which contiguous, or closely contiguous, elegies respond in various ways to one another. In all these respects Book 2 differs: not only is Book 2 itself on a huge scale, but a majority of the elegies are complex and lengthy compositions; almost all the elegies of Book 2 deeply involve the poet in a private anguish or ecstasy with Cynthia; and, corresponding to the large scale of the book itself, Propertius seems to have composed in a series of cycles, in each of which the poet progresses not through a historical sequence of events or episodes, but through a range of emotional crises ending in the death of love or a retreat into poetry. There are perhaps three such sequences of poems to be discerned: 1–11 (the poet gives Cynthia up); 12–24A (the poet resorts to prostitutes); and 24B–34 (the poet retreats into poetry). The main reason for the great length of Book 2 may be conjectured to have been that such highly dramatic sequences need large-scale treatment if they are to achieve an effect. If this view is right, then poem 2.13 comes near the beginning of a new sequence (the sequence starts with a very Hellenistic poem on the power of Cupid and the dependence of Propertius' poetry on the god; everything is secondary, there is nothing personal here; but these two themes are taken up personally in 2.13); and it may consequently be seen as programmatic not just of itself, but of a whole series of experimental poems like it in Book 2.

In poem 2.26 the poet tells Cynthia of a dream (1–20) in which he saw her shipwrecked and on the point of drowning but finally rescued by the same dolphin, probably, that rescued Arion (17–18). This is followed by a complex monologue (21–58), starting as the poet's own reflections and treating Cynthia in the third person, but then addressing Cynthia from line 44: the poet exults at Cynthia's servitude to him, and is willing even to go on a voyage with her and die at sea with her, if necessary. Most modern editors see two separate poems here.[28] But in fact the dream and the monologue are held together by several thematic anticipations. Within the dream there is a simple example of a myth used to legitimate further themes. Cynthia's hair weighing her down (4) reminds the poet of Helle (5)— he feared that the sea might adopt her name (7). Among the gods to

28. Against this view, see Macleod (1976), pp. 131–36.

whom he prays for her safety is (10) Leucothoe, who, under the name
of Ino, persecuted Phrixus and Helle into the flight that proved fatal
for Helle. Why does the poet dream of Cynthia on board a ship?
The choice of this particular myth suggests the answer: she had resolved
to leave the poet and had made accusations of persecution against him.
By way of confirmation the poet hears her confessing as she drowns
(3) that all she said against him were lies. The myth thus functions
also as a substitute for a primary statement which a reader must reconstruct.

The poet's reflections begin thus (21–28):

> nunc admirentur quod tam mihi pulchra puella
>   serviat et tota dicar in urbe potens.
> non, si Cambysae redeant et flumina Croesi,
>   dicat 'De nostro surge, poeta, toro'.
> nam mea cum recitat, dicit se odisse beatos: 25
>   carmina tam sancte nulla puella colit.
> multum in amore fides, multum constantia prodest:
>   qui dare multa potest, multa et amare potest.

'Now let them feel admiration that so beautiful a girl is in servitude to me
and that I am called master throughout the whole city. Even if a Cambyses
should return and the rivers of Croesus, she would not say: "Get out of my
bed you poet". For, as she recites my poetry, she declares that she hates rich
men (25): no girl is a more devoted lover of poetry. Fidelity is of great consequence in love, and so too is constancy: he that can give much can also love
much.'

The emphatic (21) *nunc* means that there has been a change between
the situation envisaged in the dream and that in which the poet's words
are now set: Cynthia is not leaving; both her 'servitude' and the poet's
'mastery' look back to her confession of lying (3) and to her constant
calling of the poet's name as she drowned (12). Another thematic
anticipation lies in her means of rescue: the poet prayed and the dolphin
of Arion came (17–18)—a poetic dolphin. The theme anticipates the
girl's admission (25) that poetry is more powerful than wealth. In
fact, the dream as a whole is a figure for Cynthia's real love of the poet
and of the poet's power over her.

But the dream is also itself a thematic anticipation of the poet's
declaration (29 ff.) that he would even accompany her on a sea-voyage

himself. And there is a further thematic anticipation. The dream ends with the couplet (19–20):

> iamque ego conabar summo me mittere saxo,
>   cum mihi discussit talia visa metus.

'And all the while I was trying to fling myself from the top of the cliffs, when fear dissipated the whole vision.'

Oddly enough, some commentators feel critical of the poet for not jumping to the rescue sooner. But not only is the reservation of this statement to the end merely a narrative necessity;[29] his jump is, in any case, intended not to rescue her (marine life-saving was not a recognised art in antiquity), but to join her in her horrible death. That theme anticipates and is made clear in the final couplet of the poem (57–58): if the poet has to die with her at sea, that will be an honourable death.

The connexion between the two sections of this poem is much bolder and more experimental than the connexion between 1.8.1–26 (the poet in direct address tries to persuade Cynthia not to go off to Illyria with a rival) and 1.8.27–48 (the poet exults that Cynthia— referred to in the third person—has decided not to go); in that poem, too, there is a similar change of address between its two parts. Both in the change of tone and aspect between the two parts and in the change of address 2.26 is closely analogous to 2.13. In both poems the poet has set himself the problem of uniting two disparate elements. It may in fact be, as some editors have thought, that 2.27 should continue 2.26 without break, linked by its themes of danger by sea, the North Wind, and the lover's death; but it seems impossible to demonstrate this as essential.

Very similar in structure is 2.29. This is now usually divided into two poems: a fantasy in which the poet is arrested by a band of Cupids (1–22), and a scene, described by the poet, of spying on Cynthia and of being attacked by her (23–42). But the whole is a unity: first an

---

29. Compare, for instance, Virgil's narrative of Aristaeus' visit to his mother (*Georgics* 4.333–60). The poet starts with the mother's hearing her son weeping (333–34), but he lets her take no action till she has heard it a second time (349). Meanwhile he has given himself the opportunity to describe the scene beneath the waters, list the characters, and outline the song of Clymene.

account by the poet in the form of a narrative to Cynthia of his fantasy of being arrested by Cupids the previous night (1–22); in fact, this turns out to be part of another narrative to the reader in which the poet reports what he said to Cynthia, and only then gives the necessary dramatic information, his own impressions on seeing Cynthia, what Cynthia said, and the sad ending (23–42). The fantasy-speech opens (1–2):

> Hesterna, mea lux, cum potus nocte vagarer,
>   nec me servorum duceret ulla manus . . .

'Last night, my darling, as I was wandering the streets drunk, and had no band of slaves to guide me . . .'

When the speech is ended, he says (23–24):

> mane erat et volui si sola quiesceret illa
>   visere: at in lecto Cynthia sola fuit.

'It was morning and I wanted to see if she were asleep by herself: but Cynthia was alone in the bed.'

His speech to her tells of 'last night', but the time of delivery is the morning; and, while the speech purports to show him arrested by Cupids dispatched by a Cynthia eager to make love with him, his own, somewhat mean, motive is revealed in his words to the reader: he was spying on her and used the fantasy-story as a pretext—a fact instantly recognised by Cynthia in the opening words of her attack (31). She goes on to repulse physically the poet's amorous overtures, the ground for which he had carefully prepared as a second element in his fantasy-speech. There is yet another thematic anticipation in the fantasy-speech: his own intentions were unfaithful before he was arrested, as he lets slip (14), and this is the main burden of Cynthia's attack (32): she is not unfaithful as he is (33–36). The poet's bad conscience is neatly displayed in his reaction to the sight of Cynthia (25–28):

> obstipui: non illa mihi formosior umquam
>   visa, neque ostrina cum fuit in tunica,
> ibat et hinc castae narratum somnia Vestae
>   neu sibi neve mihi quae nocitura forent.

'I was struck dumb: she never seemed more beautiful to me, not even when she was in a purple dress and going to tell her dreams to chaste Vesta to prevent anything harming either herself or me.'

The occasion he remembers as a measure of her beauty is one expressive of Cynthia's fidelity and concern for them both. This creates a perfect contrast to the drunken wantonness displayed by the poet in his fantasy-speech. And this detail, too, is a thematic anticipation of the final couplet (41–42):

> sic ego tam sancti custos deludor amoris:
> ex illo felix nox mihi nulla fuit.

'So I, the guardian of so holy a love, made a fool of myself: from that time I have not had a happy night.'

This itself is a ring-composition by opposites with the opening of the fantasy-speech.

Just as 2.26 can be seen to be related to the earlier 1.8, so 2.29 is related to 1.3 in theme and dramatic situation. But again the later poem is a much more sophisticated structure, marked by the same technique as 2.13 and 2.26 of opening with a section which is a contrast in many ways with the main body of the poem but is linked by thematic anticipation. The opening section of 2.29 is especially dramatic, because it makes use of the rare technique of beginning with a reported speech and only creating a context for that speech after it has been completed. The technique is used occasionally in epigrams: Leonidas of Tarentum (*Anth.Pal.* 7.731) used the technique dramatically to represent a suicide's self-address;[30] Philodemus (*Anth.Pal.* 5.46) used it of a lover warning his girl; and Diodorus (*Anth.Pal.* 6.243) used it, later than Propertius, of a man making sacrifice. Martial used the technique twice, and both instances turn out to be dialogues: 2.24 is not remarkable; but 8.3, where he addresses his Muse at length before giving any explanation, is more like the technique of Propertius 2.29. But, in fact, an earlier poem by a contemporary that would certainly have been known to Propertius provides the most outstanding example of the technique

---

30. Gow and Page (1965), p. 382, unaccountably interpret the epigram as 'advice from one old man to another not to cling to life'.

and its characteristic element of surprise. In Horace's *Epode* 2 a speech on the blessings of a life spent in the country extends for sixty-five lines before a final four lines declare that this was what Alfius the money-lender said just before he called in all his money. This is the quality of drama and surprise that Propertius was aiming at in 2.29.

The same structure can be seen in poem 2.30 of Propertius. There an impassioned self-address (1–12)[31] is followed by a lengthy address to Cynthia (13–40). Again modern editors generally divide this into separate elegies. The self-address opens (1–2):

> Quo fugis a demens? nulla est fuga: tu licet usque
> ad Tanain fugias, usque sequetur Amor.

'Where are you running away to—you are out of your mind: there is no escape: even though you run right to the Don, Love will follow all the way.'

He goes on to assert that it would not help to have Pegasus or to be Perseus or Mercury. This conventional use of mythology is notably marked by highly original linguistic expression. The poet is trying to escape from Love. Why? The self-address ends (9–12):

> excubat ille acer custos et tollere numquam
> te patietur humo lumina capta semel;
> et iam si pecces, deus exorabilis ille est,
> si modo praesentis viderit esse preces.

'He is a watchful guard, always awake, and he will not once let you lift your captive eyes from the ground; and, should you err, he is an amenable god, provided he sees that your penitence is instantly offered.'

There are themes here which connect with the previous poem: there the poet tried to be (41) *custos*; but that is Love's job, and the poet finds himself made subject to that *custodia*, with a longing to escape. And what of (11) *si pecces*? Again the poet's behaviour in the previous poem will supply the background. Finally, the reader can

---

31. Interpreted by Cairns (1971) as 'the flight of the beloved'. But if the question is not prejudged by assumptions about 'generic composition', the themes better suit the poet, whose love is also synonymous with the type of poetry that he has set himself to write.

scarcely move from poem 29 to poem 30 without carrying the echo of the hopeless last line (42) *ex illo felix nox mihi nulla fuit.* That would be something to run away from; but, the poet asserts, that is the last thing to do, for escape is impossible and repentance must be seen to be (12) *praesens.*

The rest of the poem displays that repentance in action (13–40): an appeal to Cynthia. But the themes are complicated by additional elements (13–26):

> ista senes licet accusent convivia duri:
>> nos modo propositum, vita, teramus iter.
> illorum antiquis onerantur legibus aures: 15
>> hic locus est in quo, tibia docta, sones,
> quae non iure vado Maeandri iacta natasti
>> turpia cum faceret Palladis ora tumor.
> num tu, dure, paras Phrygias nunc ire per undas
>> et petere Hyrcani litora nota maris,   20
> spargere et alterna communis caede Penatis
>> et ferre ad patrios praemia dira Lares.
> una contentum pudeat me vivere amica?
>> hoc si crimen erit, crimen Amoris erit:
> mi nemo obiciat. libeat tibi, Cynthia, mecum   25
>> rorida muscosis antra tenere iugis.

'Leave harsh old men to indict those parties of ours: let us, darling, pursue the course that we planned. Their ears are loaded with antique laws (15): this is the place, poetic pipe, where you should sound, you who did not deserve to be thrown to swim in the water of Maeander after the swelling made Pallas' face ugly. Surely you are not hard-heartedly preparing[32] to go through Phrygian waters and to the well-known shores of the Caspian sea (20), and to stain shared Penates with mutual slaughter and bring back terrible booty to ancestral Lares? Should I feel shame at living content with one girl? This, if it shall be counted a crime, will be the crime of Love: no one should make that an accusation against me. May it be your will, Cynthia, with me (25) to dwell in watery caves among mossy rocks.'

The old men are staunch Augustan senators who support Augustus' moral legislation and criticize the poet not only for a licentious life

---

32. The MSS here divide, more or less, between *non tamen immerito* and *num tu dure* (or *dura*) *paras.*

(13)[33] but also for not being married (23). The poet's reply to the latter charge is that his relationship with Cynthia amounts to marriage (23, *una...amica*). The reader might wonder during the opening section (1–12) where the poet imagined he was running away to in his self-address, the Don being just a symbol for a far-off place. That is to be regarded as a thematic anticipation which is remarkably completed and answered by another self-address (19–22). The idea must be supplied (and is easily supplied by a simple metonymic connexion) that another thing the old men criticized in the poet was a failure to do his duty as a patriotic soldier with the army against the Parthians (cf.elegy 3.4). This wild idea is treated by the poet as a possible means of escape from unhappy love which he had seriously considered; but he now rejects it in astonished self-address: he would be (19) *durus* to do such a thing. The way is prepared for introducing this surprising theme by the metonymic connexion between Maeander, the river of Phrygia, and (19) *Phrygias...per undas*; furthermore, the apostrophe to the pipe mediates between the address to Cynthia and the self-address. The poet adds the remarkable notion that war against Parthia would be like civil war, because, as was known at the time, Roman prisoners were being compelled to fight for the Parthians.[34] All of this thematic material, involving two cherished ideals of Augustus, is legitimated by the introduction of the (13) *senes*, who are not the *senes severiores* of Catullus 5.2 (typically disapproving conservatives), but Roman senators, committed to Augustan policies. Politically the poem stands close to 2.7, which also combines the themes of moral legislation and war against Parthia in order to reject both.

There is a further thematic anticipation (27–32):

> illic aspicies scopulis haerere Sorores
> et canere antiqui dulcia furta Iovis,
> ut Semela est combustus, ut est deperditus Io,
> denique ut ad Troiae tecta volarit avis.   30
> quod si nemo exstat qui vicerit Alitis arma,
> communis culpae cur reus unus agor?

33. For the accusation, cf. 1.12.1–2 and p. 198 below.

34. See especially Horace *Odes* 3.5. A different interpretation of lines 19–22 is given by Luck (1962) and Cairns (1971) in terms of a refusal by Propertius to undertake epic themes from the Argonaut and Theban cycles (Cairns understands the *leges* of line 15 as 'rules of epic').

'There you [Cynthia] shall see the sister Muses clinging to their rocky heights and singing of the sweet stolen loves of Juppiter long ago, how he burst into flames over Semele, how he went out of his mind over Io, and finally how he flew as a bird to the houses of Troy (30). But if there is no one at all who has overcome the weapons of the Winged One, why am I alone prosecuted on a charge that all share?'

The theme of the power of Love in the opening self-address (2, 7, 9–10) is an anticipation of the same theme here. The myths are neatly used in the particular technique that alters the movement of thought (see chap. 4, sec. 3): they start off as things Cynthia will see and hear with the poet up in the mountains, but they then supply the basis for the poet's indignant refutation of the old men's accusation from another direction. The two themes of accusation and refutation here in lines 23 and 32 form a ring-composition.

But a further theme has been introduced in anticipation: it finds its full treatment only at the end of the poem (33–40). That is the poetic dimension of the poet's relationship with Cynthia; he is a poet when he lives happily with her, but not otherwise (39–40):

> tum capiti sacros patiar pendere corymbos:
> nam sine te nostrum non valet ingenium.

'Then I shall let the sacred ivy hang down from my head, for without you my genius has no power.'

The escape, which in the opening self-address was an escape for the poet from Cynthia, becomes converted in the rest of the poem into a longed-for escape from the conventions of society and politics to two things which in Propertius are almost synonymous: poetry and a happy life with Cynthia. An unhappy life without Cynthia makes him a prey to *senes*, because, as he says a number of times, his life then becomes public and notorious. But a happy life with her enables him to refuse the dictates of conventional morality and patriotism —the latter of which would have offered him the kind of escape that he was looking for in the opening self-address. Again the two parts of the poem are highly disparate. The first concentrates in inward terms on the poet's misery and his desperate thoughts of escape. The second draws in the moral and political structure of Augustan society and resolves his misery by an appeal to Cynthia to join him in escape

from the constrictions of that society; only with her can he make that
escape, but then he has all he wants.

Poems 2.31 and 2.32 of Propertius should also be considered one
elegy on the same pattern as those examined above, though the late
MSS separated them and most editors have followed their lead. The
first section (31.1–16) shows the poet confronted with a request (by
Cynthia) for the reason for his late arrival; he explains that the golden
portico of the new temple of Apollo was opened 'by great Caesar',
and he spends fourteen lines on its description. The second section
(32.1–62) begins, responding to the theme of late arrival, with the
poet's complaints about Cynthia's absences from Rome on amorous
adventures (1–24); then he reflects that such behaviour has many
impressive precedents, and declares her free to indulge herself, as far
as he is concerned (25–62).

There are many thematic connexions here. The first couplet of the
second section is (32.1–2):

> qui videt, is peccat: qui te non viderit ergo,
>   non cupiet: facti lumina crimen habet.

'He who sees sins: so a man who has not seen you will not desire you: the
eyes are to blame for the crime.'

The last details mentioned by the poet at the end of the previous
section (31.14–16) were the deaths of Niobe's children (14), and Apollo
himself flanked by Latona and Diana (15–16). It is easy to see how
the twin themes of beauty and seeing emerge synecdochically from
these myths. In fact, the theme of 'seeing' is associative throughout
the whole poem: it is the 'sight' of the new temple that commands
the poet's attention (31.3, 5, 8, 9); it is 'sight' that leads to sexual crime
(32.1–2); the crowd 'sees' Cynthia's behaviour (32.9); Cynthia is
perhaps tired of 'seeing' the architectural splendours of Rome (32.11–
16); she is trying to escape the poet's 'eyes' (18); Phoebus will witness
to 'seeing' that her hands are pure (28)—which is also another link
with 2.31; the Hamadryads and the Sileni 'watched' Paris' love-making
(37–38); the 'seeing' of Pasiphae and of Juppiter led to lust (57–60).
And it is precisely the connexion between 'seeing' and 'beauty' that
pulls together the themes of architecture and lust (exemplified mainly
by gods): *peccare* (32.1 and 51) is to be forgiven because so many gods
have indulged it (the examples start from the myths represented on

the new temple) and because, since the gods act so, there is no reason to blame contemporary Roman girls (starting with Lesbia, 45–46) for not observing a practice (that is, chastity) that has been out of fashion since the time of Saturn (51–52).

When the poet has reproached Cynthia for her excursions (3–6), he says (7) *hoc utinam spatiere loco quodcumque vacabis*, 'I wish it were in this place that you spent all your free time': by 'this place' he means mainly the region of the new temple of Apollo that he has just described. He then ironically offers her a possible excuse, introduced by (11) *scilicet*: 'I suppose you will say you are tired of looking at Pompey's portico with its clever mechanical fountain'; the point of this is, of course, that he has just described for her a completely new portico, and the detailed description is an outstanding example of his technique in thematic anticipation—it does not achieve its full meaning till this point, and then only inexplicitly. The first section of the poem has already undermined Cynthia's supposed defence of her behaviour.

It is notable that in the juncture of themes in this complex poem the poet has produced a clash between two Augustan ideals: the new architecture, with the rebuilding of the temples, is brought into conflict with the ideal of moral legislation. It was in the same year, 28 B.C., that the new temple Apollo on the Palatine was dedicated and that the attempted moral legislation of Augustus failed.

Poem 2.33 of Propertius, divided into two elegies since Hertzberg, is a much simpler type of unity, in which the poet curses Isis and the imposition of ten days' abstinence; then he addresses Cynthia, inviting her to end the abstinence now that the ten days are complete: unfortunately she is more interested in drinking (21–44). The piece is marked as a unity by ring-composition. The first couplet is (1–2):

> Tristia iam redeunt iterum sollemnia nobis:
> Cynthia iam noctes est operata decem.

'The miserable festival is back with me again: Cynthia has now been engaged in religious service for ten nights.'

So the poet has been parted from Cynthia for ten nights, and the period of abstinence is therefore complete. The final couplet is (43–44):

> semper in absentis felicior aestus amantis:
> elevat assiduos copia longa viros.

'Women's passion is always kinder towards absent lovers: long familiarity breeds contempt of husbands who are always there.'

An optimistic exhortation: the poet hopes that his long absence will pay its usual dividends.

There is a brief pause to be observed after line 22, while the poet issues his invitation and waits for an answer that does not come. In 2.34 there is a similar technique. In the first section (1–24) the poet complains that Lynceus has tried to steal his girl; in the second (25–94) he advises Lynceus, who has, though late, fallen in love, how to deal with that situation, and especially how to use his literary talents to help himself (25–58); and, finally, the poet uses himself as an example, contrasting his own poetic interests with those of Virgil and comparing them with those of Varro, Catullus, Calvus, and Cornelius Gallus (59–94). The poet opens with unaddressed expostulation (1–8) on the folly of entrusting one's girl to the protection of Love; then he reproaches Lynceus in direct address (9–24). All of this refers to the past. The transition is then made by a single line in third-person reference (25) announcing that Lynceus has, late in life, fallen in love. Then the poet takes up direct address to Lynceus again. Of course, Lynceus' falling in love does not take place, as it were, in line 25; it has been a fact all the time the poet has been speaking. The location of the announcement is only imposed by the strategy of the narrative, as in 2.26.19–20 or 2.29.23–24: the poet wants to move from reproaching Lynceus to advising him.

The relationship between the two parts of these two poems (2.33 and 34) is very much what was suggested above as the relationship between 3.1 and 3.2, and also between 3.4 and 3.5. In 2.33 the poet gets into one poem the contrast between the severity of (and the anger aroused by) abstinence and the laxity of indulgence; in 2.34 it is the contrast between the poet's attitude of outrage at a friend's attempt to steal his girl and his indulgent advice to the same friend when he has fallen in love with some other girl, together with the scope that situation offers for exploring the literary dimension of love.

Poem 2.28 of Propertius is usually divided into two or even three elegies, but its complex structure can be seen to be held together by thematic anticipations. It opens with a prayer to Juppiter to take pity on the poet's sick girl: the death of one so beautiful will be counted a crime if Juppiter permits it. (The couplet 33–34 ought not to be transposed to follow 1–2, as is often done: quite apart from the awkwardness of 33, *hoc*, which should pick up *crimen*, the Ovidian-type witticism produced by the transposition, assuring Juppiter that his wife Juno will forgive him this kindness, is totally alien to the seriousness of the context.) Between lines 34 and 35 there is a brief pause; and then the poet announces (35–38), in an address to the reader (comparable in function to 2.34.25), that all magical remedies have failed. Then he says (39–44):

> una ratis fati nostros portabit amores
>   caerula ad infernos velificata lacus.   40
> si non unius, quaeso, miserere duorum:
>   vivam si vivet; si cadet illa, cadam.
> pro quibus optatis sacro me carmine damno:
>   scribam ego 'Per magnum est salva puella Iovem'.

'A single ship of fate will bear our love, a ship with sails set to the lakes of the underworld (40). If not on one, then I beg you have mercy on two: I shall live if she lives; if she dies I shall die. And for these hearfelt requests I pledge myself to a poem as an offering: I shall write "By the goodness of great Juppiter my girl is saved."'

There is no hint of a prayer to Juppiter after the opening couplet until this passage, and that Juppiter is the addressee is only made clear at the end. This is a clear example of thematic anticipation used to create unity. The prayer fortunately turns out to be successful, for there is another momentary pause between lines 46 and 47; then the poet prays (47–48):

> haec tua, Persephone, maneat clementia, nec tu,
>   Persephonae coniunx, saevior esse velis.

'May this clemency on your part, Persephone, remain in effect, and may you, husband of Persephone, forbear to be more stern.'

'This clemency' indicates the poet's perception that Cynthia is recovering, and the poem ends (59–62) with the poet telling Cynthia to pay her due rites to Diana and to Isis (a theme that looks forward to poem 2.33).

After the opening prayer, the poet considers the torrid summer heat as a possible cause of Cynthia's illness, but he realises that the diagnosis will not do. No: what is wrong is that Cynthia so often failed to hold the gods sacred (a theme from 2.16.47–56); in fact, her illness is due to perjury. But perhaps, he speculates, she compared herself to Venus, a jealous goddess (9–10), or disparaged Juno's temple at Argos (11) or the eyes of Athena (12)? This is, as it were, a Judgment of Paris conducted by Cynthia and with Cynthia taking the prize. The poet continues (13–16):

> semper, formosae, non nostis parcere verbis.
>   hoc tibi lingua nocens, hoc tibi forma dedit.
> sed tibi vexatae per multa pericula vitae
>   extremo veniet mollior hora die.

'Beautiful women, you have never known how to curb your words. This ⟨illness⟩ your [Cynthia's] guilty tongue caused, your beauty caused it. But on your final day a gentler hour will come to end a life harassed by many dangers.'

The poet proceeds to illustrate that cheerless proposition by a series of four *paradeigmata*: Io (17–18), Ino (19–20), Andromeda (21–22), and Callisto (23–24). The first, second, and fourth of these achieved— after death—a happy state as goddesses and as stars. The odd one out is Andromeda. A pair of commentators on her couplet say:[35] 'The poet clearly has in mind the transformation of Andromeda into a constellation, though he does not mention it.' The argument should go in exactly the opposite direction: it is notable that Andromeda is made by the poet to achieve her happiness alive and as the wife of Perseus. As has been noticed in similar cases,[36] such an oddity in a series of otherwise similar *paradeigmata* has significance: here it anticipates thematically the happy recovery of Cynthia. But there is more to these *paradeigmata*: the other three all involve Juno and her anger at Juppiter's adulteries. It now becomes clear that the 'Judgment of Paris' (9–12) is a thematic anticipation of the concentration on Juno and her anger. This section ends (25–34):

---

35. Butler and Barber (1933), p. 239.
36. For instance, 2.1.57 ff.

quod si forte tibi properarint fata quietem,
  illa sepulturae fata beata tuae,
narrabis Semelae quo sit formosa periclo,
  credet et illa, suo docta puella malo;
et tibi Maeonias omnis heroidas inter
  primus erit nulla non tribuente locus.   30
nunc, utcumque potes, fato gere saucia morem:
  et deus et durus vertitur ipse dies;
hoc tibi vel poterit coniunx ignoscere Iuno:
  frangitur et Iuno si qua puella perit.

'But if it chance that fate shall bring peace to you prematurely, that happy fate when you are buried, you will tell Semele how dangerous it is to be pretty, and she will believe you, a girl experienced through trouble of her own; and amidst all the heroines of Homer everyone will concede you first place (30). So then, as far as you can, submit yourself in your illness to destiny: both the god and the harsh day can be altered; even Juno as a wife will be able to forgive you: even Juno breaks down when a girl is dying.'

  The poet represents Cynthia's life after death as especially happy— she will, by common consent, be the most beautiful among the ranks of the beautiful dead. She will talk with Semele. This motif is thematically anticipated in the *paradeigma* of Ino, who incurred Juno's wrath by feeding Dionysus, Juppiter's son by Semele. So Juno and Juppiter enter again in this myth. This concentration on Juno, from line 11, thematically anticipates the climactic couplet of this section. The poet urges Cynthia to acquiesce in her destiny, whatever it is: gods can be changed and the day of death. Even Juno in her capacity as a wife (that is, when she is most likely to be jealous of female beauty) will be able to forgive Cynthia the combination of beauty and arrogance.[37] As a wife Juno has the best reasons (some of which have been enumerated) to feel jealous of such beauty; but, when it comes to the point that a girl is dying, Juno gives way. The clue to Juno's attitude is given in Cynthia's supposed words to Semele (27) *quo sit formosa periclo*: it is dangerous to be beautiful because Juno is jealous of the effect on Juppiter. But for a girl at the point of death she relents.

  37. Cf. line 14, where an equally vague *hoc* has to be understood from the context.

Other anticipated themes also hold the poem together. The collection of Homeric heroines (29) anticipates the wider list of heroines in lines 51–54. And Io, described in line 18 as *nunc dea quae Nili flumina vacca bibit* appears in exactly the same linguistic form at the end of the poem (61) *divae nunc, ante iuvencae*. Also, in general, the picture of the underworld in lines 27–30 is picked up in the later picture in lines 49–56. The poem is almost totally composed in secondary language, with the exception of the poet's appeal to Juppiter, based on his love of Cynthia (39–44), and the final realistic view of death (55–58), together with the expression of gratitude for recovery (59–62). The poem owes its depth to the allusiveness of the secondary language that is relieved by minimal primary expressions of emotion.

Poem 3.8 of Propertius is sometimes divided into two elegies: lines 1–34 and 35–40. But this division, too, is unjustified. The poem has a surprise opening (1–4):

> Dulcis ad hesternas fuerat mihi rixa lucernas,
>   vocis et insanae tot maledicta tuae,
> cum furibunda mero mensam propellis et in me
>   proicis insana cymbia plena manu.

'Our fight by the lamplight yesterday gave me pleasure, and all the insults of your raging tongue, when, maddened with wine, you threw over the table and flung full cups of wine at me with frenzied hand.'

The word (1) *dulcis* is an intentional surprise, but its meaning comes out in the course of the poem: first, anger in a woman is a sign of love (9–20), and, secondly, it is more fun to be in love with a woman who easily gets angry and fights (21–32). But the nature of the (1) *rixa* remains a mystery right to the end of the poem. The ending is this (33–40):

> aut tecum aut pro te mihi cum rivalibus arma
>   semper erunt: in te pax mihi nulla placet.
> gaude quod nulla est aeque formosa: doleres   35
>   si qua foret. nunc sis iure superba licet.
> at tibi, qui nostro nexisti retia lecto,
>   sit socer aeternum nec sine matre domus!
> cui nunc si qua data est furandae copia noctis,
>   offensa illa mihi, non tibi amica, dedit.

'Always I shall be at war either with you, or for you with rivals: with you peace is no pleasure. Feel happy that there is no one so beautiful: you would suffer (35) if there were. As it is you can be arrogant with complete justice. But you, who wove snares for my bed, may you have a father-in-law for ever and a house never free from her mother. And if some opportunity has been given you for stealing a night, she gave it to you, offended with me, not in love with you (40).'

The last line forms a thematic ring-composition with the opening: her offence with the poet was displayed in the *rixa* and—this was not hinted previously—by defiantly admitting the existence of a rival. What was the *rixa* about? Not about the rival assuredly: he was Cynthia's weapon. One of the symptoms which the poet lists as characterising a woman whose anger is a sign of love (9–18) is this (15–16):

> seu timidam crebro dementia somnia terrent,
> seu miseram in tabula picta puella movet.

'Or crazy dreams often make her fearful and terrified, or a girl's portrait in a painting upsets her.'

She is, that is, subject to jealousy, and this gives a clue to the opening of the poem (by synecdoche *e sequentibus praecedentia*): Cynthia was accusing the poet of being unfaithful. He gives her no reassurance till the end of the poem (35–36): she is more beautiful than any (so she has no need to fear the poet's unfaithfulness) and can continue to be as arrogant as she pleases. Her arrogance is displayed in the scene with which the poem opens, and negatively when (20) the poet wishes a 'placid girl on his enemies'. The couplet assuring her of her supreme beauty (35–36) neatly pulls together the anticipated themes of anger and jealousy and unfaithfulness.

But the jealousy which the poet diagnoses as a sign of love (15–16) in an angry woman also anticipates the poet's own jealousy, which is not revealed until the last four lines (37–40): he is jealous of the rival (who seems to have accused the poet to Cynthia of infidelity), but comforts himself that the rival is only being used by Cynthia as a pawn. The structure of the last eight lines is noteworthy. There are two points of focus (33): *tecum* and *cum rivalibus*. The former is taken up in lines 35–36, and the latter in lines 37–40. Also, while the assurance to Cynthia that she is more beautiful than any (35) takes up that aspect of the anger-theme which represented it as a symptom of love (9–20), the next line (36) *nunc sis iure superba licet* takes up that aspect of the anger-theme in which it increased the poet's pleasure in love (21–32); and, in giving Cynthia this encouragement, the poet links it with the opening theme expressed in (1) *dulcis*: he enjoys their quarrels, one of which generated this very poem.

There remain two difficult poems of Propertius which most editors (but neither Hertzberg nor Paley) have chopped into several elegies. The first is 2.18. This elegy may, in fact, be continuous with the preceding elegy, but that seems impossible to demonstrate. The elegy opens (1–8):

> Assiduae multis odium peperere querelae:
> frangitur in tacito femina saepe viro.
> si quid vidisti, semper vidisse negato;
> aut si quid doluit forte, dolere nega.
> quid mea si canis aetas candesceret annis,   5
> et faceret scissas languida ruga genas?
> at non Tithoni spernens Aurora senectam
> desertum Eoa passa iacere domo est . . .

'Continuous complaints have merely got many men disliked: a woman often breaks down when a man keeps silent. If you have seen something, always say that you have not; or if something has chanced to cause you pain, deny that it hurts. It is not as if my time of life were shining with white hair (5) and flaccid wrinkles were fissuring my cheeks. Yet Aurora did not despise the old age of Tithonus and leave him abandoned in her Eastern house . . .'

The force of (5) *quid si* with a secondary subjunctive in Latin is often that of the English 'It isn't as if . . .': that is, it dismisses a hypothesis that would have spoiled a line of argument.[38] Here there is a suppressed premise which the reader has to construct by inference; it is: '[I can afford to wait and be silent since] I am still young'. The poet expressed the opposite point of view in the triumph-poem 2.14.15–16, when he regretted that the technique of dominating a woman had

---

38. Cf. Propertius 1.9.15–34 and my remarks on this passage in Williams (1957), pp. 242–43.

come to him so late—he felt then as good as dead. But poem 2.18 takes the line that he knows the necessary technique—it is that of silently wearing the woman down—and he has the time to apply it.

At that point a *paradeigma* occurs to the poet which is related by opposite association to what he has just said. The implication of lines 5–6 is that, if he were old, love would obviously be out of the question; no time would be left. But the myth of Tithonus illustrates the opposite, and, in doing so, alters the movement of thought. The myth is explored at length in twelve lines, emphasising the pleasure that Aurora found in her association with Tithonus: her pleasures in Tithonus, aged but alive, were greater than her grief over the death of Memnon, her son. Then the poet asserts (17–38):

> cum sene non puduit talem dormire puellam
>   et canae totiens oscula ferre comae.
> at tu etiam iuvenem odisti me, perfida, cum sis
>   ipsa anus haud longa curva futura die.   20
> quin ego deminuo curam, quod saepe Cupido
>   huic malus esse solet cui bonus ante fuit.
> nunc etiam infectos demens imitare Britannos,
>   ludis et externo tincta nitore caput.
> ut natura dedit sic omnis recta figura est: 25
>   turpis Romano Belgicus ore color.
> illi sub terris fiant mala multa puellae
>   quae mentita suas vertit inepta comas.
> deme: mihi certe poteris formosa videri;
>   mi formosa sat es si modo saepe venis.   30
> an si caeruleo quaedam sua tempora fuco
>   tinxerit, idcirco caerula forma bona est?
> cum tibi nec frater nec sit tibi filius ullus,
>   frater ego et tibi sim filius unus ego.
> ipse tuus semper tibi sit custodia lectus,   35
>   nec nimis ornata fronte sedere velis.
> credam ego narranti, noli committere, famae:
>   et terram rumor transilit et maria.

'So beautiful a girl felt no shame in sleeping with an old man and showering kisses so often on his grey hairs. But you are tired of me even when I am young, unfaithful woman, although you too are sure to be a bent old crone in no long time (20). Why do I not cut short my worrying since Cupid is often wont to be unkind to the one to whom he was previously kind?

Even now you are insanely imitating the painted Britons, and playing about, your head stained with some foreign dye. As nature formed them so are one's looks at their best (25): Belgian dye is disgraceful on a Roman face. May many ills befall that girl in the underworld who in her folly deceitfully alters her hair. Remove ⟨the make-up⟩: I assure you that you will have no difficulty in appearing beautiful to me—to me you are beautiful if only you come to me often (30). Do you think that, because some girl has stained her temples with blue paint, for that reason blue looks are good? Since you have neither brother nor a son, let me be your brother and let me be your only son. Let your own bed be your guardian (35), and cease wanting to display yourself with your face covered with make-up. I shall believe the gossip that speaks of you, so do not sin: rumour leaps across both land and sea.'

The myth of Tithonus is not only used by negative association with what has preceded it, but it is also used to alter the movement of ideas (see chap. 4, sec. 3). So from the idea that Aurora was not ashamed of her aged husband comes the idea that Cynthia is tired of the poet even in his youth—the idea of (19) *odisti* picking up the theme of (1) *odium* from which the poem begun. From that is generated the opposite idea: Cynthia will soon be an old hag herself. Both ideas were generated from the myth, but thereby the movement of thought has been altered and the opening resolution deliberately forgotten (1–4).

However, that theme is now (21–22) picked up in a different form; for the poet's reflection that Cupid changes can only be of small—though philosophical—use as far as the poet's own situation is concerned, but it enjoins silence on him and, at the same time, relieves his feelings against Cynthia to reflect that she will soon inevitably be unsuccessful in love.

What has Cynthia been doing? That now appears (23–32): daubing on outlandish make-up. In line 23, *nunc etiam* picks up (20) *anus*: she is doing it 'even now'—the time will come when she will be old and such aids will be necessary. And (20) *anus* is picked up again in (27) *sub terris*, as the poet looks forward to her death. The explanation of all this does not come until lines 35–36: line 35 is an exhortation to be faithful (her bed will be her 'guardian' if it admits only the poet), while line 36 tells her not to behave like a prostitute—the purpose of sitting about in public, made-up (cf. poem 1.2). The poem ends with a ring-composition, for lines 37–38 are another version of the opening of the poem (1–4): that gave one reason for keeping silent; then lines 21–22 gave another; but the final couplet amounts to saying: '(I may say nothing but) do not sin: gossip about you is sure to reach me and I will believe it'.

There is a further thematic anticipation in the poem. When in lines 33–34 the poet asks to be Cynthia's brother and son, he is alluding to the type of family-love (*pietas*) which Catullus treated as one aspect of ideal love between a man and a woman in poem 68. But here the theme of 'your only son' has been anticipated in Aurora's loss of her only son Memnon (16).

The poem reveals itself only at the end. The opening resolution not to complain raises a question that is not answered till line 30: Cynthia does not come to the poet. Cynthia's pursuit of lovers is contrasted with the poet's single-minded love and devotion (33–34). Then the theme of old age enters very obliquely and is unexpectedly expanded so that it includes the ultimate fate of both Cynthia and the poet, and so provides a framework for the attack on her and for the poet's own declaration of his devotion—a devotion that will survive old age (so that now, as it were, the poet is Aurora and Cynthia, Tithonus). The poem is a subtle unity that deliberately draws in disparate themes and solves the consequent problem of coherence by the technique of thematic anticipation and the use of *paradeigmata* to alter the movement of ideas.

The other difficult poem, 2.22, is usually treated as two elegies and divided at line 42, so that lines 43–50 form a brief separate elegy. The poem seems to begin with the poet regretfully confessing his interest in every girl he sees (1–14):

> Scis here mi multas pariter placuisse puellas;
> scis mihi, Demophoon, multa venire mala.
> nulla meis frustra lustrantur compita plantis;
> o nimis exitio nata theatra meo,
> sive aliquis molli diducit candida gestu   5
> bracchia, seu varios incinit ore modos.
> interea nostri quaerunt sibi vulnus ocelli,
> candida non tecto pectore si qua sedet,
> sive vagi crines puris in frontibus errant,
> Indica quos medio vertice gemma tenet.   10
> quae si forte aliquid vultu mihi dura negarat,
> frigida de tota fronte cadebat aqua.
> quaeris, Demophoon, cur sim tam mollis in omnis?
> quod quaeris, 'quare' non habet ullus amor.

'You know that yesterday many girls were equally delightful to me; you know, Demophoon, that many troubles come my way. No streets are trodden in vain by my feet; o theatres, too perfectly designed for my destruction, whether a girl parts her white arms in a supple movement (5), or sings in harmony a lilting tune; meanwhile my eyes seek to have themselves wounded, whether some beautiful girl sits with her breast uncovered, or long hair strays over her clear forehead, clasped by an Indian jewel at the top of her head (10). If any of them had chanced, with unyielding face, to deny me anything, chill moisture kept flowing down my white face. You inquire, do you, Demophoon, why I am so susceptible to all? Well, you can ask: Love never admits of "Why?"'

What does the poet mean by (1) 'yesterday'? One editor asserts:[39] 'The context shows that this must mean "of late", and further that this extended meaning of the word must have been regular in daily speech'. But there is not the slightest evidence of this. It would seem reasonable to use 'yesterday' either to contrast the past with the present (that is, 'yesterday' as distinct from 'to-day'), or to mean a precise date, but not at all to mean 'recently' (that is, a period of time which includes 'to-day'). The poet is obviously not contrasting the past with the present since his troubles continue; so he must mean that 'yesterday' Demophoon had a special opportunity to see the poet's predicament with his own eyes. That autopsy was yesterday, but Demophoon made the further observation (2) that a lot of trouble comes (not just came yesterday but continues to come) to the poet in that way; the 'trouble', however, is not yet explained. The following present tenses (3–10), then, must be historic presents, vividly recreating yesterday's scene. This interpretation is confirmed by the curious nature of the scene described: streets and theatres seem to be combined. That combination would uniquely suit the *ludi compitalicii* which were held by Octavian after his triple triumph in 29 B.C. and apparently on some later occasions too.[40] Theatrical side-shows were erected in the streets and the festival was of the type that spreads over a whole town or city. The poet's eyes therefore meet with constant temptation. Lines 11 and 12 then appear to move towards defining (2) *mala*. For the expression of his emotional distress, the poet moves back into the precision of past tenses. But the definition is unexpected: jealousy, the difficulty of

39. Camps (1961–67), ad loc.
40. For details, see ibid., pp. 151–52.

making a choice, the hazards of managing many affairs at once—all these explanations would seem reasonable in the circumstances. The paradox was, however, that with so many girls to choose from the poet made no choice, and that, just as all delighted him equally (1), so each refusal was of the same value and hurt him to the same extreme extent. Demophoon might well ask 'Why?' But the poet has only this answer (15–24):

> cur aliquis sacris laniat sua bracchia cultris   15
>   et Phrygis insanos caeditur ad numeros?
> uni cuique dedit vitium natura creato:
>   mi fortuna aliquid semper amare dedit.
> me licet et Thamyrae cantoris fata sequantur,
>   numquam ad formosas, invide, caecus ero.   20
> sed tibi si exilis videor tenuatus in artus,
>   falleris: haud umquam est culta labore Venus.
> percontere licet: saepe est experta puella
>   officium tota nocte valere meum.

'Why does a man cut his arms with sacred knives, and practise surgery on himself to the mad rhythms of a Phrygian pipe? To each as he was born Nature gave a vice: to me Fortune gave that of always being in love. Though the fate even of the singer Thamyras befall me, never, grudging creature, shall I be blind to pretty girls (20). But if you are thinking that I am thin with frail limbs, you are wrong: love-making has never caused me trouble. You can ask: a girl has often experienced the exercise of my powers a whole night through.'

There is a skilful synecdoche in the use of the *paradeigma*: Thamyras challenged the Muses to a singing contest; if he won, he would sleep with all nine: if he lost, he would be deprived of whatever they decided. He lost, and they deprived him of his sight. Only the second element in the wager is mentioned, but the first is what makes the *paradeigma* significant in the context.

The movement of ideas then veers (21) to anticipate a thought that might (metonymically) occur to Demophoon: he is assured of the poet's physical capacity, despite his skinny appearance. But the evidence he offers is oddly only that of one girl. What is more, to show that love-making need not weaken a man, he goes on now to deploy the examples of Juppiter with Alcmena (25–28) and of Achilles with

Briseis and of Hector with Andromache (29–34). Each of these involves only one woman. The poet then appears to offer another example (35–36):

> aspice uti caelo modo sol modo luna ministret:
> sic etiam nobis una puella parum est.

'See how at one time the sun, at another the moon, services the sky: in the same way also one girl is not enough for me.'

The ideas have again veered from physical capacity to the need for more than one girl. But the reason for the poet's needing more than one is totally unexpected: if one girl for some reason refuses him, then there is another to take her place (37–40). This is a long way from the abandoned plurality of the poem's opening, and must raise a question about the meaning of that opening. It was argued above that (1) *here* means a specific occasion and that the description of the occasion suggests a specific event. But the poet's (2) *mala* turn out not to be those connected with the managing of a plurality of affairs, but are caused by a girl's refusal. The poem ends according to the MSS (41–50):

> nam melius duo defendunt retinacula navim,
>   tutius et geminos anxia mater alit.
> aut si es dura, nega: sin es non dura, venito!
>   quid iuvat haec nullo ponere verba loco?
> hic unus dolor est ex omnibus acer amanti   45
>   speranti subito si qua venire negat.
> quanta illum toto versant suspiria lecto,
>   cum recipi quae non venerit ipse vetat!
> et rursus puerum quaerendo audita fatigat,
>   quem quae scire timet quaerere facta iubet.   50

'For two cables are better for ensuring a ship's safety, and an anxious mother is safer if she rears twins. "Either, if you are hard-hearted, say no: but if you are not hard-hearted, come!" What good is it to waste these words? This is the sharpest pain a lover feels (45): if a girl suddenly says she is not coming when he expects her. What sighs then toss him all over the bed as he himself gives orders that she who did not come be not admitted; and tires out his slave by asking over again things he has been told, and bids him find out what has happened when he fears to know it.'

There are uncertainties in the text of the last few lines, but its drift is clear. The sudden apostrophe to a girl in line 43 is characteristic of the poet, and it takes up and modifies the *mala* expressed in lines 11–12; for here the trouble is not openly expressed refusal, but failure to keep a promise (that is, a concealed refusal). Commentators seem to assume that line 44 is also addressed to the girl, and have difficulty since they can find no parallel to the idiom. But if this is the poet's own hopeless reflection, addressed to himself, there is no difficulty: 'Why does he waste these words?'—the girl takes no notice and says what she pleases. But the real pain is to have a girl say yes and then not come. That is the real reason why he needs more than one girl. These are the real (2) *mala*. It is not, after all, that he is a Lothario, but that he longs for true love and cannot find it, even though he was prepared to love every girl at the *ludi compitalicii*.

The movement of the poem is from a unique occasion, when his friend Demophoon accompanied him, to the way in which that unique occasion symbolises the poet's life. The unique occasion produced *mala* that were also unique to it: particular kinds of refusal. What troubles the poet's life in general is not simple refusal, but the type of refusal that is concealed by an apparent promise. Every stage in the poem modifies the previous stages. The anticipated theme of (2) *mala* is picked up and redefined several times; finally the wording of the address to the girl in line 43 echoes, but varies, the wording of the first definition of *mala* in line 11. The poem ends in a ring-composition on the theme of *mala*, now defined in detail. Another anticipated theme is that of plurality, which also goes through a series of stages beginning with apparent promiscuity, then being deceptively linked to the poet's physical capacity, before ending by becoming the only—and very uncertain—insurance the poet can find against the pain described in lines 45–50. In a sense, the final element of the ring-composition is formed by the opposite to the opening: there it sounded as if *mala* arose from the fact of plurality, but at the end it emerges that plurality arises out of *mala*. The true love, exemplified by the figures of Achilles and Hector, always eludes the poet.

One poem of Horace is on a scale to be considered in this context. For Horace's great ode to *Fortuna* (1.35) is held together by an intricate interweaving of anticipated themes. The poem has been seriously mis-interpreted by modern commentators and is worth detailed analysis. Two aspects of the goddess are portrayed, and these two aspects are outlined in the opening stanza (1–4):

> o diva, gratum quae regis Antium,
> praesens vel imo tollere de gradu
> mortale corpus vel superbos
> vertere funeribus triumphos . . .

'O goddess that rules over delightful Antium, present and ready either to elevate from the lowest grade a mortal body, or to overthrow proud triumphs by funerals . . .'

The goddess can exalt or she can destroy. Those were, of course, the normal attributes of the capricious power of Chance as Hellenistic philosophers used the concept to symbolise the unpredictability of life. But the *Fortuna* of this ode is not capricious; she has a moral dimension that is hard to illustrate in cult. It is to be seen, however, in the common proverb that Terence uses in the form (*Phorm.* 203) *fortes Fortuna adiuvat.*[41] It expresses the idea that a man's fortune is directly related to his character and behaviour—crudely, god helps those who help themselves. Cicero uses the idea in discussing the Stoic paradox (*paradoxa Stoic.* 34) that all wise men are free but all fools are slaves; he declares: 'to the wise man Fortune herself, who is said to possess the greatest power of all, gives way—since, as the wise poet said, "Fortune is moulded for each man by his own character"'.[42] The corollary to this is that *Fortuna* rewards virtue when she exalts, and punishes vice when she destroys. This aspect of *Fortuna* became crucial at the time when men like Cicero began to turn against Julius Caesar, and it can clearly be seen if one compares Cicero's readiness in 46 B.C. to attribute the good-will of *Fortuna* to Caesar (*pro Marc.* 19) with what he wrote privately to Cornelius Nepos:[43] 'The quality of being fortunate (*felicitas*) is nothing but the prosperity that comes from honourable conduct; or, to define it another way, the quality of being fortunate shows *Fortuna* as the supporter of good counsels—and a man who does not follow those can in no way be fortunate. Therefore in the accursed and impious counsels that Caesar follows there can be no *felicitas*. More fortunate, in my judgment, was Camillus in exile than Manlius at that time, even if—and that is what he really wanted—he had been able to

---

41. For the range of this proverbial form, see Otto (1890), p. 144.
42. For this aspect of *Fortuna* in Roman thought, see Weinstock (1971), p. 113.
43. Quoted by Ammianus Marcellinus 21.16.3—*frag. epist.*: II ad Cornelium Nepotem 5 (Watt).

be king.' The political analogy at the end shows clearly the motivation of Cicero's attack on Caesar. But the important fact for understanding Horace's ode is that, in such contexts, *Fortuna*'s actions are the result of moral judgments.[44]

The next three stanzas focus on *Fortuna*'s capacity for destruction and on men's fear of her:

> te pauper ambit sollicita prece 5
> ruris colonus, te dominam aequoris
>   quicumque Bithyna lacessit
>   Carpathium pelagus carina;
>
> te Dacus asper, te profugi Scythae,
> urbesque gentesque et Latium ferox 10
>   regumque matres barbarorum et
>   purpurei metuunt tyranni,
>
> iniurioso ne pede proruas
> stantem columnam, neu populus frequens
>   ad arma cessantis, ad arma 15
>   concitet imperiumque frangat.

'You are flattered with anxious prayer (5) by the poor farmer as mistress of his land, you are flattered as mistress of the sea by anyone who challenges the Carpathian strait in a Bithynian ship; of you are the rough Dacians terrified, of you the run-and-fight Scythians, and cities, and races, and proud Latium (10), and the mothers of barbarian kings, and purple-clad tyrants lest with violent foot you bring crashing down the supporting pillar and the assembled people stir the hesitant with the cry "to arms, to arms" (15), and break their [the tyrants'] power.'

The fear of *Fortuna* dominates first farmers and sailors, both subject to the elements; then it dominates the enemies of Rome on the northern frontier, then all cities and races of men, then Rome itself (10)—this aspect of the fear covers the success or failure of military operations. Finally, it dominates kings and tyrants. For the safety of kings their mothers are afraid (the poet thinks of someone like Atossa), but tyrants are frightened for themselves. It is only when the poet's vision has

---

44. Something of this moral dimension can be seen very occasionally in Greek poets: for instance, in the hymns to *Tyche* at the opening of Pindar *Olympian* 12 and in the anonymous fragment quoted by Stobaeus, Page *Poet.Mel.Graec.* 1019.

focused on political power and then has moved from the more or less legendary Atossa to that particular aspect of political power which is designated by the opprobrious name of tyranny that the poet digresses to specify the nature of the fear: it is of a popular uprising, with the approval and assistance of *Fortuna*. Here is the first clearly moral judgment by *Fortuna*: it is political and the action taken is violent and destructive. The poet expresses the tyrant's point of view, but there is no doubt of his attitude: he approves the feared action of *Fortuna*.

There follows the most difficult section of the poem (17–28):

> te semper anteit saeva Necessitas,
> clavos trabalis et cuneos manu
>   gestans aena, nec severus
>   uncus abest liquidumque plumbum;   20
>
> te Spes et albo rara Fides colit
> velata panno, nec comitem abnegat
>   utcumque mutata potentis
>   veste domos inimica linquis.
>
> at vulgus infidum et meretrix retro   25
> periura cedit, diffugiunt cadis
>   cum faece siccatis amici
>   ferre iugum pariter dolosi.

'In front of you always walks pitiless Necessity, carrying in her bronze hand beam-sized nails and wedges, nor is the cruel hook absent nor liquid lead (20); Hope ever attends you and rarely seen Honesty veiled in a white cloak, and neither denies her companionship whenever, with changed clothing, in hostility you leave the homes of the powerful. But the faithless mob and the dishonest whore (25) draw back, and, when the casks are drained lees and all, friends run away in all directions, too treacherous to bear their share of the burden.'

The fearful aspect of *Fortuna* has been the theme so far, and in lines 17–20 this reaches a climax. But most modern commentators suppose that Necessity is pictured as carrying the tools of the building trade to symbolise the idea that 'the structure that Necessitas rears is designed to last'.[45] If so, the symbolism is empty as far as this poem is concerned, since the concept of the decrees of Fate as eternal (such as is found in

45. Nisbet and Hubbard (1970), p. 395.

carm.saec. 25–27) is simply neither used in the poem nor relevant to its ideas. The details here would be merely decorative, and Lessing's criticism would be fully justified. But if *Necessitas* is in the building trade, why is she (17) *saeva* (the reading now generally accepted in preference to the variant *serva*)? Why, too, is her hand (19) *aena*? Why is the *uncus* designated (20) *severus* if it is only a building clamp? And why, finally, is the lead (20) *liquidum*? The latest commentators, after quoting a series of passages in which nails are used as emblems of fixity, declare:[46] 'These passages are sufficient to refute the old notion (seen, for instance, in Lessing and in Gray) that Horace is referring in this stanza to instruments of torture or violence.' This said, they proceed to explain away the other difficulties. Having explained (18) *cunei* as 'dowels used to hold together blocks of stone', they comment: 'The nature of the *cunei* strongly recommends Campbell's conjecture *aenos*, which also has the merit of giving all the implements a balancing adjective'. So the problem of her bronze hand is side-stepped. No comment is offered on *severus*. On the liquid lead they say: 'O. Keller (*Epilegomena zu Horaz* 1879, p. 22) points out that we should not think of the lead as liquid when it is being carried by Necessity; he compares the dedication of "lucida funalia" at 3.26.6 f.' There is no doubt that Roman poets could use epithets ornamentally, and that may be true in *Odes* 3.26. But, while it is the sole function of torches to be *lucida* even if they happen to be extinguished at the moment of speaking, it is the function of lead, if it symbolises stone-work designed to last for ever, to be solid. Taken with the other adjectives, the picture intended by the poet must be that of an executioner,[47] with the nails and wedges used to fasten criminals (to the cross, for instance) and the hook and liquid lead used to extract confessions preliminary to execution.[48] To *Fortuna* and *Necessitas*, as pictured in this poem, mortals are creatures without legal rights, subject to summary torture and execution (for which the various instruments are metonymic).

Taken in this way, the picture is metonymically related to the fear that all peoples of the world feel towards *Fortuna*. Moreover, she is pictured as moving in procession on the way to execution, with all the instruments ready for use. The horrifying portrait gathers up the

46. Ibid., p. 394.
47. And her hand is a metal claw of unfeeling brass.
48. See especially Pöschl (1970), pp. 57–61, with references.

themes of the preceding stanzas into a climax at the half-way point of the poem.

A further metonymic movement of thought takes the poet to a picture of other attendants of *Fortuna*, this time beneficent. The misinterpretations that have been imposed on this passage can be seen in rows of commentaries and articles since Bentley first expressed difficulty in 1711. It will be sufficient here to note the most recent commentators. On (24) *inimica* they say:[49] 'This word introduces the most extraordinary confusion. Up to this point Horace suggests that the Fortuna of the family shares the disaster that befalls the man. But *inimica linquis* gives a totally different picture: Fortune is now a deity independent of the house, who has gone off and left the great man in the lurch.... In such contexts the faithful friend ought to be praised precisely because he does *not* accompany Fortune.... For Horace's sake one would be glad to believe that the text is corrupt. Bentley considered *inimica vertis*; one could then imagine the true friends as staying in the ruined house, as opposed to the false friends who fly. But *comitem* strongly supports a verb of motion like *linquis*, and the inconsistency of *inimica* with *mutata vesta* still remains.... Campbell suggested *manicata* ("in chains") for *inimica*; one would sooner try *lacrimosa* or something of the kind. Then we should have to assume that the great man is going into exile accompanied by his true friends.' In their introduction to this ode, they comment on these lines: 'The next stanza is scandalously confused.'

The confusion of commentators, however, stems from the assumptions they make. Since *Fortuna* 'leaves' (24, *linquis*) the house, the assumption is made that 'Fortune in such passages is not a capricious and independent deity; in Roman cult different families had their own separate *Fortuna*.' Then *mutata . . . veste* is taken to mean that *Fortuna* is 'in mourning', and so 'the Fortune of the house shares the suffering of the great man'. If all that is assumed, then of course *inimica* comes as a most unwelcome surprise. But, as was pointed out above, *Fortuna* in this ode is a deity of terrifying power who both rewards and punishes. To represent her as rewarding a family, the poet has applied the idea of the Roman family cult of *Fortuna* to picture her as residing in the house, presiding over it with her attendants, Hope and Honesty. That had two poetic advantages for him. First, it enabled him to picture her

49. Nisbet and Hubbard (1970), pp. 396–97.

decision to punish the house as a scene of movement, a procession parallel to that of *Necessitas* and *Fortuna* in the previous stanza. Second, it set up the contrast between the faith and loyalty of *Fortuna*'s attendants to her, and the faithlessness of the great man's attendants (25, *at*) to him. The value of this contrast to the poet lay in its enabling him to show (not tell) why *Fortuna* came to condemn the house.

A house filled with *vulgus infidum*, *periurae meretrices*, and 'friends' who are there to help to drain the wine-casks (lees and all, in their greed) is morally depraved. So *Fortuna*, from being the presiding deity, becomes an *inimica*, and her clothing, from being festive, becomes funereal—not because she herself is 'in mourning', but because she has passed sentence of death (here is a clear thematic connexion with lines 3–4). The moral depravity of the house is of the type which moralists professed to find widespread in the late Republic, and which Cicero, for instance, urged Julius Caesar to put right, as a matter of the first importance (*pro Marc.* 23): 'It is for you alone, Caesar, to bring back to life all those things that you see lying shattered and prostrated, as was inevitable, by the very shock of war: courts must be instituted, Honesty must be recalled, lust must be stamped out, child-bearing must be encouraged—all the things that have slipped and disintegrated must be constrained by severe legislation.' All of this Augustus undertook, and in his condemnation here of a particular type of immorality, Horace was expressing an Augustan viewpoint that often recurs in his *Odes*. This is only one of several Augustan themes in this ode. For *Fortuna*, with her attendants *Spes* and *Fides*, is portrayed as setting Augustan standards.

The execution-procession (17–20) is made to precede the condemnation of the house, not only because of the metonymic connexion between the world's fear of *Fortuna* and the grim portrait of her attendant, but also because the terror can be poetically re-activated by the one word (24) *inimica*, taken together with *mutata . . . veste*. But the exit-procession also introduces the more beneficent aspect of *Fortuna* in the person of her attendants, Hope and Honesty, and prepares for the prayer with which the poem climactically ends (29–40):

> serves iturum Caesarem in ultimos
> orbis Britannos et iuvenum recens   30
>   examen Eois timendum
>   partibus Oceanoque rubro.

eheu! cicatricum et sceleris pudet
fratrumque. quid nos dura refugimus
　　aetas? quid intactum nefasti   35
　　　liquimus? unde manum iuventus

metu deorum continuit? quibus
pepercit aris? o utinam nova
　　incude diffingas retusum in
　　　Massagetas Arabasque ferrum.   40

'May you keep Caesar safe as he prepares an expedition against the Britons, the furthest people of the world, and also the new (30) swarm of young men, a cause of fear to the regions of the East and to the Indian Ocean. Alas! we repent the woundings and the crimes and ⟨what we did to⟩ our brothers. What sin have we, an unfeeling age, recoiled from? What wickedness (35) have we left untried? From what have our youth restrained their hands through respect for the gods? What altars have they spared? O that you might reforge our blunt swords on a new anvil for use against the Massagetae and the Arabs (40).'

The prayer is a ring-composition: the expeditions for whose success the poet prays (29–32) are picked up by the expedition in which he prays for *Fortuna's* participation. That ring-structure encloses a lengthy outpouring of the nation's repentance for the crime of civil war. The connexion of thought is close to that of *Odes* 1.2: the crime of civil war will be expiated by expeditions against threatening external enemies.[50] Many themes from the earlier part of the ode are picked up here. Outstandingly, lines 33–38 function as an act of confession and repentance; that theme connects with the character of *Necessitas* as executioner and torturer. *Fortuna* is being asked to regard the foreign expeditions as appropriate expiation for the sin of civil war. She is also being asked to accord her favour to Augustus, and that picks up the theme of *Fortuna's* power to exalt (2–3). Another anticipated theme is first sounded by (4) *triumphos*, then by (10) *Latium ferox*; the patriotic theme opens and closes the final prayer (29–32 and 38–40). Again the fear that (10) 'proud Latium' felt was realised in *Fortuna's* (unspoken) condemnation of Rome for civil war and exemplified in defeats which the expeditions mentioned in the prayer are to avenge. Finally, the type of civil uprising which the tyrant fears (14–16) prefigures the civil

---

50. See p. 13 above, and Pöschl (1970), pp. 64–66.

war (33–38) for which the poet offers an act of contrition. This should be regarded as that type of thematic anticipation which is a synecdoche *e sequentibus praecedentia*, such that, when the reader has grasped lines 33–38, he goes back to modify his understanding of lines 13–16. For within that general statement of the tyrant's fear can be seen the particular case of Julius Caesar, whose desertion by the *Fortuna* he had so assiduously cultivated, resulting from his pretensions to unconstitutional rule, together with the consequent civil dissension, led to the fifteen years of civil war which the poet explicitly repents on behalf of the nation. The date of the poem is certainly about the year 27 B.C., when fears of renewed civil war were still alive and were compounded by the failure of Augustus' proposed moral legislation, and when attention was being deliberately diverted towards foreign enemies.

The unity and coherence of this great ode depends on recognition of the intricate pattern of thematic connexions and the essentially metonymic mode of the movement from one idea to the next.

CHAPTER VI

TECHNIQUES OF
METONYMY AND
SYNECDOCHE

It has been noted above that many relationships between the secondary forms of expression and the primary ideas (whether expressed or not), which are principally metaphoric, have nevertheless, in another aspect of their relationship, a metonymic mode. This is true of *paradeigmata*, in cases where the larger context entails an understanding of unmentioned elements in the *paradeigmata*. It is also true where an anticipated theme requires a later context for its full understanding. Both of these relationships are, strictly speaking, synecdochic and of the type *e sequentibus praecedentia*.

The concern of this chapter, however, is with techniques of metonymy or synecdoche whereby, in virtue of the fact that a motif has the characteristic of belonging to at least two fields of ideas, the poet uses it to alter the movement of ideas from the one field to the other by a process of metonymy. This is the technique that Catullus used in poem 68 to move from Troy as the scene of the Trojan War to Troy as the scene of his brother's death, or to move from the love of Laudamia to the exploits of Hercules by means of the word *barathrum*. In the mode of synecdoche it is the technique by which Horace juxtaposed the expulsion of the Tarquins and the suicide of Cato in order to evoke the ideal of Republican constitutionality and resistance to tyranny as an element of Augustan idealism. In *Odes* 1.12 the figure also works in the major context of the poem in a metaphoric mode, since an analogy is being implicitly established between the historical thesis presented by the poet's shaping of Roman history and the rule of Augustus.

Several instances of this type of metonymy have already been noticed in poems of Propertius, where a complex structure is held together by thematic anticipation. In poem 2.13, the subject of the

poet's funeral is reached in line 17 by a synecdochic movement from
(16) *Iovis inimicitiae*: here the larger field of Juppiter's hostility can
contain within it the possibility of the poet's death. In 2.22.19–20,
the myth of Thamyras is connected as a *paradeigma* to the immediate
context by the unmentioned element of the wager that involved, on
one side, the singer's desire to sleep with each of the nine Muses (on
the other—as it turned out—deprivation of sight). In poem 2.30 the
movement from the pipe as a symbol of the love-poet and his activity
to the war against Parthia is made by means of the accidental geographical connexion that the pipe was thrown by Athena into the
Maeander, a river of Phrygia, and the poet designates the seas, through
which the fleet must sail to reach the Parthians, as Phrygian waters;
and the deliberation of the epithet shows the poet consciously creating
the metonymic link. This is exactly the technique of the movement
from the Trojan War to his brother's death in poem 68 of Catullus.

It is worth noting here that symbolism may be metonymic in
nature. In poem 2.15, Propertius, rejoicing after the night of love-
making with Cynthia, feels that he will be immortal if there are many
such nights (39–54):

> si dabit haec multas, fiam immortalis in illis:
>   nocte una quivis vel deus esse potest.   40
> qualem si cuncti cuperent decurrere vitam
>   et pressi multo membra iacere mero,
> non ferrum crudele neque esset bellica navis,
>   nec nostra Actiacum verteret ossa mare,
> nec totiens propriis circum oppugnata triumphis   45
>   lassa foret crinis solvere Roma suos.
> haec certe merito poterunt laudare minores:
>   laeserunt nullos pocula nostra deos.
> tu modo, dum lucet, fructum ne desere vitae:
>   omnia si dederis oscula, pauca dabis.   50
> ac veluti folia arentis liquere corollas,
>   quae passim calathis strata natare vides,
> sic nobis, qui nunc magnum spiramus amantes,
>   forsitan includet crastina fata dies.

'If she shall give me many such, I shall become immortal in them: in a single
such night any man can become even a god (40). If only all men were de-

sirous of passing their life like that, and of lying with their limbs weighed down by much wine, there would have been neither cruel swords nor warships, nor would the waters of Actium have been tossing our bones about, and Rome, beleaguered so often all about by her own triumphs (45), would not have become weary letting down her hair in mourning. This at least the next generation can rightly praise in you and me: our cups injured no gods. But you therefore, while it is light, do not abandon the harvest of life: if you give all your kisses, you will give only a few (50). And as leaves drop from withered garlands and you see them fallen and floating in the wine-cups, so for us, who now breathe great confidence of our love, perhaps to-morrow will bring the close of our lives.'

Here in line 42 wine is a symbol of love-making, related to it by contiguity and so a metonymy for it: to drink wine is a symbol for making love. This is picked up in line 48: 'the poet's cups caused offence to no god' means that the poet's love-making was innocent in a way that war—and especially civil war—was not. This symbol is then beautifully picked up in the simile in such a way that the abandoned cups, with withered leaves floating in them, symbolise the ending of love by death. This is an unusually extended metonymy, and here it is designed to lead into the climactic simile.

1. *Propertius*

Poem 1.16 is a highly original shaping of the traditional theme of *paraclausithyron*, the lover before the closed door of his mistress's house. Its form is based on that of Catullus 67, and consists throughout of a speech made by the door which has constantly been subjected to the humiliation of having to listen to a lover prostrate before it. The poem opens (1–2):

> Quae fueram magnis olim patefacta triumphis,
>   ianua Tarpeiae nota pudicitiae . . .

'I who had once been opened to famous triumphs, a door known to the chastity of Tarpeia . . .'

Commentators go to extraordinary lengths to explain this away by assuming that either the reference is merely geographical, or is to a

Tarpeia who really was chaste, or else they resort to emendation. This is because such a mythological reference is taken to be simply exemplary, and 'the Tarpeia of the story told later by Propertius in 4.4 would not serve as a symbol of *pudicitia*'.[1] But the reference to 'the chastity of Tarpeia' enacts the movement of the whole poem. The door has fallen on very evil times, and the house is occupied by a woman of the most scandalous behaviour. But the door could actually remember the time when Tarpeia was a chaste Vestal virgin. By a process of synecdoche, quite similar to that of Horace *Odes* 1.16 and the reference to Thyestes instead of Atreus, the failure to mention Tarpeia's *impudicitia* ironically anticipates the later development of the poem. The technique is a combination of thematic anticipation, analogy, and synecdoche.

There is a fairly simple example of metonymy of ideas in the moving final poem of Book 1. The poet purports to answer a question by Tullus as to his origin and family (1.22):

> Qualis et unde genus, qui sint mihi, Tulle, Penates,
> quaeris pro nostra semper amicitia.
> si Perusina tibi patriae sunt nota sepulcra,
> Italiae duris funera temporibus,
> cum Romana suos egit discordia civis,   5
> (sic mihi praecipue, pulvis Etrusca, dolor,
> tu proiecta mei perpessa es membra propinqui,
> tu nullo miseri contegis ossa solo),
> proxima supposito contingens Umbria campo
> me genuit terris fertilis uberibus.   10

'You ask me, Tullus, in the name of our long-standing friendship, what my rank is, from whom descended, and where is my ancestral home. If you know Perusia, the grave of our country, that place of death in those days of pain for Italy, when their own discord drove Roman citizens to destruction (5)—so, soil of Etruria, are you especially painful to me: you allowed the limbs of my kinsman to be flung out unburied, you cover his pitiful bones with no soil—where Umbria, rich in fertile land, runs bordering on it and the plain lies just below, there was I born.'

The mention of Perusia in this poem is a metonymy of the same type as that used by Catullus in poem 68 to move from the Trojan

---

1. Camps (1961–67), ad loc.

War to his brother's death. A private connexion linked Perusia in Propertius' mind with his own region of Assisi—a connexion which the previous poem worked out.[2] A further contiguity links civil war and the death of his kinsman. The geographical facts are public but irrelevant; no one would need to define Assisi by referring to Perusia. Two fields of ideas intersect privately in the death of the poet's kinsman, and the poet uses that point of intersection to move from the one to the other. There is an exciting sense of arbitrary, but perfectly controlled, movement in such associations of thought.

A similar metonymy, though much more surprising, concludes poem 2.9, which was previously examined for the technique of arbitrary assertion of similarity (pp. 73 ff.). The poem concerns a rival and uses the concept to define the nature of the poet's love for Cynthia. It ends (41–52):

> sidera sunt testes et matutina pruina
> et furtim misero ianua aperta mihi,
> te nihil in vita nobis acceptius umquam;
> nunc quoque erit, quamvis sis inimica, nihil.
> nec domina ulla meo ponet vestigia lecto: 45
> solus ero, quoniam non licet esse tuum.
> atque utinam, si forte pios eduximus annos,
> ille vir in medio fiat amore lapis!
> non ob regna magis diris cecidere sub armis
> Thebani media non sine matre duces,   50
> quam, mihi si media liceat pugnare puella,
> mortem ego non fugiam morte subire tua.

'The stars are witnesses for me and the morning frosts and the door secretly opened to my pitiful pleas—that nothing in life has ever been dearer to me than you; and even now nothing shall be, though you feel at enmity with me. Nor shall any mistress leave her tracks in my bed (45): I shall live alone since I cannot be yours. And, if I have indeed led a devoted life, may that man of yours turn to stone in the midst of love-making. Not more deadly was the combat over the kingdom in which the Theban leaders fell, with their mother in the middle [intervening to stop them] (50), than ⟨that combat in which⟩, if it should be allowed me to fight with my girl in the middle, I should not shrink from undergoing death to the accompaniment of your death too!'

2. See Williams (1968), pp. 172–81.

This whole passage is sometimes treated as a separate poem, sometimes only lines 49–52; or lacunae are assumed at either or both places.
None of this is justified. The poem is a unity, with a ring-composition
between the rival mentioned (in third-person reference) in the opening
couplet, and then, by a characteristically bold Propertian change of
addressee, apostrophised in the last line. There is nothing unlikely in
the poet's thoughts turning in line 47 from the expression of his own
eternal devotion to use that devotion (47, *pios*) as the basis of a prayer,
which has a close parallel in poem 76 of Catullus, against his rival. The
rival's lack of *pietas*, the basis of lines 23–28, is another example of
thematic anticipation used to hold together a complex structure.

The similarity that exists between the exemplum (49–50) and the
conclusion which the poet bases on it (51–52) is that, as Eteocles and
Polynices both died fighting one another, so the poet is ready to die
along with his rival in single combat. The similarity is closer drawn,
however, by a surprising metonymy of the type that Catullus used in
poem 68 to move from the love of Laudamia to the labours of Hercules.
There it was the relationship between the metaphorical and literal
meanings of *barathrum*; here it is the relationship between two senses
of *medius* or *in medio esse*. The one sense means literally 'between, in
the middle, intervening'; and that is the sense in which Iocasta, their
mother, was *media* in the combat of the two brothers. But in the case
of Cynthia the sense of *media* is 'that which is placed in the middle,
a stake, a prize'.[3] What the poet is doing here is close to what he was
seen to be doing in poem 2.8.21 ff (see p. 86). There, realising as he told
the story of Antigone and Haemon that their situation differed from
the one he posited for himself and Cynthia, he emended, as it were,
his own situation to fit by resolving to murder Cynthia. Here he emends
his own situation to fit the triangle Eteocles-Polynices-Iocasta by setting
Cynthia in a linguistically similar, but semantically different, situation.

What is even more surprising, however, is the movement of ideas
from line 48 to line 49: from the rival's being petrified to the Theban
duel. This is achieved by a metonymic movement from the word (48)
lapis which can be regarded as covering the contiguous ideas of 'impotent' and then (deriving from the Gorgon's petrifying gaze) 'dead';
though it is also possible—and perhaps simpler—to analyse the move-

---

3. So Augustus in a letter to Tiberius (Suetonius *Aug.* 71.2): *in singulos talos
singulos denarios in medium conferebat*; he refers to a stake on a throw of dice.

ment as one from the metaphorical sense of *lapis* as 'unable to move, impotent' to the literal sense by which *lapis* is the normal word for 'gravestone,' and so capable of making 'dead' an idea contiguous with 'impotent'. From there the poet moves to the idea of killing his rival, but starting from, not ending with, the unexpected exemplum of the Theban duel.

Poem 2.1 contains a series of metonymic movements. Its large-scale structure is: 1–46, literature, leading into: 47–78, life. At the point where the first section ends, the final couplet (45–46) forms a ring-composition with the opening couplet on the theme of the poet's own particular subject-matter. The two sections contrast in another respect: the first sounds as happy and confident as the second is fore-boding and gloomy.

The poem opens with the poet explaining (1–16) that his relationship with Cynthia is not only the inspiration of his poetry but, in a sense, actually is his poetry. Then (17) an address to Maecenas is made as the poet explains that, if he had been given the talent for epic, he would not have written of Greek myths or even of earlier Roman history, but of (25–26):

> bellaque resque tui memorarem Caesaris, et tu
> Caesare sub magno cura secunda fores.

'I should have recorded the wars and deeds of your ⟨admired⟩ Caesar, and next after great Caesar you would have been my second subject.'

There follows a list of battles in the civil wars (27–34), and the poet then asserts (35–38):

> te mea Musa illis semper contexeret armis,
>   et sumpta et posita pace fidele caput:
> Theseus infernis, superis testatur Achilles,
>   hic Ixioniden, ille Menoetiaden.

'My Muse would always have linked you with those feats of arms, stalwart spirit both when peace was adopted and also when it was set aside: Theseus in the underworld, Achilles on the earth here above, testify, the former to the son of Ixion, the latter to the son of Menoeteus.'

This forms an elegant ring-composition of a type that has frequently been noted above in Propertius, who uses the figure to insert, as it were, a complete section, forming its own unity, into a coherent context. Here lines 35–36 respond to line 26, and lines 37–38 to (25) *tui . . . Caesaris*. The passage is frequently ruined by editors who suppose a lacuna after line 38, or who transpose lines 37–38 elsewhere. What happens here is that the myths are substituted, as often, for the primary statement: that is, instead of the primary statement's being illustrated by the myths so that they are subordinated to it by a particle asserting similarity, the myths stand independently and the primary statement has to be reconstructed by analogy: Pirithous was to Theseus and Patroclus to Achilles ⟨as Maecenas is to Augustus⟩. What is particularly elegant here is that the poet uses Greek myths of a kind that could provide material for the epic type of poetry he is refusing to write, just as he leaves Caesar and contemporary history to return to asserting his incapacity for epic from a different direction.

The movement from the first to the second section of the poem is this (45–48):

> nos contra angusto versantes proelia lecto:
>   qua pote quisque, in ea conterat arte diem.
> laus in amore mori: laus altera si datur uno
>   posse frui: fruar o solus amore meo!

'My subject is the battles that I fight on a narrow bed: let each man spend his day on the exercise of the skill that he can. It is a glory to die in love: it is another glory if a man is permitted the ability to enjoy one love:[4] oh! may I alone have the enjoyment of my love.'

Here (46) *diem* is a synecdoche for *vita*, and by an association of contiguity which is also metonymic, the poet's thoughts turn to death, and specifically to death in love. And so the fame the poet hopes to win for his poetry (the theme of the first section of the poem) is translated into the fame he hopes to win from his love-affair. This section, too, is enclosed in a ring-composition in which the full meaning of death in or from love is made clear only in the last line of the poem (78); and this line itself, by a ring-composition of opposites, echoes in the word *dura* the word (2) *mollis* of the opening couplet of the whole poem. The smaller of these ring-compositions (47–48 and 78) is also of the type which is based on thematic anticipation.

The movement of ideas in this second section of the poem needs close analysis (47–56):

---

4. On this phrase, see Williams (1969), p. 485.

laus in amore mori: laus altera, si datur uno
    posse frui: fruar o solus amore meo!
si memini, solet illa levis culpare puellas,
    et totam ex Helena non probat Iliada.   50
seu mihi sunt tangenda novercae pocula Phaedrae,
    pocula privigno non nocitura suo,
seu mihi Circaeo pereundum est gramine, sive
    Colchis Iolciacis urat aena focis,
una meos quoniam praedata est femina sensus,   55
    ex hac ducentur funera nostra domo.

'It is a glory to die in love: it is another glory if a man is permitted the ability to enjoy one love: oh! may I alone have the enjoyment of my love. If I remember, she is wont to find fault with fickle girls, and because of Helen disapproves of the whole *Iliad* (50). Whether I must taste the cups of the step-mother Phaedra, cups not designed to injure her step-son, or whether I must perish by the herbs of Circe, or if the Colchian woman should heat her cauldron on the hearths of Iolcus, since one woman has stolen away my senses (55), from this houses shall my funeral be conducted.'

The curious phrasing of lines 47–48, starting from the idea of death in love, posits that death on the faithfulness of the girl. Her faithfulness is then tentatively asserted on evidence that seems less than convincing (49–50), and is even expressed with ironic humour. The myths that follow are substituted for an unspoken primary statement that any attempts to weaken the poet's faithfulness against his will are certain to fail. But the myths do not simply replace that statement; they start from it and modify it substantially. For only the myth of Phaedra and Hippolytus substitutes for the idea of an assault on his faithfulness. The myths of Circe and Medea draw in the themes of death and destruction. A synecdochic movement supplies the connexion of thought: the drugs of Phaedra were not intended to harm Hippolytus, but he did, in fact, perish as a result of the passion that prompted the drugs. So the following two myths are substituted for a modified form of the primary statement: If I have to undergo a death that is forced, or otherwise brought on me, I am and will remain faithful (55) and will therefore die in her house (56). The change in the myths motivates a synecdochic movement from love to death. There is here also a thematic anticipation, since there is no indication of why or how the poet might die; that will only come with the last line of the poem (78), though the question is deliberately aroused in the mind of the reader by line 56.

From there the ideas take another turn (57–70):

> omnis humanos sanat medicina dolores:
>> solus amor morbi non amat artificem.
> tarda Philoctetae sanavit crura Machaon,
>> Phoenicis Chiron lumina Phillyrides,   60
> et deus exstinctum Cressis Epidaurius herbis
>> restituit patriis Androgeona focis,
> Mysus et Haemonia iuvenis qua cuspide vulnus
>> senserat, hac ipsa cuspide sensit opem.
> hoc si quis vitium poterit mihi demere, solus   65
>> Tantaleae poterit tradere poma manu;
> dolia virgineis idem ille repleverit urnis
>> ne tenera assidua colla graventur aqua;
> idem Caucasia solvet de rupe Promethei
>> bracchia et a medio pectore pellet avem.   70

'Medicine can heal all human ills: Love alone feels no love for the physician of its illness. Machaon healed the limping legs of Philoctetes; Chiron, son of Phillyra, the eyes of Phoenix (60); and the god of Epidaurus with Cretan herbs restored the dead Androgeon to his ancestral hearth; the youth from Mysia by that same Thessalian spear from which he had received the wound received assistance too. If anyone shall be able to relieve me from this deep affliction (*vitium*), by himself (65) he will be able to place the apples within the grasp of Tantalus; he will also fill casks full from the virgins' urns and stop their soft necks being bowed low with endless water-carrying; he will also free the arms of Prometheus from the Caucasian rock and will drive the bird from the centre of his breast (70).'

From the idea of death in line 56 the poet's thoughts shift by a metonymic movement to the contiguous idea of illness. The proposition that love alone cannot be cured is illustrated by four myths, one of which goes far beyond the others. Philoctetes and Telephus had festering wounds and Phoenix went blind, but Androgeon actually died. As on other occasions in Propertius, the odd exemplum resonates beyond its immediate context (see p. 142). Here the theme of death, which the poet left at line 56 but will take up in the final section of the poem (71–78), is introduced in a myth, apparently invented by Propertius, which shows that even death can be cured, though love cannot. The myths here not only illustrate; they permit the surprising conversion of *amor* into *vitium*, and this movement of thought is parallel to that which converted (57) *dolores* into physical defects. The assertion that this *vitium* is incurable is not made in these words, but is translated instead into a series of ἀδύνατα. Consequently—and this too is left to be extracted from the myths—the disease of love itself becomes deadly. This concept then permits the final movement of the poem (71–78):

> quandocumque igitur vitam mea fata reposcent
>   et breve in exiguo marmore nomen ero,
> Maecenas, nostrae spes invidiosa iuventae,
>   et vitae et morti gloria iusta meae,
> si te forte meo ducet via proxima busto,   75
>   esseda caelatis siste Britanna iugis,
> taliaque illacrimans mutae iace verba favillae:
>   'Huic misero fatum dura puella fuit'.

'Whenever, then, my fate shall demand its due of my life, and I shall become a brief name on a tiny stone, Maecenas, hope and envy of our youth, true glory both for my life and for my death, if by chance your path shall take you close by my tomb (75), halt your British chariot with its carved yoke, and, weeping over my unanswering ash, speak words like these: "For this poor fellow a hard-hearted girl was his fated death."'

The praise of Maecenas takes up an important theme anticipated in the first half of the poem, and when the poet strangely says that Maecenas will be his real glory both in life and death, he means that the place Maecenas will occupy in his poetry, as well as the encouragement he gives, will ensure fame for his poetry even after his own death. This connexion of thought also serves to tie together the major themes of literature (1–46) and life (47–78). The other theme of the final section is the poet's death. The movement had been made from dying in love (47) to dying from love (unspoken in 57–70), but the nature of the disease and the manner of death have not been explained. What has happened is that the transition to the poet's death has been legitimated by the four myths (59–64). This theme is then brought to a climax in the explanation of his death, a brooding theme that will hang over the whole of the second book: Cynthis's hardness of heart will be the cause of his death.

Finally, there is an interesting movement of thought in poem 3.1, which, though it has the proportion of analogy and the shape of enthymeme, has also, in the way in which a stage of the argument is omitted, something of the technique of synecdoche. The poet moves from speaking of his poetic aims and achievements to the fame that will be his (21–36):

> at mihi quod vivo detraxerit invida turba,
> > post obitum duplici faenore reddet Honos.
> omnia post obitum fingit maiora vetustas:
> > maius ab exsequiis nomen in ora venit.
> nam quis equo pulsas abiegno nosceret arces,   25
> > fluminaque Haemonio comminus isse viro,
> Idaeum Simoenta Iovis cum prole Scamandro,
> > Hectora per campos ter maculasse rotas?
> Deiphobumque Helenumque et Pulydamanta et in armis
> > qualemcumque Parim vix sua nosset humus.   30
> exiguo sermone fores nunc, Ilion, et tu
> > Troia bis Oetaei numine capta dei.
> nec non ille tui casus memorator Homerus
> > posteritate suum crescere sensit opus.
> meque inter seros laudabit Roma nepotes: 35
> > illum post cineres auguror ipse diem.

'But whatever the envious crowd shall detract from me in my lifetime, Honour will pay me as my due with doubled interest after my death. Time makes everything bigger after death: after the funeral a name becomes enlarged on men's lips. For who could have got to know of the citadel battered by the wooden horse (25), and the rivers that went to do battle with the Thessalian man, Idaean Simois together with Scamander, offspring of Juppiter, and the wheels that thrice stained Hector across the plains? And Deiphobus and Helenus and Polydamas and Paris, sorry creature in arms—their own country would hardly know of them (30). Small talk would there have been about you now, Ilion, and about you, Troy, twice captured by the god created on Oeta. Even Homer, the famous historian of your fall, found his work to increase among posterity. And Rome shall laud me among her late descendants (35): I myself am the prophet of that day after my death.'

Commentators generally seem to understand the poet as expressing the commonplace that even great events need a poet to make them memorable. They then see that this proposition has little to do with the poet's argument, and assume that the poet, realising this fact as he plodded through the enumeration of lines 25–32, grabbed hold of Homer in lines 33–34 to lever himself gratefully back on track. Nothing of the sort: the poet's line of argument is much more interesting, and deliberately leads into the unexpected climax with Homer. He starts with the assertion of his own fame after death (proposition A). He then moves to the theme: who would have known about Troy? (proposition B^1) From that he leaps to: Homer's fame grew after death (proposition A^1). He ends with: my reputation will be posthumous (proposition A). The introduction to B^1 gives the clue to its interpretation: (23) *fingit maiora*. The events of Troy were unimportant, minor happenings; they only grew in reputation because of Homer and posterity. But Homer himself also enjoyed the same growth in fame after death. The original idea here is that there is a reciprocal posthumous growth in reputation both of poet and of subject-matter. What the poet has done here has not only been to reverse the order of A^1 and B^1—which serves to postpone the explanation (almost indefinitely, if the poet but knew it)—but also to omit proposition B altogether (that the poet's fame grows mutually with that of his subject-matter)—except for the brief suggestion in line 35.

The strongest argument for treating elegies 3.1 and 3.2 as a single elegy is that the link between poet and subject-matter, mutually ensuring immortality (proposition B), is postponed from this section of 3.1, where he establishes the setting for the idea, to 3.2.17–26, where the poet makes it explicit for Cynthia and for himself. Seen in this way, it is a particularly interesting example of thematic anticipation. The element of synecdoche here lies in the fact that the lengthy exposition of proposition B^1 compels a reconstruction of the unstated proposition B such that the proportionality between A^1/B^1 and A/B is properly maintained. That reconstruction cannot be undertaken with confidence until the lines of what is usually regarded as the next poem (3.2.17–26) have been read. This is a procedure of the familiar type *e sequentibus praecedentia*.

2. *Tibullus*

In poem 1.1 Tibullus pictures a life of simplicity for himself in the country:

> non ego divitias patrum fructusque requiro
>   quos tulit antiquo condita messis avo.
> parva seges satis est; satis est requiescere lecto

si licet et solito membra levare toro.
quam iuvat inmites ventos audire cubantem   45
   et dominam tenero continuisse sinu,
aut, gelidas hibernus aquas cum fuderit Auster,
   securum somnos imbre iuvante sequi.

'I do not ask for the riches of my ancestors and the fruits which the stored harvest produced for my grandfather long ago. A small crop is sufficient; it is sufficient if I may sleep on a bed and rest my limbs on my own accustomed couch. What a delight it is, lying in bed, to hear the vicious winds (45) and to hold my mistress in my loving bosom, or, when the south wind in winter has poured out its chill waters, to sleep on carefree, lulled by the rain.'[5]

Here the glancing mention of (46) *domina*, an anticipated theme of great importance in this poem, is legitimized by the metonymic association of *lectus* and *torus* with love-making. So the poet moves from ideas of simplicity and sufficiency to pleasures—among them erotic pleasures—that are also simple. The decisive step, however, was made in line 43 when the poet moved from the idea of a small harvest to the idea of bed: that metonymic movement is mediated by the unspoken idea of work, the condition of self-sufficiency, and the metonymically related idea of honest weariness.

There is a much more complex series of metonymic movements in poem 1.7. The poet is celebrating his patron Messalla's triumph in 27 B.C. and recalls a series of campaigns in which he himself served under Messalla. These are organised into balanced sections, each introduced by a different narrative formula. First Tibullus uses the formula *testis est* (9–12); then the formula *an te . . . canam*? (13–16); and finally the formula *quid referam*? (17–22). This last series goes beyond the previous two for an extra couplet, and the poet takes off from that (21–52):

qualis et, arentes cum findit Sirius agros,
   fertilis aestiva Nilus abundet aqua?
Nile pater, quanam possim te dicere causa
   aut quibus in terris occuluisse caput?
te propter nullos tellus tua postulat imbres,   25
   arida nec pluvio supplicat herba Iovi.

5. The reading here is that provided by the Paris *excerpta*; the Ambrosianus has *igne*. For a discussion, see Galinsky (1973), pp. 161–62.

te canit atque suum pubes miratur Osirim
    barbara, Memphiten plangere docta bovem.
primus aratra manu sollerti fecit Osiris
    et teneram ferro sollicitavit humum,   30
primus inexpertae commisit semina terrae
    pomaque non notis legit ab arboribus.
hic docuit teneram palis adiungere vitem,
    hic viridem dura caedere falce comam:
illi iucundos primum matura sapores   35
    expressa incultis uva dedit pedibus.
ille liquor docuit voces inflectere cantu,
    movit et ad certos nescia membra modos:
Bacchus et agricolae magno confecta labore
    pectora tristitiae dissoluenda dedit: 40
Bacchus et adflictis requiem mortalibus adfert,
    crura licet dura compede pulsa sonent.
non tibi sunt tristes curae nec luctus, Osiri,
    sed chorus et cantus et levis aptus amor,
sed varii flores et frons redimita corymbis,   45
    fusa sed ad teneros lutea palla pedes
et Tyriae vestes et dulcis tibia cantu
    et levis occultis conscia cista sacris.
huc ades et Genium ludis centumque choreis
    concelebra et multo tempora funde mero: 50
illius et nitido stillent unguenta capillo,
    et capite et collo mollia serta gerat.

'And how, when the Dog-Star fissures parched fields, fertile Nile overflows
with summer water. O father Nile, for what reason or in what lands can
I say that you have hidden your head? Because of you your land does not ask
for rain (25), nor does withered grass supplicate Juppiter the rain-god. The
foreign youth, taught to bewail the bull of Memphis, sing of you and revere
their own Osiris. Osiris was the first to fashion a plough with skilful hand and
to harass the soft soil with iron (30); first, too, to entrust seed to the inexperienced earth and to gather apples from unrecognised trees. He it was who
taught how to wed the pliant vine to stakes, and to lop its green foliage with
pitiless pruning-hook; to him the mature grape first gave sweet juices (35)
when crushed by untaught feet. That fluid showed men how to modulate
their voices in song, and directed ignorant limbs in patterned movements.
Bacchus provided the means for farmers' hearts, worn with heavy toil, to be
parted from their misery (40); and Bacchus brings peace to mortals in affliction, though their legs sound to the clank of harsh fetters. Not your style are

miserable worries and grief, Osiris, but dancing and song and carefree love, and variegated flowers and the brow bound with ivy (45), and the yellow cloak reaching to delicate ankles and cloth of Tyre and the pipe sweet for song and the wicker chest privy to the sacred emblems. Come hither and celebrate the Genius with games and a hundred dances and soak our temples with lots of wine (50); and let ointment drip from his gleaming hair, and let him wear soft garlands on his head and neck.'

Here the campaigns are so ordered that Egypt comes as the climax and so, by metonymy, draws in the Nile. The river, in turn, metonymically suggests the eternal question of its source (25–26). Another simple metonymic movement then associates the Nile and Osiris, the chief Egyptian god. The river is now dropped; the poet concentrates on Osiris and his invention of various kinds of agriculture (29–32), including viticulture (33–34). That leads to wine (35–36), and wine to the modes of celebration in song and dance (37–38). Since the poet is moving to Rome, the explanation of various associated powers of wine is attributed to Bacchus so that Bacchus and Osiris become identified. The poet can now return to Osiris, since he has been respectably Romanized, and elaborate the modes of celebration (43–48), with a final appeal to the god to come to the celebration of Messalla's birthday, where prominence is given to wine (50). These movements by metonymic association are at the same time surprising, since they are unpredictable, and also executed with grace and confidence as if the movement of ideas was entirely natural.

There is a similar movement in poem 1.10, where the poet curses war but is forced to go off on a campaign. Peace is contrasted (45–56):

> interea pax arva colat. pax candida primum
>   duxit araturos sub iuga curva boves:
> pax aluit vites et sucos condidit uvae,
>   funderet ut nato testa paterna merum;
> pace bidens vomerque nitent, at tristia duri
>   militis in tenebris occupat arma situs.   50
> rusticus e lucoque vehit, male sobrius ipse,
>   uxorem plaustro progeniemque domum.
> sed Veneris tunc bella calent, scissosque capillos
>   femina, perfractas conqueriturque fores;
> flet teneras subtusa genas; sed victor et ipse   55
>   flet sibi dementes tam valuisse manus.

'Meanwhile let Peace cultivate our fields. Fair Peace was the first to guide oxen under curving yokes to plough; Peace nurtured vines and stored the juices of the grape so that the father's wine-jar could pour wine for his son; in Peace the hoe and ploughshare shine, but in darkness rust creeps over the savage weapons of the cruel soldier (50). And the farmer, far from sober himself, transports wife and children home on his wagon. But the wars of Venus then flare up, and the woman complains of hair torn and doors broken down. She weeps with bruises on her soft cheeks; but the victor actually (55) weeps also that his hands in their insanity found such strength.'

Here the metonymic association is made with the concept of wine. For wine, as conceptually used here by the poet, belongs to, or creates, two fields of ideas: as one of a series of the benefits of Peace it connotes an absence of war; but as one of the main stimuli of love it connotes the presence of a different type of war. Or, to put it differently, the two opposed fields of peace and of war intersect at the point where wine belongs to both. That point of intersection is neatly managed by the poet. For an idea which is metonymically associated with Peace is that of the country festival—hence (51) *e luco*; but wine was an evident part of such festivals—hence (51) *male sobrius ipse*. At that point comes the connexion with 'the wars of Venus'. Such a passage, simpler in technique than any of Propertius, shows clearly how interested poets of the time were in the possibilities of metonymic association for poetic composition.

Tibullus 2.1 is also about a country festival, and the poet describes the scene under the guise of organising it; then his thoughts turn to the various valuable contributions to human life made by country gods and festivals in their honour. In the course of this, after speaking of the origins of dancing and drama, he turns to the household (59–72):

> rure puer verno primum de flore coronam
>   fecit et antiquis imposuit Laribus.   60
> rure etiam teneris curam exhibitura puellis
>   molle gerit tergo lucida vellus ovis.
> hinc et femineus labor est, hinc pensa colusque,
>   fusus et adposito pollice versat opus:
> atque aliqua adsiduae textrix operata minervae   65
>   cantat, et a pulso tela sonat latere.
> ipse quoque inter agros interque armenta Cupido
>   natus et indomitas dicitur inter equas.
> illic indocto primum se exercuit arcu:

ei mihi, quam doctas nunc habet ille manus! 70
nec pecudes, velut ante, petit: fixisse puellas
gestit et audaces perdomuisse viros.

'It was in the country that a slave-boy first made a garland from spring
flowers and put it around the ancestral Lares (60). It was in the country, too,
that a gleaming sheep wore a soft fleece on its back to create work for gentle
girls. From here, too, is derived a task for women, from here the wool and
distaff, and the spindle turns the work by the application of a thumb; and a
weaver, devoting herself to the endless work of Minerva (65), sings, and the
warp resounds as the weights are struck. Cupid himself, the story goes, was
born in the fields and among the herds and the untamed mares. There first
he exercised with his unskilled bow—alas for me! what skilled hands he has
now (70)! And he does not now, as before, aim at animals: he delights to
pierce girls and to subdue bold men to his will.'

There is a delicate combination here of metonymic movement
with thematic anticipation. In the course of enumerating various people
whose lives are bound up with the arts and inventions of the country
gods, the poet comes naturally to (61) *tenerae puellae*, but only as mem-
bers of a work-force. His thoughts linger over the tasks of spinning
and weaving, women's work. Then, by an unstated metonymic connexion, Cupid appears, but as himself, at first, a worker in the countryside—no longer, however: his pleasure now is (71) to wound *puellae*
and—by the most obvious metonymy—strong men. The erotic topic
is now at the poet's command and persists for the rest of the poem
(73–90). The teasing thematic anticipation of (61) *tenerae puellae*, especially in the suggestive adjective, is cleverly held off for another
twelve lines.

There is another interesting movement of thought in poem 2.3,
where editors since Lachmann usually now assume a lacuna (where
Heyne did not). In this poem the poet's mistress has left him for a wealthy
lover, with whom she is living in the country. This situation opens up
all the poet's favourite themes, and he pictures his willing slavery and
demeaning toil if he could be there with Nemesis. He recalls Apollo's
servitude to Admetus, and reflects (29–42):

felices olim, Veneri cum fertur aperte
servire aeternos non puduisse deos. 30
fabula nunc ille est; sed cui sua cura puella est,
fabula sit mavult quam sine amore deus.

at tu quisquis is es, cui tristi fronte Cupido
    imperat ut nostra sint tua castra domo,
ferrea non venerem sed praedam saecula laudant;   35
    praeda tamen multis est operata malis.
praeda feras acies cinxit discordibus armis:
    hinc cruor, hinc caedes mors propiorque venit.
praeda vago iussit geminare pericula ponto,
    bellica cum dubiis rostra dedit ratibus.   40
praedator cupit immensos obsidere campos
    ut multa innumera iugera pascat ove.

'Happy the men of olden times when, they say, the eternal gods were not ashamed of openly being slaves to Venus (30). He [Apollo] is now a scandal: but the man who really loves his girl prefers to be a scandal than a god without love. But you—whoever you are—whom Cupid with angry face commands to set up your camp in my house,[6] the ages of iron value loot, not love (35); yet loot is the cause of many ills. Loot arms savage battle-lines with hostile weapons: hence blood, hence slaughter and death speeds up. Loot bids men double their perils on the moving ocean when it fits rams of war on unstable ships (40). The man of loot lusts to occupy unmeasured plains so that he may graze many acres with unnumbered sheep.'

Here the poet turns suddenly with disgust to his rival (33), now mentioned for the first time. But the address *at tu* does not here herald an imperative; it merely singles out this creature as the addressee for the following attack. As in poem 1.10, the fields of war and love intersect in the metaphorical application of fighting terms to love-making. The words *imperat* and *castra* in line 34 set up the field of warfare in the metaphorical sense, but the metonymic movement to (35) *praeda* shifts the field to that of real warfare and explicitly excludes love (*non venerem sed praedam*). The argument then takes up *praeda* in the literal sense as a cause of war. This figures the rich rival as a barbarous soldier; but in lines 40 ff., with *praedator* and the military term *obsidere* allowing the military images to taper off, the greed and destructiveness of the rich man are attacked directly. What is particularly delicate here is the metonymic movement from (34) *imperat* and *castra* to *praeda* (which also involves transfer from the metaphoric to the literal field), for the prime target of the poet's attack is his rival's wealth. The assumption

6. This is the point at which a lacuna is assumed.

of a lacuna here is perfectly designed to ruin that skilful movement of thought.

3. *Horace*

Metonymic and synecdochic connexions of ideas are fairly frequent in the *Odes* of Horace and even in his *Satires* and *Epistles*. Most of these are quite straightforward, although the metonymic link may depend on an association that is unfamiliar to a modern reader. For instance, at the end of the great ode to Maecenas, 3.29, the poet asserts his own independence from *Fortuna*: she loves to be capricious, but he will enjoy her while she stays with him, and if she shakes her swift wings, he will give up everything and look for a new wife in undowried but honourable Poverty (49–56). Then follow two stanzas picturing the poet on a merchant ship, caught in a storm, quite happily abandoning the rich cargo and climbing into the 'lifeboat' (53–64). The metonymic relationship between the concept of *Fortuna* and the picture of the ship is illustrated by a frequently occurring emblem depicting *Fortuna* with a rudder:[7] it was a familiar fact to the ancient world that great wealth could be made—or lost—on a single voyage. That was the most striking emblem to them of the power of *Fortuna*. The humour of the portrait of *Fortuna* as a wife obtaining a divorce (to be replaced in her office by Poverty) is nicely balanced by the portrait of the poet in a tiny dinghy, destitute but safe, as the unexpected climax of the poem. That quality of unexpectedness and unpredictability is what the poet gained from skilful use of metonymic connexions.

It is unnecessary to examine a series of detailed passages; all that will be attempted here will be to indicate briefly some of the typical forms that these connexions take.

Odes 2.13 starts with three stanzas of curses on the wretch who planted the tree that has almost fallen on the poet's head (1–12). Then two stanzas explain how unexpected death always is and always has been: sailors fear the seas, soldiers arrows and the Parthians, the Parthian Romans—(19–20) *sed improvisa leti / vis rapuit rapietque gentes*, 'but the violence of death has always snatched, and always will snatch, mankind away without being foreseen'. The poet continues (21–28):

7. See, for instance, Weinstock (1971), pp. 123–27.

> quam paene furvae regna Proserpinae
> et iudicantem vidimus Aeacum
>   sedesque discriptas piorum et
>   Aeoliis fidibus querentem
>
> Sappho puellis de popularibus,
> et te sonantem plenius aureo,
>   Alcaee, plectro dura navis,
>   dura fugae mala, dura belli.

'How near I came to seeing the kingdom of dark Proserpina and Aeacus passing judgment and the separate abodes of the good and Sappho on Aeolian strings singing sadly of the girls of her people, and you, Alcaeus, intoning more richly with your golden plectrum the ills of shipboard hard to bear, of exile hard to bear, and of war hard to bear.'

Here there is a nicely unexpected metonymic movement from the idea of death to that of the underworld and so to the poet's two dead Greek predecessors, Sappho and Alcaeus. It is an arbitrary, even whimsical, movement, yet completely convincing poetically at each stage, from the cursing of the tree and the unexpectedness of death to the sudden appearance of the two poets.

The poem ends (29–40) with a portrait of the effect the two poets have on their audience in the underworld. And this closure displays a characteristically Horatian touch. First the poet sees the shades listening in silence to both his great predecessors, but the mob is more tightly shoulder to shoulder (32, *densum umeris*) around Alcaeus. And what wonder they listen so intently (33) since even Cerberus and the Eumenides are charmed. Prometheus himself and Tantalus are lulled into forgetfulness of their agony (37–38). Finally (39–40):

> nec curat Orion leones
> aut timidos agitare lyncas.

'Nor is Orion interested in pursuing lions or timid lynxes.'

The ending is a perfectly devised *diminuendo*, with Orion metonymically related to Prometheus and Tantalus as a sinner; but his totally different activity produces the gently falling closure, with lions succeeded by the tamer *timidas . . . lyncas*. An almost identical *diminuendo* occurs in *Odes* 3.4, where the list of dead Giants is closed by (79–80) *amatorem trecentae | Pirithoum cohibent catenae*, 'three hundred chains hold

fast the lover Pirithous'. This unexpected figure is connected metonymically with the Giants through his ancestry, but his intended act of
violence against Persephone was quite unlike that of the Giants against
Juppiter. Similar again is the *diminuendo* in *Odes* 4.7. The theme is that
nothing helps against death; no power can release one from the underworld (25–28):

> infernis neque enim tenebris Diana pudicum
>   liberat Hippolytum,
> nec Lethaea valet Theseus abrumpere caro
>   vincula Pirithoo.

'For neither does Diana release the chaste Hippolytus from the darkness
below, nor can Theseus break the Lethaean chains from his dear Pirithous.'

Here the metonymic movement from Hippolytus to his father
Theseus is even more surprising, but the gentle closure is perfectly
timed, with the mortal friend replacing the goddess. The effect of the
ending of *Odes* 2.19 is an example of the same technique. The part
played by Bacchus in defending Juppiter against the Giants' assault is
treated as an example of the god's prowess in war (21–24). Then the
poet reflects on a wrong opinion (25–32):

> quamquam choreis aptior et iocis
> ludoque dictus non sat idoneus
>   pugnae ferebaris: sed idem
>   pacis eras mediusque belli.
>
> te vidit insons Cerberus aureo
> cornu decorum leniter atterens   30
>   caudam et recedentis trilingui
>   ore pedes tetigitque crura.

'And yet you were alleged to be more fitted for dancing and laughter and
play, and were considered unsuited to battle: but you were the same in the
midst of peace and of war. Cerberus looked on you adorned with a golden
horn, and did not harm you, but, gently wagging his tail (30), he nuzzled
with his triple-tongued mouth your feet and your legs as you moved away.'

The connexion between the final legend, in which Bacchus descended to the underworld to bring back his mother Semele, and what
precedes is metonymic: the idea of courage connects both. But again

the *diminuendo* is perfectly conceived, with the picture of the monster fawning as the god moves quietly away. This is the opposite of a ring-composition, since the ending contrasts dramatically with the wild dithyrambic opening (there is a similar contrast in 2.13). The end of *Odes* 1.10 uses much the same technique, where the picture of Mercury in the underworld contrasts deeply with the humour of the earlier part of the poem, and the connexion is made by a striking synecdochic relationship between the dead Hector (who is not mentioned in the previous stanza describing Priam's mission to Achilles) and the (17) *piae . . . animae* in the underworld. The metonymic relationship between the themes of death and the underworld works powerfully in Horace's poetry and sustains a recurring note of melancholy that contrasts as much with the heroic pessimism of Virgil as with the self-indulgent melodrama of Propertius.

The puzzling ode 3.2 can be viewed as constructed by means of a series of surprising metonymic movements. Lines 1–6 portray the ideal young Augustan soldier, crusading against the Parthians:

> Angustam amice pauperiem pati
> robustus acri militia puer
>   condiscat et Parthos feroces
>   vexet eques metuendus hasta
>
> vitamque sub divo et trepidis agat   5
> in rebus.

'Let the sturdy boy learn through hard military service to suffer pinching Poverty as a friend, and let him harass the proud Parthians, a horseman to be feared for his spear, and let him spend his life under the open sky and surrounded by danger.'

The poet then views him through the eyes of a king's mother and of a prince's betrothed, both anxious that their man should not encounter so fearful a hero (6–12):

> illum ex moenibus hosticis
> matrona bellantis tyranni
>   prospiciens et adulta virgo
>
> suspiret, eheu, ne rudis agminum
> sponsus lacessat regius asperum   10
>   tactu leonem, quem cruenta
>   per medias rapit ira caedis.

'Let the wife of the warring tyrant, looking at him [the Roman youth] from enemy walls, and ⟨with her⟩ let her grown-up daughter sigh—alas!—lest her royal betrothed, inexperienced in battle, should provoke that lion, dangerous to touch, whom bloodthirsty rage spurs through the middle of the carnage.'

This scene retreats from the opening reality into a Homeric τειχοσκοπία by a type of double synecdoche (for the relationship starts from the contiguity of the Homeric scene—the connecting idea being war—not its similarity); by this means the substitution of the Homeric scene for the Parthian reality has the effect of also converting the young Augustan soldier into a Homeric hero (with a hint at an epic lion-simile to describe him in lines 10–12). That movement now (13–16) allows the poet to reflect on the Homeric ideal of courage in war as it was perpetuated by later Greek elegiac poets:

> dulce et decorum est pro patria mori:
> mors et fugacem presequitur virum,
>   nec parcit imbellis iuventae   15
>   poplitibus timidove tergo.

'Desirable and glorious is a death for one's country: death even follows after the man who runs away, and does not spare the knees and back of a spiritless youth.'

At this point another metonymic movement, easy for the Roman mind, from military virtue to civic virtue draws in a picture of *Virtus* as a candidate for the Roman consulship, but not subject to the whims of mass voters. Rejected, but with 'untarnishable honour', she achieves immortality by a route otherwise denied (17–24):

> Virtus repulsae nescia sordidae
> intaminatis fulget honoribus,
>   nec sumit aut ponit securis
>   arbitrio popularis aurae;   20
>
> Virtus recludens immeritis mori
> caelum negata temptat iter via,
>   coetusque vulgaris et udam
>   spernit humum fugiente penna.

'Virtue, recognising no disgrace in defeat at the polls, shines with untarnishable honours, and does not take up nor put down the axes ⟨of office⟩ at the whim of popular favour; Virtue that opens up heaven to those undeserving to die explores a route along a path ⟨usually⟩ denied, and disdains the vulgar mobs and the damp earth with escaping wing.'

Here *Virtus* is pictured as a candidate for the consulship because what is intended by the poet is not *Virtus* in general but the specific qualities required of the good citizen in contemporary Rome. This theme is metonymically related to the preceding theme: military and civic virtue are contiguous ideas. The point being made here is that such *Virtus* is not defined in terms of a poll among the masses. Not only might the ideal citizen fail to be elected to the consulship, but the very ambition to achieve the consulship as such ought to be irrelevant to him. It is no mere coincidence that the poet's portrait inevitably recalls the character of Cato,[8] for what is in question here is the ideal of political behaviour in the early years of Augustus and the advertised return to Republican constitutionality. This ideal was closely associated with the ideal of Roman military supremacy in the world at large, so that the metonymic movement involved here was simple.

What is remarkable in the poet's portrayal of both ideals is that the basic characteristic in both is self-denial: poverty endured as a friend and a readiness to surrender his life are the qualities of the soldier as seen by the Roman analyst (he is a magnificently different creature in the eyes of the terrified enemy); a readiness to deny himself the fruits of popularity and to look for immortality within himself are the qualities of the good citizen. (The poet, of course, assumes the good citizen to be a man of substance and position, a senator; lesser citizens were not worth talking about.) Both virtues are curiously unspectacular: ambitious men were dangerous; discipline and conformity to agreed ideals were what were needed. The final ideal is equally unspectacular (25–32):

---

8. Cato's pleasure in rejection at the polls became a commonplace: cf. Seneca *epist. moral.* 104.33: *vides honorem et notam posse contemni: eodem quo repulsus est die in comitio pila lusit* ('you realise that honour and disgrace can be despised: on the very day that he [Cato] was rejected at the polls, he played ball'); or Pliny *Nat.Hist.praef.* 9: *cum apud Catonem illum ambitus hostem et repulsis tamquam honoribus inemptis gaudentem ... pecunias deponerent candidati* ('since the candidates deposited their money with Cato, that foe of corruption, that man who rejoiced in electoral defeat as an honour not bought with money ...').

est et fideli tuta silentio   25
  merces: vetabo qui Cereris sacrum
    vulgarit arcanae sub isdem
      sit trabibus fragilemque mecum

solvat phaselon. saepe Diespiter
  neglectus incesto addidit integrum: 30
    raro antecedentem scelestum
      deseruit pede Poena claudo.

'There is a sure reward for faithful silence: I shall not allow the man who has published the rite of secret Ceres to be under the same roof-beam or to cast off a frail boat in my company. Often the Sky-Father, when disregarded, has coupled an innocent with a guilty man ⟨in destruction⟩ (30); not often has Vengeance abandoned a guilty man through lameness of foot—though he has got a start on her.'

Here the poet has quoted almost word for word a famous saying of Simonides that was often on Augustus' lips: ἔστι καὶ σιγᾶς ἀκίνδυνον γέρας, 'there is also a sure reward for silence'. What is important here is that, as in the case of the quotation from Alcaeus that opened *Odes* 1.18 (see p. 120), the poet has added a significant adjective. For the addition of *fidele* to *silentium* has the effect of approximating the virtue intended to that of *Fides*. Here the movement of ideas is synecdochic, for *Fides* is a part of the good citizen's armoury of virtues, and *fidele silentium* is itself synecdochically related to *Fides*. But the poet's assertion is brief and riddling; and the apparently explanatory expansion which follows, unlike that which follows (13) *dulce et decorum est pro patria mori* (itself a simple enough assertion), does not enlighten. For immediately the poet swerves away[9] into a condemnation of those who profane mysteries, which belongs to the age-old commonly shared Greek and Roman religious taboos and which is signalled as being outside the sphere of the contemporary political ideas of the rest of the poem by the antique form of Juppiter's name, *Diespiter*, and by the Greek concept of Ἄτη in *Poena*. The relationship between this taboo-silence and *fidele silentium* is metonymic and of a type similar to the metonymic movements that Catullus in poem 68 pivoted on the words *Troia* and *barathrum*: that is, *silentium* means one

---

9. For this type of poetical swerving away from an excess of immediate reality, see Williams (1968), pp. 165–68.

thing in the first context and something else in the second, but both meanings can be covered by the one word *silentium* (though it has to be qualified by *fidele* in the first context).

This series of connexions indicates that the poet probably chose the word *silentium* because it provided the possibility of the movement of ideas rather than because it precisely described the intended virtue. In that case, the deliberate addition of *fidele* may be read, if taken in conjunction with the preceding *Virtus* (17–24), as designed to convey a condemnation of senatorial opposition to Augustus and, in particular, of the rejection of the moral legislation in 28 B.C. Augustus could have expressed that rejection as a failure of *Fides* in his opponents, basing his claim on the 'universal consent' by which he was 'in complete control of the whole state' (*res gestae* 34.1) until the end of 28 B.C. Those senators who succeeded in blocking his moral legislation, perhaps at a stage prior to any formal attempt to pass it and so by private expressions of dissent, were *infidi*. The sense of *Fides* here is that of 'loyalty' as in *Odes* 1.35.21 or 1.24.6–7 *Iustitiae soror / incorrupta Fides* (cf. *carm.saec.* 57 and *Odes* 4.5.20). Metonymically related, but distinct, is the sense in *Odes* 1.18.16, *arcanique Fides prodiga, perlucidior vitro*, but it is by that very metonymic leap that the poet concludes the poem, swerving aside into ideas that have no direct relevance to a political situation. So the 'loyal silence' of line 25 is the loyalty that is expressed by silent acceptance of directives from a man to whom one is bound by oath, and this is taken up and transformed into the silence that refuses to divulge rites that one is under religious oath to keep secret.

That sort of swerving aside, as if the poet could not stand too much reality, is characteristic of Horace's treatment of political themes, especially in *Odes* 1–3. It can be seen at the end of *Odes* 1.12 where, from more or less factual reflection on Augustus' power, the poet swerves away into traditional religious ideas. Here, and in other similar structures, for instance in *Odes* 3.3 or 4.5 or 4.15, a metonymic movement of ideas places the poet in a nonpolitical context that has no factual relevance to the contemporary situation. In *Odes* 3.2, the swerve aside at the beginning of the poem from Roman military reality into Homeric romanticism is paralleled by the swerve aside at the end which relieves the poet from further definition of the poetic reality behind *fidele silentium*. In all of these examples the unexpectedness of the swerve derives from, and is controlled by, the metonymic relationship between the ideas.

CHAPTER VII

THE OBJECTIVE
FRAMEWORK

The technique to be examined in this chapter bears some resemblance to T. S. Eliot's concept of the 'objective correlative' (see p. 31), in that its effect is to permit the poet to focus, or appear to focus, his attention on some ostensible field of ideas and yet to create an unmistakable sense that the poem can only achieve its full meaning if another semantic dimension is taken into account at the same time. But it differs both in the extent of the reconstruction of the unspoken field that is entailed by a proper reading of the poem and also in the complexity of the relationship between the field that actually appears in the poem and the unspoken field. There are four particular characteristics of the technique.

First, it is not true of it, as it is true of some types of allegory, that the object of interpretation is to penetrate a disguise for which the 'real' meaning is then substituted and the disguise is, as it were, discarded. Instead, the ostensible field of the poem excites a sense of the unspoken field so that the poem acquires a new dimension that co-exists with the immediately perceptible dimension. Seen from the poet's view-point, it is a technique for transforming subject-matter which, from whatever motive, he is unwilling to treat directly. Secondly, the process is one by which the poet achieves a certain objectivity. He insulates himself from direct involvement in the unspoken field, as Catullus, for instance, insulates himself by using the myth of Laudamia in poem 68. Thirdly, the proportionality between the two fields always turns out to be more complex than can be described by simply naming or even exhaustively plotting the two fields, and this is another way in which the technique differs from simple allegory. In the simplest form, the poet, in relation to the ostensible field, has a different persona from that which he wears in relation to the unspoken field. The proportionality is always between two relationships. Fourthly, there is always an element in the poem which can be regarded as fulfilling the function of an index of proportionality between the two fields. It is a pointer to the reader, showing him how he can make the transference from the one field to the other and what is the relationship between them.

Dramatic monologue is often an example of the technique in its simplest form. In a more complex form the poet selects a field of discourse that is easily recognised to be analogous and sometimes even associated with the unspoken field, so that transfer is relatively simple. In this form, the poet can be regarded as processing a subject for poetic treatment by setting it in a framework to which it does not normally belong but to which it can be seen to be related either metaphorically or metonymically. In the most complex form, not only are the two fields unpredictable in their relationships to one another, but there is also an element of the arbitrary in the poet's decision to associate them no less than in the manner in which he associates them. In this form, transfer from one field to the other demands a risky leap of the imagination, and not only can the transfer never be in the least complete, but the very dimness with which the unspoken field is viewed is a powerful factor in the success of the technique. For suggestiveness is the essence of this poetic technique. In each case what I have called the 'framework' constitutes the immediately perceptible field of the poem, and I have designated it 'objective' because an essential function of it is to insulate the poet from the unspoken field, to save him from what could be a disturbing or embarrassing subjectivity.

Although this technique differs in important ways from allegory, what Quintilian says of one type of allegory is relevant (8.6.54): 'In that type [of allegory], however, in which the meaning is contrary to what is said, there is irony: they call it *illusio*. Comprehension of it comes by way either of the delivery or of the speaker's character or of the nature of the subject; for if any of these is at variance with the words, it is clear that the speaker's intention is different from what he says.' Quintilian is, as usual, analysing in terms of a speech, but his criteria for grasping the framework are close to what I have called above the 'index of proportionality'. Most relevant, however, is what Quintilian says of a figure that is called by no other name than *schema* or *figura* (9.2.65–66):

Related to, or identical with, this [*emphasis*] is a figure that we use very greatly nowadays. For I must now turn to that type which is of very frequent occurrence and on which I am certain comment is expected from me. It is that whereby we wish something that we do not say to be understood by a type of inference [*per quandam suspicionem*]; this something is certainly not contrary to our words, as in irony, but it is a secondary meaning and is left to be discovered, as it were, by the listener. As I said above,[1] rhetoricians nowadays pretty well restrict the word *schema* to this figure, and it is from it that *controversiae figuratae* derive their name. Its use is threefold: first, if it is quite unsafe to speak openly; second, if it is not fitting; the third type is that which is employed just for charm and which gives more pleasure by its very inventiveness and variety than if the expression had been direct.

Quintilian continues with his analysis of the three types (67–75, 76–95, and 96–99). He gives the briefest attention to the third (which is the most interesting) because he is always thinking in terms of a speaker and an audience, sometimes in a real court but usually in a declamation-school. He recognises the closeness of this type of figure to allegory (9.2.92): 'The whole procedure of saying one thing and wishing another to be understood is similar to allegory'.[2] This type of figure is discussed at greater length by the author of chapters 8 and 9 of the *Ars Rhetorica* that has come down in the tradition falsely under the name of Dionysius of Halicarnassus. That writer's analysis is also threefold and is close to that of Quintilian. But even Quintilian's analysis, designed as it is to process the figure for the use of an orator, allows one to see something of the potentiality of this figure for the poet. On the other hand, the vagueness of his analysis and the restriction of his examples to quotations of a few sentences at most (in which the relationship between what is said and what is intended to be understood is childishly simple) show how intractable to analysis in his traditional categories the rhetorician would have found even simple poetic exploitation of the figure. His only recourse was to regard it as a type of allegory in which a disguise had to be penetrated by whatever violence was most easily available.

1. The reference is to 9.1.14.
2. It can readily be seen from Quintilian's analysis that what I am calling 'the objective framework' has a relationship to what I have called 'secondary language' (chap. 2, sec. 4) that is analogous to the relationship between allegory and metaphor.

1. *Dramatic Monologue and Related Techniques*

Whereas in Book 2 Propertius usually confronts Cynthia directly in a dramatic situation, in Book 1 he often uses a technique of dramatic monologue that involves him in direct confrontation with a third party rather than with Cynthia. The way in which this technique works may be seen from poem 1.4. The situation appears in lines 1–4: Bassus is trying to part the poet from Cynthia by praising other girls to him, but the poet wants to spend the rest of his life in his 'accustomed servitude' to Cynthia. The poet asserts that her beauty exceeds that of Antiope and Hermione and of all mythical heroines (5–14). To make this ostensibly personal statement, however, he withdraws into secondary language; the only statement that is primary in form is contained in the final two couplets of this section (11–14):

> haec sed forma mei pars est extrema furoris;
>   sunt maiora quibus, Basse, perire iuvat:
> ingenuus color et multis decus artibus et quae
>   gaudia sub tacita ducere veste libet.

'But this beauty is the least cause of my passion; there are more important things over which, Bassus, it is my pleasure to die: the good breeding of her complexion, the distinction that comes from great artistic talent, and the joys I love to prolong under the unrevealing coverlet.'

Cynthia, then, is of gentle birth, artistic, and good at making love. The statement, though primary in form, is as detached and unrevealing as the secondary language that preceded it. The next couplet (15–16) asserts that the more Bassus tries to part them, the more both of them stand firm by their mutual pledges. That makes the transition to Cynthia (17–24): she will not only be faithful, but will be angry with Bassus and seek to harm him in every way. The poems ends with couplets of mixed assertion and prayer (25–28):

> non ullo gravius temptatur Cynthia damno
>   quam sibi cum rapto cessat amore decus—
> praecipue nostro. maneat sic semper, adoro,
>   nec quicquam ex illa quod querar inveniam.

'By no loss is Cynthia more gravely assailed than when her beauty is forced to be idle because a love has been stolen from her—especially mine. I pray that it may remain so for ever, and that nothing to grieve me may befall me from her.'

The ostensible field of the poem is Bassus' relationship with the poet, but this functions as an objective framework for the important field of the poet's relationship with Cynthia. The index of proportionality between the two fields is to be found in an unspoken element in the dramatic situation. Why is Bassus trying to persuade the poet to leave Cynthia? An oblique hint appears in lines 19–22: he wants Cynthia for himself. But once that hint is taken it colours everything the poet says about Cynthia: his confidence in their mutual pledges, his assertion that she is more shattered by the loss of his love than that of any other (tentatively expressed so that serious doubt is evoked), and his final prayer. All suggest that the relationship is in reality far less stable than his representation of it to Bassus.

There are two reasons why the reader of this poem and of those that follow is led to realise and explore a secondary field (that is, in this poem, to go beyond the primary field by asking why Bassus is trying to get the poet to leave Cynthia). The first is inherent in each poem itself: a sense is created that the poet has chosen to compose in the form of a monologue addressed to a carefully selected male friend precisely because he thereby achieves a certain kind of detachment from an obsessive emotional problem—that is, an important issue is being deliberately left unexpressed and is yet allowed to appear somewhere behind the poem; the careful choice of addressees allows a variety of viewpoints on that problem, while insulating the poet from direct emotional involvement in it. The second reason arises from the ordering of the poems in Book 1: the three opening poems allow partial and puzzling, though direct, glimpses of the very strange relationship that exists between the poet and Cynthia and which the first poem declared was the origin of his poetry. That poetic sense of curiosity, once aroused in the reader, carries over into the poems that follow so that there is a constant awareness of the poet's emotional obsession lying behind the dramatic occasion that constitutes the primary field. In 1.4 the awareness of a secondary field leads to a sensing of the poet's doubts and fears that are not expressed directly in the primary field; as a result, in this poem the two fields are seen to stand in inverse relationship to one another: what is said positively in the primary field must be understood with a negative twist in the secondary, and the index of proportionality provides the responsive reader with a clue for that procedure.

The next poem (1.5) explores a similar situation from a different point of view in a closely responding poetic form (even to the degree of having the address to Gallus in the final couplet, whereas the address to Bassus was in the first couplet). Here Gallus, who is openly trying to seduce Cynthia, is told to desist, on the curious ground that he could not possibly wish to undergo the torture that the poet has been compelled to undergo. Here the overt field is the relationship between the poet and a friend who is trying to seduce his girl. The unspoken field is again the relationship between the poet and Cynthia. The poet purports to give Gallus an account of this latter field, but since this has an obvious and admitted purpose in the overt field (to stop the seduction), how is the reader intended to sense the reality? The index of proportionality here is provided by a couplet (9–10) that also functions as the explanation of the poet's opening outburst:

> quod si forte tuis non est contraria votis,
> at tibi curarum milia quanta dabit!

'But if she happens to accede to your desires, yet what thousands of pains she will give you!'

This is reinforced by the following (27–30):

> non ego tum potero solacia ferre roganti,
> cum mihi nulla mei sit medicina mali;
> sed pariter miseri socio cogemur amore
> alter in alterius mutua flere sinu.

'I shall not then be able to solace you when you ask me, since I have no cure for my own suffering; but the two of us, joined in an equally unhappy partnership of love, will be compelled to weep together on each other's bosom.'

So the poet has no means of telling whether Cynthia will be unfaithful or not, and if she is, then Gallus will be as helpless as the poet. Here, then, in contradistinction to the previous poem, the two fields are closely related: in spite of the rhetorical motive (to prevent the girl's seduction), transfer from the ostensible field to the unspoken field is more or less direct, and this latter field is related to the former by synecdoche. The relationship of this to the previous poem is completed by the fact that what the poet says of Cynthia in 1.5 seems, as it were, to be a definition of *assueto ... servitio* (1.4.4), which, therefore, instead of being taken as a conventional metaphor, can be regarded on the evidence of poem 1.5 (*e sequentibus praecedentia*) as another index of proportionality, enforcing the inverse relationship between the two fields in 1.4. In both poems the area of the unspoken field that is evoked by the ostensible field is small in relation to the area of the field in reality; revelation is not only detached and at a considerable remove, but it is also fractional.

Poem 1.6 involves a double relationship in the ostensible field. Tullus has invited the poet to accompany him to Asia (with his uncle, the proconsul of 30–29 B.C.); the poet is ready to go to the ends of the earth with Tullus, but must refuse because of the hurt his departure would cause Cynthia. This complex situation is used to contrast Tullus' relationship to the state (and fame and public service) with the poet's to Cynthia. The unspoken field is again the reality of the poet's love-relationship. In the ostensible field the poet suggests a willing deference to his girl's wishes. But the index of proportionality between the two fields appears in words that the poet uses of his own situation, such as (25) *iacere*, 'lie prostrate'; (26) *multi ... periere*, 'many have died' (the poet wishes to be one); and *duro sidere*, 'an unkind star'. It is to be seen also in the analogy drawn between Tullus' relationship to the state and the poet's to his girl: the poet's sense of compulsion and inescapable destiny explores yet another area of that reality which the poet avoids confronting directly.

In poem 1.7 the epic poet Ponticus despises the poetry of Propertius (a fact that only becomes clear in the last couplet, 25–26). The poet warns him that love-elegy has its function and that Ponticus will come to understand that Propertius is no (21) *humilis poeta* in reality, and will actually place him at the head of Roman literary geniuses (22). Here the ostensible field is the relationship between epic poetry and love-elegy; the unspoken field is again the relationship of the poet with Cynthia. The index of proportionality lies in the concept that the lover is compelled by the rigours of his situation to write a particular type of poetry (5–8):

> nos, ut consuemus, nostros agitamus amores
>   atque aliquid duram quaerimus in dominam;
> nec tantum ingenio quantum servire dolori
>   cogor et aetatis tempora dura queri,

'I, as usual, am occupied with the theme of my love-affair, and search for some weapon against the harshness of my mistress; and I am compelled to be a slave not so much to inspiration as to pain, and to mourn the sufferings of my life.'

Here yet another area of the unspoken field is explored, and it is one that is of great importance to this poet; but it is an obscure and difficult area, and the poet has taken full advantage of the opportunities this technique offered him for oblique treatment. This area of the field is that which concerns the relationship between love and poetic inspiration, and it has two aspects, both of which appear here and elsewhere:[3] the first is that the poet-lover is compelled to a particular subject-matter and form; the second is that such poetic composition helps the poet—not only psychologically but also practically. The point that the index of proportionality enforces is that love is inevitably painful and inescapable: lovers, no less than poets, are born, not made. But the idea is also expressed that this type of poetry is difficult and requires a long apprenticeship (19–20). It is an imaginative and suggestive treatment of the relationship between poetry and life.

The following poem, 1.8, functions as an illustration in action and reality of the principles asserted in 1.7. Cynthia is deserting the poet and going off to Illyria, perhaps with a propraetor (in which case her situation closely parallels that of the poet in 1.6). The poet addresses her in anguish (1–26). There is a pause during which she agrees to stay with the poet, who then expresses his ecstasy in soliloquy (27–46). Here his address to her is poetry in action (1–26), as his references to it in his soliloquy show: (28) *assiduas non tulit illa preces*, 'she could not withstand my continuous prayers', and (40) *sed potui blandi carminis obsequio*, 'but I was able ⟨to move her⟩ with the help of winning poetry'. It is very noticeable that this poem which, unlike the others examined, directly confronts the poet's relationship with Cynthia and immediately presents primary experience, is almost totally composed

---

3. Notably in elegy 1.1: see pp. 34 ff. above.

in secondary language. This device is used by the poet as a substitute for the objective framework (as also in poem 1.1).

Poem 1.9 returns to Ponticus and the ostensible field presents him in the most abject state: he is enslaved to a slave-girl. The index of proportionality which relates this to the unspoken field of the relationship between the poet and Cynthia is this couplet (7–8):

> me dolor et lacrimae merito fecere peritum:
> atque utinam posito dicar amore rudis!

'Pain and tears have conferred on me well-earned expertise—but would that I could only divest myself of love and be called ignorant.'

In poem 1.10 the poet has seen Gallus and Gallus' girl making love. Here the index of proportionality between this ostensible field and the real field consists in (4) *o quotiens votis illa vocanda meis*, 'o that night [of your love] so often to be invoked in my prayers', and in 27–30:

> at quo sis humilis magis et subiectus amori,
>   hoc magis effectu saepe fruare bono.
> is poterit felix una remanere puella
>   qui numquam vacuo pectore liber erit.

'But the more servile you are and enslaved to love, so much the more are you likely to enjoy success. That man will be able to stay happy with one girl, who shall never be free [i.e. always be a slave], his heart always full ⟨of her⟩.

Here, as in 1.4, the relationship between the two fields is inverse: in Gallus is portrayed all that the poet is not.

Poem 1.11 is addressed to Cynthia: she has left the poet and is in Baiae. He apologises for his anxieties about seducers and about being forgotten. Here the two fields are extremely close and may be expressed thus: the ostensible field concerns a careful portrait of a solicitous lover and of his girl, who may be in danger. The secondary is the relationship of a lover to a girl who has abandoned him and is not to be trusted. The index of proportionality is to be seen in lines like 17–18:

> non quia perspecta non es mihi cognita fama,
>   sed quod in hac omnis parte timetur amor.

'It is not that you are not well known to me to be of unblemished honour, but because, in a situation like this, one fears every kind of love.'

I am inclined to think, though it cannot be demonstrated certainly, that the main MSS are right in marking no division between this elegy and the next. There is a characteristic shift to speaking of Cynthia in the third person as the poet addresses an accuser (1–2):

> quid mihi desidiae non cessas fingere crimen
> quod faciat nobis conscia Roma moram?

'Why do not cease trumping up against me an accusation of idleness—that Rome keeps me hanging about and well knows why?'

The ostensible field is that of the poet confronted by this accusation. The nature of the accusation, slyly hinted at in the word *conscia*, can only be inferred from the poet's answer: it is that he is dissolutely idling about the capital, indulging erotic pleasures, instead of doing his duty abroad with the army. The poet explains that Cynthia is as far from his bed as one end of the world from the other. All has changed: he was happy and envied, but that great love has disappeared in a moment (12). Now he is alone. A man can be happy weeping in his girl's presence, or, when rejected, becoming another's slave (15–18). Neither course is open to him: (20) *Cynthia prima fuit, Cynthia finis erit*. The unspoken field here is that of the poet and his view of the world he lives in; and the index of proportionality is supplied by the surprising (implied) assumption he makes that his explanation about Cynthia's being absent fully answers the accusation made against him. Even his poetry fails—this is the implication of (14) *cogor et ipse meis auribus esse gravis* ('and I am compelled to be a burden to my own ears') taken with (6) *nec nostra dulcis in aure sonat* ('and her sweet voice sounds no longer in my ear'). The values of the poet's life are derived from, and depend on, the close interrelationship of love and poetry. The two elegies, taken together, show poetry failing in action (in 1.11) and the way in which this affects the poet's view of life. Taken together, the two elegies are a precise contrast to poem 1.8: there the appeal of the poet succeeded and he rejoiced; here it has failed and his life has collapsed.

In poem 1.13 the ostensible field is that of Gallus at last totally enslaved by a girl. As in the previous poem to Gallus (1.10), this field stands in inverse relationship to the unspoken field of the poet and Cynthia. The index of proportionality is provided by the contrast between Gallus, who rejoices at the poet's misfortune (the same misfortune as in 1.12), and the poet, who wishes Gallus well (4 and 33–36). The reconstruction of the unspoken field is all too easy.

The ostensible field of poem 1.14 is that of Tullus luxuriantly enjoying his wealth, while the unspoken field is again that of the poet and Cynthia. The index of proportionality here is provided by the last couplet (23–24):

> quae mihi dum placata aderit, non ulla verebor
> regna vel Alcinoi munera despicere.

'As long as she will be pleased to aid me, I shall not hesitate to despise the kingdom and treasure of Alcinous.'

The poet has asserted (7–14) that love is wealth beyond avarice; and there wealth functioned as a metaphor. Here love appears in the form of the capricious goddess whose favour needs imploring in a prayer (*placata* and *aderit*); if she accedes, literal wealth is to be despised —with the implication that, if she does not, literal wealth like Tullus' is useless. The sad meaning of this for the poet's life—that is, the unspoken field—just momentarily appears at the margin of the poet's vision.

In poem 1.15 the two fields are the poet's expressed view of his relationship with Cynthia on the one hand and the reality of that relationship on the other.[4] The only index of proportionality between those two fields is provided by the unspoken events in the dramatic monologue: there is a pause after line 24 while Cynthia protests her innocence, and again after line 38 while she pales and weeps. The poet finally collapses, and the unspoken field is left a mystery. What was the reality? Was the poet wrong in his accusations? All we know is that once again he surrendered; but the function of this technique is to confront the reader with this unspoken field and increase the depth of the poem.

In all of these poems the analysis used above has demonstrated the poet speaking of one field of ideas in such a way as to suggest

---

4. For interpretation of this poem, see pp. 64 ff. above.

another, closely related, field which the poem is thereby made to include within its frame of reference. In each case it has been fairly easy to define the unspoken field, though it is a characteristic of the technique that the reader can only apprehend that field more or less dimly; he cannot know its details. But in some types of poetry where this technique seems to be used it is by no means easy even to define in outline the unspoken field. There is just the sense of another field to increase the depth and resonance of the poem. That is the case with a number of odes of Horace. One relevant ode (1.18) has already been analysed from a different point of view (pp. 118 ff.), but ought to be recalled and set among the odes that are now to be examined as examples of this technique.

Odes 1.9 has long given trouble to commentators:

> Vides ut alta stet nive candidum
> Soracte, nec iam sustineant onus
>   silvae laborantes, geluque
>   flumina constiterint acuto;
>
> dissolve frigus ligna super foco   5
> large reponens atque benignius
>   deprome quadrimum Sabina,
>   o Thaliarche, merum diota.
>
> permitte divis cetera, qui simul
> stravere ventos aequore fervido   10
>   deproeliantis, nec cupressi
>   nec veteres agitantur orni.
>
> quid sit futurum cras fuge quaerere et
> quem Fors dierum cumque dabit lucro
>   appone, nec dulcis amores   15
>   sperne puer neque tu choreas,
>
> donec virenti canities abest
> morosa. nunc et campus et areae
>   lenesque sub noctem susurri
>   composita repetantur hora,   20
>
> nunc et latentis proditor intimo
> gratus puellae risus ab angulo
>   pignusque dereptum lacertis
>   aut digito male pertinaci.

'Do you see how Soracte rears white with deep snow and the toiling woods can no longer sustain their burden and the rivers have come to a halt with the sharp frost (4)? Dissipate the cold by heaping logs on the hearth, and be more generous in drawing off the four-year-old wine, o Thaliarchus, from its Sabine jar (8). Leave all else to the gods; for, once they have stilled storm-winds battling over the boiling ocean, the cypresses are no longer shaken nor the aged ash trees (12). Forbear to ask what is going to happen to-morrow, and credit to your account each day that Fortune shall give you, and do not spurn the pleasures of love and dancing while you are young (16), as long as surly grey keeps off your fine hair. Now is the time for an interest in the Campus Martius and the piazze and gentle whisperings just before nightfall at the agreed hour (20), and in a girl's delightful laughter that gives her away as she hides in a secret corner, and in the pledge snatched from her arm or from her scarcely resisting finger.'

This poem has been severely handled. One critic has said:[5] 'But we have to admit that as a whole the poem falls short of the perfection reached by Horace in many of his odes. Its heterogeneous elements have not merged into a harmonious unit. Line 18 *nunc et campus et areae* and what follows suggest a season wholly different from the severe winter at the beginning.' The most recent commentators say:

'Horace is not describing a particular scene; rather he has composed a picturesque Christmas-card, based on Alcaeus, and containing among more conventional elements a single feature of familiar topography. The second stanza is likewise based on literature rather than observation.... The third stanza also provides surprises for the over-literal reader. Horace implies, even if he does not state, that a storm is raging; this is inconsistent with the clear, cold day at the beginning of the poem. In the first stanza the trees bend under their load of snow; in the third they are shaken in the high wind. The contradiction may be derived from Horace's sources.... Horace's advice to Thaliarchus also contains some confusion. First of all he seems to imply "The storm will soon blow over, and with it our troubles". However, in the last three stanzas he advises: "Enjoy yourself while you can; you will not always be able to". He has included two themes of Greek poetic moralizing which on close inspection seem inconsistent...."[6]

5. Fraenkel (1957), p. 177.
6. Nisbet and Hubbard (1970), p. 117.

Yet they end by saying: 'This is a great poem.' And this seems to be the instinctive reaction of critics; they only become dismayed by the results of their analysis and then feel obliged to modify their appreciation.[7]

This is a dramatic monologue of a type familiar in Horace. The first stanza sets a scene perfectly adapted for drinking in front of a fire. The second stanza arranges for the fire and the wine. There is a pause at this point while Thaliarchus carries out the poet's orders. When he has completed his tasks, he is told: 'Leave all else to the gods'. It is important that the scene be visualised, so that the final four stanzas are placed in their proper setting. They are not an accompaniment to the poet's orders, nor does the drinking begin after the poem has ended. The drinking begins as the poet says, 'Leave all else to the gods'; and all that he says thereafter is said as they enjoy the pleasures of fire and wine together. The philosophical reflections and advice arise from and blend with the setting: these pleasures belong to this occasion, other pleasures to another. The ostensible field of the poem is the relationship of the poet to this highly particular setting. The setting may be even more particular than it seems, though I do not insist on the point since it cannot be demonstrated with certainty and may offend lovers of the poem.

For critics have been puzzled by the social implications: if Thaliarchus is the host, why does the poet order him about?[8] But if Horace is the host, then the orders can be considered to be given to the younger man. The latter seems right. But who is Thaliarchus? He is addressed with the emotional *o*, and this should not just be dismissed as a Grecism that goes with his Greek name.[9] It sounds as if Thaliarchus might be a beloved of the poet's who has reached that time in life when, by a convention recognised at least in ancient literature, a youth shifts his interest from men to girls.[10] If so, the advice he is given is highly specific to his circumstances, and the occasion then becomes emotionally charged and momentous for the poet.

The poem is dominated by weather. A still winter's day opens it, everything frozen and dead. The power of the gods is illustrated by

7. The analysis in West (1967), pp. 1–12 is, however, a conspicuous exception.
8. Ibid., pp. 6–7.
9. See Nisbet and Hubbard (1970), ad loc.
10. See Williams (1968), p. 557, and *Odes* 1.4 (Lycidas).

the image of a storm. The latest commentators say of this: 'It may be asked why in our passage Horace should choose this relatively unimportant manifestation of divine omnipotence. The explanation surely lies in the óde's literary ancestry; it seems to have been a conventional feature in sympotic poems to say "a storm is raging outside, but the gods will still it, and with it our present troubles".... In our poem Horace keeps the traditional reference to storms, though strictly speaking it does not suit the weather of the first stanza'.[11] This must be wrong. There are no 'present troubles' in the meteorological sense, and it was only their importation that caused inconsistency to be found. The completion of Thaliarchus' tasks allows the reference to the gods: as men they have done all they can and need; everything else is up to the gods. The illustration of their power by the storm-image is not only metonymically related to the first stanza and so contrasted with it, but it also suggests metaphorically and symbolically the gods' power over the emotional storms of human life. It has another function: it unexpectedly climaxes in *cupressi* and *veteres ... orni* and therefore in metonymic associations with death and old age. This is taken up at the end of the next clause; for the single word *virenti* is metaphorical of spring and consequently draws *canities*, a metonymy for old age, into a metaphorical suggestion of winter, echoing the first stanza. Finally, *sub noctem*, with its implications, suggests the heat of summer. From the dead cold of winter, through raging storms, through spring contrasted with winter, the poem reaches the heat of summer.

Throughout, the poet's thoughts concentrate on his friend, but the unspoken field of the poem makes itself felt as the relationship of the poet to life in general. The index of proportionality—the means, that is, by which the mind can transfer from the one field to the other and is indeed invited to make that transfer—consists in the opening generalisation of the poet's talk (9) *permitte divis cetera*, together with the contrast between (17–18) *virenti* and *canities morosa* (for no doubt is possible that the poet counts the latter state as his own). Perhaps, too, the metonymic contrast between winter's dead coldness and the storms also suggests the cooling of a once passionate affair. At any rate, the poem's horizons open out to include a portrait of the poet himself and of a life of which Thaliarchus and his past and future are only a part. Paradoxically, the greater the poet's success in making

11. Nisbet and Hubbard (1970), p. 121.

the ostensible field particular to a vividly specific occasion, the wider and more excitingly general is the sweep of the unspoken field and the stronger the pressure exerted by that field on the reader to make the transfer and reconstruct its outlines in imagination. To put it crudely, the technique provided Horace with the means to process certain moralising observations about life so that they transcend that didactic condition to make a poem in which far more is suggested than the words immediately convey.

It is an inadequate account of this poem to say that it starts in a particular situation and then moves out into general reflections. If the interpretation of the poem given above is correct, that transition never takes place in the primary field; in fact, the primary field is one of extreme specificity in every detail, and it is that uniqueness of the occasion that must first engage the reader's attention. On this level, all the poet's reflections are specific to this particular setting and its participants. It is only after the poem has been understood on this level that certain key phrases and contrasts invite the reader to sense the much more general field of human life and relations in which a morally coherent series of attitudes to mortality and old age is suggested, and, with that, something of the personality of the speaker. It may seem artificial to distinguish the two fields so sharply in this poem, and this method of analysis will certainly lose its usefulness if pushed too far. But it will serve well as a way of escaping from the old view (often repeated) that sees Horace as making poetry out of hackneyed moralising commonplaces which he disguised by a perfunctory and unconvincing pretence at a dramatic setting (itself often lifted directly from a predecessor like Alcaeus). The truth is quite otherwise. The problems of the moral life were one of the abiding sources of poetic inspiration for Horace, and the technique of the highly specific dramatic monologue was devised by him as a means of suggesting (not expressing) moral attitudes of a high generality. But each poem is to be appreciated and enjoyed in both aspects—or fields, as I have called them—and it is the function of the analysis offered above to account for the sense of depth which is the most important feature of the technique as Horace used it. The poet was himself aware of the wider field of his moral reflections and included that awareness as an element in his composition; the indexes of proportionality are a means of pointing to its existence and of suggesting a faint outline of some of its features.

The way in which a personal moral view of life is objectified by

the technique of dramatic monologue can be seen also in *Odes* 1.11 on
a very small scale:

> Tu ne quaesieris, scire nefas, quem mihi, quem tibi
> finem di dederint, Leuconoe, nec Babylonios
> temptaris numeros. ut melius, quicquid erit pati,
> seu pluris hiemes seu tribuit Iuppiter ultimam
>
> quae nunc oppositis debilitat pumicibus mare
> Tyrrhenum: sapias, vina liques, et spatio brevi
> spem longam reseces. dum loquimur, fugerit invida
> aetas: carpe diem, quam minimum credula postero.

'Please do not enquire—the knowledge is forbidden—what end the gods
have appointed for me or for you, Leuconoe, and do not make use of Baby-
lonian horoscopes. How much better to endure whatever will come, whether
Juppiter has assigned us more winters or whether this is the last which is at
this moment weakening the Etruscan sea against the rocks that block its path.
Be sensible, strain the wine, and prune back your far-reaching hopes within
short limits. As we are speaking, grudging time will have flown by. Harvest
the day, placing the least possible trust in the morrow.'

The specific situation is created here by the girl's odd name and
her trust in astrology. The poet's order to the girl to strain the wine
functions in a similar way to the same motif in *Odes* 1.9: they are
drinking together. The poet's words address the immediate situation,
which is, of course, erotic, as is the delicately implied invitation in
the final two lines. But the synecdoche which figures winter specifically
by one of its characteristic features and the metaphors from viticulture
in the last three lines[12] provide an index of proportionality to open
up a general vision of life and man's proper attitude to it, of which
the actual words of the poem only touch on one small part.

The same technique can be seen also in *Odes* 1.20, which is not to
be interpreted as an invitation. There the poet is entertaining Maecenas,
and as he pours the wine, he explains its particular interest, going on
to draw the important contrast with the wines to which Maecenas
is accustomed. Here the index that makes a bridge to a general view
of life is provided by the picture of Maecenas' reception in the theatre

---

12. See West (1967), pp. 58–64.

and the luxury of his way of life. The unspoken field is that of the poet's own attitude towards life and ambition. Very much the same unspoken field surrounds *Odes* 3.8, where again Maecenas is entertained, and where, too, the whole poem consists of the poet's conversation as they drink.[13] There the bridge to the unspoken field is provided by the poet's very personal reason for celebrating the Matronalia.

In all of these poems the tone is more or less serious. But the technique can also be used light-heartedly, as in *Odes* 1.36:

> Et ture et fidibus iuvat
> placare et vituli sanguine debito
>   custodes Numidae deos,
> qui nunc Hesperia sospes ab ultima
>
>   caris multa sodalibus,   5
> nulli plura tamen dividit oscula
>   quam dulci Lamiae, memor
> actae non alio rege puertiae
>
>   mutataeque simul togae.
> Cressa ne careat pulchra dies nota,   10
>   neu promptae modus amphorae,
> neu morem in Salium sit requies pedum,
>
>   neu multi Damalis meri
> Bassum Threicia vincat amystide,
>   neu desint epulis rosae   15
> neu vivax apium neu breve lilium.
>
>   omnes in Damalin putris
> deponent oculos, nec Damalis novo
>   divelletur adultero
> lascivis hederis ambitiosior.   20

'With both incense and strings and with the due blood of a calf it is our pleasure to placate the gods who guard Numida. He now, safely back from farthest Spain (4), shares out many kisses to his beloved friends, to none more than to charming Lamia, remembering a boyhood spent under his leadership (8) and the toga assumed on the same day. Let this happy day not lack a Cretan mark, and let there be no holding back from the wine-amphora that has been broached, nor resting of feet ⟨as they dance⟩ in the Salian way

---

13. See Williams (1968), pp. 103–07, and (1969), pp. 70–74.

(12), and let deep-drinking Damalis not outdo Bassus in the Thracian sconce, and let roses not be absent from our festivities nor unwithering celery nor the short-lived lily (16). Everyone shall hang languishing eyes on Damalis, and Damalis, more entwining than lascivious ivy, shall not be plucked away from her new lover.'

Here the third and fourth stanzas show the host giving his instructions for the gay party which has just begun. It is in honour of Numida and is immediately preceded by a sacrifice in thanks for his safe return. The poet executes the sacrifice by simply announcing it. Numida has just arrived and is still kissing his friends—hence the present tense (6) *dividit*. Various difficulties disappear if the extreme specificity of the dramatic monologue is fully appreciated, and the way the action progresses throughout the poem. For instance, the latest editors comment on lines 13–14:

'It is not clear why Horace should say "Let heavy drinking Damalis fail to defeat Bassus". Even if Bassus is also a heavy drinker (see below), one would naturally expect the man to defeat the woman. *neu vincat* would, it is true, be consistent with a prolonged and evenly balanced contest. . . . Even so, the transmitted reading seems to divert our attention a little too much from the spectacular Damalis to the unimportant Bassus. . . . One might suggest reading *Damalin* and *Bassus*; yet this spoils the elegant variation *Damalis . . . Damalin . . . Damalis*. The text would make sense if one emended *neu* (12) to *et* (accepting Janus's transposition); yet one is reluctant to give up a single *neu*.'[14]

If the immediacy of the situation is realised, there is no difficulty in seeing that the poet's way of speaking has the effect of issuing a teasing, light-hearted challenge to Bassus, who is present.

But it has another point also. The reference at the end of the quotation above to 'Janus's transposition' refers to doubts about lines 13–16: 'The sequence of these lines causes some doubt. Janus, and independently Peerlkamp, proposed that 13–14 should be placed after 15–16. On this hypothesis the two references to Damalis are brought together, and (what matters more) the unimportant flowers are given less emphasis. There is something to be said for this proposal; though in an ode which shows signs of imperfection one cannot be certain'.

14. Nisbet and Hubbard (1970), pp. 404–05.

This cannot be right. There is a nice economy of names in the poem, while the presence of a large number of people is suggested. The mention of Damalis in the drinking context is an example of that type of thematic anticipation which lets a theme just appear that will turn up later in a more important setting. So here the name of Damalis teases the mind for a moment till she appears again to figure in the final, erotic stage of the party; she is the girl of Numida in whose honour the party is being held. Nor are the flowers unimportant: they not only symbolise lavishness, but also suggest a resonance with human life in general, especially in their epithets. And their placement at just this point has significance: they separate, by their static display, the early stages of the party with the drinking and playful contests, from the final stage to which the poet-host looks forward in future tenses—the stage of love-making.

In fact, the very detailed specificity of the poem to one particular occasion succeeds in creating a suggestive impression of the field of life and society at large, of which this is an instantaneous miniature. The bridge to that wider field is provided by the concrete detail about Lamia and the friendship between him and his exact contemporary and companion, Numida. And, as in many of Horace's odes, the very tension between things Greek and things Roman, brought together in the same poem, itself functions as a support for the index of proportionality. The Greek details surround a Roman core consisting of Lamia, Numida's return from Spain, and the sacrifice owed for his safety. This may not be a great poem, but it does bring alive the sense of belonging to a particular age and society; and it even suggests something of the values and attitudes of that society in the indirect and imaginative way that is characteristic of this technique. The same type of analysis should be applied to *Odes* 1.18, already examined above.

Similarly light-hearted are the odes 3.19 and 3.28.[15] In both, Roman details provide the index of proportionality: in 3.19 it is the toast proposed to Murena, who has just been co-opted to the college of augurs (10–11), and in 3.28 it is the occasion of the Roman festival of the Neptunalia. The analysis of the poems offered above shows that the incorporation of Roman details in essentially Greek settings is not random or whimsical: the details function as a bridge from

15. For details, see Williams (1968), pp. 115–18, 120–21, and (1969), pp. 108–12, 141–43.

the ostensible field of the poem which is constructed from traditional and conventional elements to a larger field which lies quite outside the poem as it appears on the page.

There is another type of Horatian ode to which this analysis can be usefully applied. The relationship between poem 34 of Catullus and *Odes* 1.21 is well known. But Catullus' poem is a genuine prayer addressed to Diana; in fact, it is so puzzling when compared with the rest of his work that one is tempted to consider a real occasion for its composition. In view of the request for help for the Roman state with which it ends, it might have been composed, on official request, for ceremonies connected with a disaster—for instance, the loss of Crassus and the legions at Carrhae in 53 B.C.[16] But however that may be, Horace's poem is at a remove. In the first three stanzas he addresses a choir of boys and girls, directing them to sing of Diana and Apollo; in the last stanza he explains to them that Apollo, moved by their prayer, will save the people of Rome and their *princeps* Caesar from war, famine, and disease and will transfer those plagues to the Parthians and Britons. Here the ostensible field is that of the poet directing a prayer to Diana and Apollo, but the unspoken field is that of the relationship of poetry to society: that is, the social and political function of poetry. (This is a field that interested Horace, and he treated the theme discursively in the letter to Augustus, *Epistles* 2.1.118–38.) Here the index of proportionality between the two fields is provided by the address to the choir and the Roman details in the last stanza. Not only can the unspoken field of this poem be grasped more clearly than usual with the help of *Epistles* 2.1, but the effect of the technique can be gauged with some precision from the rather bewildering impression that the poem of Catullus makes on a reader (as distinct from the impression it might make when performed by a choir).

Horace went so far as to use this technique in the hymn which he wrote for actual performance by a choir. The *carmen saeculare* ends, not with requests to Apollo and Diana, but with statements in the indicative that the gods are in fact performing as the choir prayed they would (61–72). The final stanza is this (73–76):

16. In that case, it would have its analogue in the ceremonies prescribed by the *decemviri sacris faciundis* in 217 B.C. (Livy 22.1.18), in 207 B.C. (Livy 27.37.7), and in 200 B.C. (Livy 31.12.5–6). In 207 B.C. the poet was Livius Andronicus and in 200 B.C., P. Licinius Tegula.

> haec Iovem sentire deosque cunctos
> spem bonam certamque domum reporto,
> doctus et Phoebi chorus et Dianae
> dicere laudes.

'That Juppiter is of this mind and all the gods, I bring home with me the good and certain hope, a choir trained to sing the praises both of Phoebus and of Diana.'

Here the self-conscious statement by the choir relates two fields: the one (that of the *carmen saeculare*) is that of the relationship between a prayer and the gods; the other, unspoken, field is that of the relationship between poetry and society. In this way the poem functions as a political manifesto of the Augustan regime in the year 17 B.C. The technique emphasises the tension between the form of the poem (a prayer implying that the gods are responsible for social and economic progress) and the reality within which it functions (the recognition that everything depends on Augustus). The index of proportionality between the two fields is provided by the choir's statement in their own name as Roman citizens.

The inspiration of the *carmen saeculare* formed the subject of two further odes. One of them, *Odes* 4.3, is a hymn of thanks to the Muse. The other, *Odes* 4.6, is an elaborate Pindaric request to Apollo for inspiration (1–28).[17] In the rest of the poem the poet acknowledges the receipt of inspiration (29–30) and then instructs the choir in their hymn (31–40): his instructions are almost totally hymnic (with just a passing reference to crops), except for a command to keep time to the correct musical beat as he gives it. Then comes a surprise ending (41–44):

> nupta iam dices 'ego dis amicum,
> saeculo festas referente luces,
> reddidi carmen, docilis modorum
> vatis Horati'.

'Soon, when you are a married woman, you will say: "I, when the century brought round the sacred day, sang a song acceptable to the gods, well trained in the rhythms of the poet Horace."'

17. See Williams (1968), pp. 61–65.

By a surprising synecdoche, he addresses the choir of boys and girls in the person of one girl, and looks forward to her marriage. It is no accident that the marriage-legislation of Augustus, passed only the previous year, is one of the most important themes of the *carmen saeculare*. But here the theme is introduced charmingly and lightly. The effect of the stanza, however, is once again to create a bridge from the ostensible field of the poem (the composing of a hymn) to the unspoken field of the social function of poetry, so that the act of the poet is effectively set in a wider social and political context.

In his use of the technique to handle the hymnic form, Horace detaches himself (and, in the *carmen saeculare*, the choir) from a specificially religious commitment: the poet is talking about one thing in a particular way, but he is also meaning something else which the reader can only sense by taking the bridge, as it were, from one field to the other so that both are apprehended at once. This deliberate detachment of himself from the act of composition is also effected in *Odes* 4.6 by the appeal for inspiration and the announcement of its receipt: this is the bridge between two worlds—the real world and the world of the poem—which are related by the medium of inspiration. The use of this technique is particularly important in *Odes* 3.4.1–8, because there it functions as the index of proportionality between the myth of the battle of the Giants (42–80) and the political reality that lies behind it but is not mentioned.[18] The technique is also used in two thematically similar poems about poetic inspiration: the simpler is *Odes* 2.19 where the vision of Bacchus (1–8) gives the poet the right to compose poetry about him. In *Odes* 3.25, also addressed to Bacchus, the poet feels himself receiving the inspiration to political poetry.[19] In both poems the immediate field is that of the poet confronted by a divine presence, and the unspoken field is that of the poet confronted by the need to compose a poem on a particular topic. In *Odes* 2.19 the index of proportionality is provided by the detached appeal to posterity (2) *credite posteri*;[20] in 3.25 it is the surprisingly specific mention of 'great Caesar' (3–6).

The technique in all of these poems, while generally classifiable as coming within the scope of what Quintilian calls *figura* or *schema*,

18. See Williams (1968), pp. 268–70 and (1969), pp. 44–54.
19. See Williams (1968), pp. 67–70 and (1969), pp. 128–31.
20. Williams (1968), pp. 68–69.

is also related to the technique which he calls *fictiones personarum* (in translation of the Greek προσωποποιίαι). He says of this figure (9.2.29 ff.):

'They both vary and lend animation to oratory in an admirable way. By means of them we display the thoughts of our opponents as if talking to themselves[21] (they will, however, only escape disbelief if we shall represent them as saying things that it would not be absurd for them to have thought); and we credibly introduce our own conversations with others or of others among themselves and we create *personae* that are suited to advise, blame, complain, praise, or pity.... Indeed there are those who reserve the term προσωποποιίαι for cases in which we invent both persons and words, and who perfer to call imaginary conversations between men διαλόγοι, which some Latin writers term *sermocinatio*. But I, following the normal practice, have called both by the same name. For it is certainly true that words cannot be invented without our also inventing them for a particular *persona*'.

The complexity of dramatic monologue in Propertius and Horace arises from the fact that both poets combine this technique of *sermocinatio* with that of *figura* or *schema*. In all cases the relationship between the ostensible field of the poem and the unspoken field is metonymic and synecdochic.

2. *Substitution of a Related Field*

Analysis of this technique can well begin with poem 50 of Catullus:

> Hesterno, Licini, die otiosi
> multum lusimus in meis tabellis,
> ut convenerat esse delicatos:
> scribens versiculos uterque nostrum
> ludebat numero modo hoc modo illoc,   5
> reddens mutua per iocum atque vinum.
> atque illinc abii tuo lepore
> incensus, Licini, facetiisque
> ut nec me miserum cibus iuvaret
> nec somnus tegeret quiete ocellos,   10
> sed toto indomitus furore lecto

21. Cf. Quintilian 7.2.6 and Lausberg (1960), sec. 154.

versarer, cupiens videre lucem
ut tecum loquerer simulque ut essem.
at defessa labore membra postquam
semimortua lectulo iacebant,   15
hoc, iucunde, tibi poema feci
ex quo perspiceres meum dolorem.
nunc audax cave sis, precesque nostras,
oramus, cave despuas, ocelle,
ne poenas Nemesis reposcat a te—   20
est vehemens dea: laedere hanc caveto.

'Yesterday, Licinius, having nothing to do, we amused ourselves a lot on my writing-tablets after we had agreed to be wanton: each of us, composing verses, played now in this metre, now in that (5), mutually rewarding each other in our playfulness and drinking. And from there I came away on fire with your charm, Licinius, and wit, so that in my longing neither food interested me nor did sleep close my eyes in peace (10), but, uncontrollable in my passion, I tossed and turned over the whole bed, longing to see the dawn so that I could talk with you and be together with you. But after my limbs, tired out with their suffering, lay half-dead on the bed (15), this poem, dear one, I composed for you so that, with its help, you could understand my passion. Now please do not be haughty, and, I beg you, do not spurn my prayers, darling, lest Nemesis demand retribution from you (20)—she is a powerful goddess: take care not to injure her.'

Here the language of love—in this case homosexual love—is clear throughout.[22] For (2) *ludere* is frequently used of love-play; (3) *delicatos* covers 'the whole range of uninhibited behaviour from wilfulness . . . to irresponsible pleasure-seeking, frivolity, dissipation and sensuality';[23] (6) *reddens mutua*, (8) *incensus*, loss of appetite and of sleep, (11) *indomitus furore*, tossing on the bed, the desire to be with the beloved, limbs exhausted by *labor*, (17) *dolorem*, (18) *preces*, (19) *ocelle*, and the threat of vengeance for repulse—all of these belong to the language of physical passion. The poem has sometimes been taken literally in the sense that Catullus is actually expressing a physical passion for Calvus; or, on the contrary, it has been taken as evidence of the overheated language of affection in this precious circle of poets. Certainly lines 6–20 can be understood as a declaration of physical passion, and that

22. See Macleod (1973), p. 294.
23. Fordyce (1961), p. 216.

is their obvious interpretation. But the poem is not a real letter to
Calvus; it is intended for the world as well, as the opening lines show
by creating a setting that Calvus would not have needed to be reminded
of. In its language the main field of the poem seems to be that of
homosexual passion, but the opening lines, which prepare for that
field, also contain an index of proportionality to another field—that
of the composition of poetry.

To oversimplify, the poem is about the excitement of extempore
poetic composition in inspiring competition with an extremely talented
and poetically experienced friend. Nothing is said about the nature
of that inspiration nor of the poetic ideals that the two shared; only
a hint is given of the subject-matter in (3) *delicatos*, (4) *versiculos*, and
(5) *ludebat*: it was erotic poetry. The reader is left to reconstruct the
field of poetic composition by sensing its proportionality with the
field of physical passion. That is not simple, since the proportionality
is between the feeling of physical passion of a man for a man, on the
one hand, with its heat and frustration and longing, and, on the other,
a poetic inspiration that involves the presence and poetic activity of
another poet, together with technical aspects such as metrical experimentation. This actual poem itself exemplifies what it is talking about,
and it carries within it the generation of its own inspiration. It is in
itself an enactment of the working of poetic inspiration. In this way
it is similar to *Odes* 2.19 and 3.25 of Horace, though its form is quite
different. Its self-mocking humour adds another dimension to confusion,
but the poem wonderfully succeeds in suggesting the attitudes to life
and to literature in this talented coterie.

The index of proportionality here—the reference to poetic composition—is specific to this poem, but the poem, in fact, appeals to
an unmentioned and much wider index of proportionality that was
inherent in a Roman attitude to one of their fundamental social
institutions. This was the way in which Romans of the last century of
the Republic used words like *amare*, *amor*, *amans* of their feelings for
their *amici*. This meant that homosexual love provided a ready framework for treating a personal relationship with an *amicus*. The availability
of this framework, essentially inspired by and derived from Greek
homosexual poetry, can be seen in the younger Pliny's reference to
an epigram (a Greek literary genre) of Cicero addressed to his freedman
and secretary, Tiro. Pliny is, as often, self-consciously defending his
own practice of writing naughty or erotic verses. He describes how he

had read to him Asinius Gallus' polemical comparison of his own father (Asinius Pollio) with Cicero, in the course of which an epigram of Cicero's to Tiro was quoted. Pliny then took a siesta, but, unable to sleep, felt inspired to compose in hexameters (*Epist*.7.4.5–7):

intendi animum contraque opinionem meam post longam desuetudinem perquam exiguo temporis momento id ipsum, quod me ad scribendum sollicitaverat, his versibus exaravi:

> Cum libros Galli legerem, quibus ille parenti
> ausus de Cicerone dare est palmamque decusque,
> lascivum inveni lusum Ciceronis et illo
> spectandum ingenio, quo seria condidit et quo
> humanis salibus multo varioque lepore
> magnorum ostendit mentes gaudere virorum.
> nam queritur quod fraude mala frustratus amantem
> paucula cenato sibi debita savia Tiro
> tempore nocturno subtraxerit. his ego lectis
> 'cur post haec' inquam 'nostros celamus amores
> nullumque in medium timidi damus atque fatemur
> Tironisque dolos, Tironis nosse fugaces
> blanditias et furta novas addentia flammas?'

transii ad elegos; hos quoque non minus celeriter explicui, addidi alios facilitate corruptus.

'I set my mind to it and, unexpectedly after being long out of practice, in a mere moment of time I sketched out in verses the very thought that had provoked me to write:

"As I was reading the books of Gallus in which he dared to take the palm and glory from Cicero and award them to his father, I discovered the wanton *jeu d'esprit* of Cicero that is noteworthy for that same genius with which he composed serious works and also demonstrated that the minds of great men delight in polished jokes and wide-ranging humour. For he complains that, with malice prepense, Tiro had deceived his lover [i.e. Cicero] and cheated him at night of a few kisses that had been promised him after dinner. After reading this, I said to myself: Why conceal my loves [or, my love-poems] and timidly avoid publishing them? Why not admit that I too know the tricks of a Tiro, and a Tiro's flirtatious charms and the deceits that add fuel to the fires?"

I went on to elegiacs: these too I composed with no less speed; I composed more, lured on by my own facility.'

Clearly Cicero in the epigram treated Tiro as his beloved. There is a whole series of poems by Catullus,[24] extending the theme through his collected work, that deal with what seems an erotic triangle composed of the poet, the young man Juventius, and the pair Furius and Aurelius (poems 15, 16, 21, 23, 24, 28, 47, 48, 81, and 99). Catullus was proud to publish what Cicero probably kept private, and these poems, with their scurrilous and scatological wit, should be regarded as an example of the way in which the framework of homosexual love could be used to process, as it were, personal relationships (whether truly homosexual or not) for humorous poetic treatment. In all of this, the index of proportionality goes unexpressed because it was inherent in Roman social language and attitudes; and it is that fact that has laid this poetry open to widespread misinterpretation in modern times. But this is the poetry of a coterie, dependent on the intimate acquaintance of individuals and primarily addressed to them rather than to the world at large.

Catullus, however, also invented a more serious and more influential framework. He uses it when he treats the relationship between himself and Lesbia as if it were one between a man and his wife.[25] But that is to oversimplify. The essence is expressed in poem 109:

> Iucundum, mea vita, mihi proponis amorem
>   hunc nostrum inter nos perpetuumque fore.
> di magni, facite ut vere promittere possit,
>   atque id sincere dicat et ex animo,
> ut liceat nobis tota perducere vita
>   aeternum hoc sanctae foedus amicitiae.

'You promise me, darling, that this love of ours will be a joy to us and will last between us for ever. Great gods above, cause her to make that promise truly and speak sincerely and from her heart, so that our whole life through we may be able to prolong this eternal bond of sacred friendship.'

The word *foedus* belongs to marriage, and also the concept of the eternal bond. But there is another element both here and in other uses by Catullus of this framework. The index of proportionality goes unmentioned, but essentially it inheres in the pun on the word *amica*

---

24. See especially the treatment by Macleod (1973), pp. 294–303.
25. See Williams (1958), pp. 23–25.

'girlfriend'[26] which links the relationship also to the social institution
of *amicitia*.[27] In fact, the framework is constructed out of a conflation
of the institutions of marriage and *amicitia*. This corresponds to the
division of love into the two constituent elements (in poem 68 and
in other poems) of *pietas* and physical passion (see pp. 57–61). It allows
the poet to represent himself as both the *amicus* and the husband of
Lesbia, and to demand from her, and measure her conduct against,
all the obligations that are owed both by a wife and by an *amicus*.
By this means he can also bring the powerful Roman concept of *fides*
to bear on their relationship, especially in poem 76 where it is combined
with the idea of *foedus*. From this framework stems the striking contrast
(poem 85) *odi et amo* by way of the idea that Lesbia's conduct constitutes
an *iniuria* which excludes *bene velle* on the poet's part, while increasing
amare (72.7–8; 75.3–4). This framework has enabled Catullus to process
his relationship with Lesbia for a number of different poetic treatments.

Propertius used this framework to compose only one poem (3.20);
but it is a very important poem since it probably treats the first night
that the poet spent with Cynthia, and he represents this as preceded
by a sort of elaborate marriage-ceremony.[28] The framework was
widely available to him and he makes use of it, almost exclusively as
a framework of marriage, in many references which make appeal to
it merely by a choice of key words such as *uxor*, or *solus*, or *unus*, or
by viewing the *foedus* between them as eternal.[29] It is by means of this
type of casual appeal to the framework that *Odes* 1.13 of Horace, too,
suddenly shifts into an unexpected seriousness and depth of tone in
the final stanza.[30]

Horace uses the technique of substituting one field for another
with particular success in his *Epistles*. For instance, in *Epistles* 1.7,
addressed to Maecenas, the poet's relationship to Maecenas is translated
into terms of the relationship of a dependant with a great man as that
relationship was envisaged by Hellenistic Greek philosophers and used

---

26. Quintilian's comment is worth quoting (9.2.99): 'The most trivial form ⟨of
figure⟩ is that derived from one word, although Cicero uses it against Clodia: "Especially since everyone thought her everyone's girl-friend [*amicam*] rather than anyone's
enemy [*inimicam*]".'

27. See Reitzenstein (1912).

28. For details, see Williams (1968), pp. 413–17.

29. On these marriage-ideals, see Williams (1958), pp. 22–25.

30. See Williams (1968), pp. 563–65.

by them for discussions of ethical problems.[31] That Greek field is specified in these words (37–38):

> saepe verecundum laudasti, rexque paterque
> audisti coram, nec verbo parcius absens.

'You have often praised me for being respectful, and have been called "Lord" and "Patron" to your face—and not a syllable less behind your back.'

This is the type of relationship that is portrayed throughout the poem. But a fine index of proportionality is supplied by the surprisingly realistic portrait of the poet and his regrets (25–28):

> quod si me noles usquam discedere, reddes
> forte latus, nigros angusta fronte capillos,
> reddes dulce loqui, reddes ridere decorum et
> inter vina fugam Cinarae maerere protervae.

'But if your wish is that I shall leave you in no circumstances, you must give me back my strong lungs, my black hair growing low on to my forehead, you must give me back my capacity for winning talk and pleasant laughter and for lamenting over wine a refusal by the usually forward Cinara.'

The framework devised by the poet enabled him to treat an intimate relationship with some objectivity, so that emotions would be held at a distance and he might seriously concentrate on the vital question of how, under temptations and difficulties, a man can achieve independence from material goods and comforts.

In *Epistles* 1.19, the idea that Horace's *Odes* have been ill-received by critics is used as a framework within which the poet can address Maecenas on the topic of the originality of the *Odes*. Here the index of proportionality is provided in amusing lines which show the poet very vulnerable to a critic's accusations that his real interest is in Augustus' reception of his poetry and that, in fact, he is supremely confident that he alone has true poetic inspiration (43–45). Again the value of the technique lies in the objectivity which it provides.

As a final example, the end of *Epistle* 2.1 may be considered. There the poet addresses Augustus on the value of poetry to the Roman

---

31. For details, see Williams (1968), pp. 19–23, 566–68.

princeps. The framework for the discussion, however, is the relationship of Alexander to the poets who surrounded him and provided him with the desired type of panegyric.[32] Within this framework are set Virgil and Varius. It is true that the poet agrees that poets like Choerilus were bad, whereas Virgil and Varius are very good—and that is turned into a compliment to the good judgment of Augustus (245). But the clear implication remains that Virgil and Varius are to be recommended to Augustus as panegyrists. This, however, is simply the working of the framework and not to be taken as the poet's real estimate. The framework enabled him to objectify for public discussion what was in effect a personal relationship, and it relieved him of the necessity of making a true critical estimate of Virgil's poetry from the point of view of Augustus. A clear index of proportionality between the reality and the framework is given in these lines (245–47):

> at neque dedecorant tua de se iudicia atque
> munera quae multa dantis cum laude tulerunt
> dilecti tibi Vergilius Variusque poetae.

'But Virgil and Varius, poets loved by you, do not disgrace your judgment of them nor your gifts which they received to the great renown of the giver.'

These words give the reader the means of sensing, rather than reconstructing, the field of the real relationship of Augustus with Virgil and Varius; for that the poet has substituted the field of the relationship between Alexander and Choerilus, which is itself paradigmatic of the relationship between writers and Hellenistic kings. But just as Augustus was not to be regarded as a Hellenistic king, so Virgil and Varius were not to be seen as the sort of writers which a relationship with such a king implied. The distance between the two fields is great, and the proportionality between them is only to be sensed by a sympathetic imagination.

3. *Large-scale Association of Distantly Related Fields*

It has been seen that the effect of substituting a related field was essentially to process for poetic treatment a subject that could be analysed

---

32. See Williams (1968), pp. 71–75, 77, 160.

as a relationship between two elements, by talking not about it but about a more familiar relationship associated with the suppressed relationship by a mode usually of metaphor but sometimes of metonymy. In all cases the two fields, even if from a certain point of view distant, could yet be regarded as readily associated, and the only problem was to divine the intended proportionality between them. Now it remains to consider the association by means of this technique of fields that are distant, not only in the sense of not being normally associated, but, more important, in the sense of there being a distinct element of the arbitrary in the decision to associate them. There are three major works to be considered from this point of view: Virgil's *Eclogues* and his *Georgics*, and the *Ars Poetica* of Horace. This is not to be taken as in any way a systematic treatment of any of these works; only those parts of them or elements in them will be considered that are of interest in examining the technique of the objective framework.

A number of the *Eclogues* seem clearly to be, in some sense, about poetry, poetic composition, the relationship between poetry and society, the relationship of different modes or genres to one another, sources of inspiration, and so on. But for this purpose Virgil used various adaptations of what I have called the objective framework, sometimes derived from Theocritean *Idylls*, sometimes not. *Eclogue* 6 is a conspicuous example of a non-Theocritean framework.[33] It begins with Apollo's firm direction of the poet (who has been thinking about trying epic) back to pastoral poetry (1–12), and it ends (82–86) with Silenus taking up the themes that Apollo sang by the Eurotas. In between, there is the capture of Silenus (13–26) and the song (that is, poetry) of Silenus (31–81), which is not quoted but is described or summarized by the poet in his own words; that song is framed by two descriptions (27–30 and 85–86) of the incredible effect it had on a listening world. The very appearance, and certainly the capture, of Silenus would have created a specific expectation in the minds of readers. The legend of his capture had been used by Aristotle in a famous passage of his *Eudemus*, and by Cicero in his *Tusculans* and in his now lost *Consolatio*.[34]

The message of Silenus, captured and tortured by Midas, was deadly serious: 'the best thing for human beings is not to be born;

---

33. In what follows, the discussion in Williams (1968), pp. 243–49 is assumed.
34. On this, see especially Hubbard (1975).

the second best is to die as soon as possible'. This was interpreted philosophically in terms of a Platonic distinction between the world of the soul (the unchanging world of the Forms and of Being) and the world of the body (the world of flux and change and of Becoming). But the expectation of anything so deeply serious is immediately modified in *Eclogue* 6 by the amusing manner of Silenus' capture here, his own laughter, and his suggestively sexual promise to the nymph who takes part in his capture. The *pueri*, the instigators of his capture, had often been cheated by him of promised poetry; no torture is needed, he knows what they want and instantly promises poetry. What then remains of the expectation is that this philosopher, now turned poet, will have something important to say. So commentators have tried to extract a coherent message from the odd collection of topics that range from the formation of the world to various episodes of peculiar love and metamorphosis; each successive commentator, however, convinces only himself. But the poet has insulated the reader from Silenus' words. This was poetry that virtually brought the world to a standstill (no wonder Silenus performed so rarely and reluctantly), and the poet gives only a mere thematic summary in his own words; this at times degenerates almost to a catalogue, but throughout displays a wonderful dexterity in varying the structural forms of narrative. It is in itself a brilliant example of the way in which Hellenistic poetic technique tried to give new life by means of novel treatment to the worn themes of Greek mythology.[35]

Hence the ostensible field of the poem is that of Silenus and the themes of his poetry (we know nothing of his technique since that is explicitly Virgil's). The unspoken field is difficult to define. It is certainly not something like the question 'Was ist im Grunde die wahre Poesie?' That hypothesis is demonstrated to be false by what is clearly one index of proportionality—the opening. The relationship of this to the prologue to *Aitia*[2] of Callimachus has long been recognised—and misinterpreted. When Apollo appeared to Callimachus, he asserted the superiority of the short, refined poem as an absolute value. But, when he appears to Virgil, he asserts that a shepherd ought to fatten his sheep but keep his poetry slim (4–5): that is, Apollo asserts that, as long as Virgil is a pastoral poet, epic themes and style are unsuited to him. This clearly leaves it open to Virgil, when he ceases to be

35. See Williams (1968), pp. 239–43.

Tityrus (an activity defined by lines 1–2), to turn to epic poetry. Apollo's veto is thus based neither on Virgil's incapacity nor on an absolute judgment about what is 'true poetry'. The unspoken field must be much more restricted, such as 'the poet and the source of his material', or 'the poet and the problem of the relationship between theme and genre'. These are problems that Virgil faces, for instance, in *Eclogue* 4, where he apologises in the opening lines for thematic material that normally lies outside the range of pastoral. Also, at the very end of *Eclogue* 5, Menalcas gives away as a present the pipe that taught him *Eclogues* 2 and 3 (and, of course, 5). The poet who placed *Eclogue* 6 to follow *Eclogue* 5 seems unlikely to have failed to notice the effect of what appears to be a symbol for abandoning pastoral poetry, or, rather, one particular type of it, when that symbol is immediately followed by a pastoral poet's attempt to treat non-pastoral themes.

The other index of proportionality is provided by a feature which recurs in a number of other *Eclogues* and has an effect, equivalent to that in drama of a breaking of the dramatic illusion. At a climax in his song Silenus describes the transumption of Cornelius Gallus to the summit of Helicon, where he is presented with the pipes of Hesiod, while 'the choir of Phoebus' rises to honour him. This episode is parallel to the rather less honorific encounter of the poet with Apollo at the beginning, not only in the common element of Apollo, but also in the fact that this episode, too, has a Callimachean background in the original opening to the *Aitia* in which the poet had a Hesiodic dream of meeting the Muses on Helicon. The two episodes are also inversely related. Gallus is found (64) *errantem Permessi ad flumina* 'wandering along the streams of Permessus'. This was interpreted by Propertius (2.10.25–26):

> nondum etiam Ascraeos norunt mea carmina fontis
> sed modo Permessi flumine lavit Amor.

'For not yet do my poems know the fountains of Ascra, but Love has only bathed them in the stream of Permessus.'

Here is Hesiod in the reference to Ascra, and Propertius interprets Permessus as a lower level of poetry, that of love-elegy. There is no reason not to accept this as a correct contemporary interpretation of the passage in *Eclogue* 6 (the whole concept being, no doubt, original to Virgil), and it may well be that Gallus himself had used Permessus as the symbol for the inspiration of his love-poetry. In Virgil the Muse takes Gallus up Helicon, the choir of Phoebus rises in his honour, Linus presents him with the pipes of Hesiod (who led stiff trees down mountains by his poetry) and the instruction (72–73): 'You are to sing the origin of the Grynaean grove with these, so that there may be no grove on which Apollo prides himself more'.[36] Unlike the poet, then, whom the veto of Apollo held within his humble genre, Gallus is promoted by the inspiration of Apollo and his attendants to practise a higher kind of poetry, while Virgil must stay within the humble genre of pastoral in spite of his aspirations to epic.

How does the episode of Gallus fit into the song of Silenus? There are three principles of organisation in the song of Silenus. The first is mainly chronological.[37] The treatment moves from the formation out of four elements of the world in the void to the separation of land and sea, earth and sky; then the growth of vegetable and animal life, the creation of mankind by Pyrrha, the age of Saturn, and Prometheus' theft and punishment. Here a final chronological movement (marked by the poet's comment 43, *his adiungit*) leads to the second principle— love, with the myth of Hylas and Hercules. The myths (connected by the theme of love) of Pasiphae and of the daughters of Proetus (45–60) introduce the third principle—transformation (already seen in the stones of Pyrrha). The myth of Atalanta (61) contains both principles of love and transformation; so does the myth of the sisters of Phaethon (62–63), except that love is there modified to sisterly love (*pietas*). At this point Gallus appears and the connexion is created by a modification of both principles: Gallus is a forlorn (*errantem*) lover and he is transformed by the admiration of Apollo and the Muses. The episode of Gallus (64–73) is followed by the two episodes of Scylla (74–77) and Philomela (78–81), which display again the sheerly physical aspects of love and transformation. The song ends with an inclusive formula that stresses the theme of love (82–84).[38] This is not to explain away the episode of Gallus; nothing could be more surprising than the sudden appearance of the living poet in a mythical context, and it has received fairly general

36. This, too, is an echo of Callimachus' hymn *To Delos*, lines 269–73: οὐδέ τις ἄλλη / γαιάων τοσσόνδε θεῷ πεφιλήσεται ἄλλῳ / ... ὡς ἐγὼ Ἀπόλλωνι ('nor shall any place be loved so much by any god ... as I am by Apollo').

37. Though it also contains a strong element, by anticipation, of the third principle, transformation.

38. See Williams (1968), pp. 239–43.

condemnation as inappropriate and bizarre. But it is to insist that, on reflection, a reader can discern links, all metonymic in mode, that connect the Gallus-episode to the surrounding myths.

There is no reason to doubt Servius' information that Cornelius Gallus actually did write a poem on the oracle of Apollo at Grynium, based on a work of Euphorion. In that case, Virgil should not be regarded as offering advice to Gallus on how to write such a poem, but as celebrating a poem which had already been written. The words in which the pipes are presented by Linus are notable: he says (69–70) *hos tibi dant calamos (en accipe) Musae | Ascraeo quos ante seni*, 'The Muses present these pipes to you (here, take them) which previously they gave to the old man of Ascra'.[39] Gallus, then, is being designated as *Hesiodus redivivus*, and Hesiod was the poet admired in preference to Homer by poets in the circle of Callimachus who wrote aetiological poems of the type here enjoined on Gallus.[40] So Gallus has been transformed from a love-poet to being the composer of an admired type of Alexandrian poem, in which he has achieved a distinction to equal that of the most revered model of Alexandrian poets. It may be added, too, that there is a clear connexion between Gallus' reception by the Muses and the encounter with them which Hesiod recalls as having taken place below Helicon, as he was tending his sheep (*Theogony* 22–34). Hesiod plays a central part in the episode.

The episode of Gallus functions in two complementary ways within the song of Silenus. First, it demonstrates that the master-poet Silenus recognises Gallus as a fellow-poet of comparable stature. Secondly, it adds a dimension that makes the song of Silenus immediately relevant to contemporary poetry. Its third function lies in the poem as a whole: together with the poem's opening, it provides an index of proportionality between the two fields of the poem. Virgil took a risk in advertising the song of Silenus so enthusiastically—it held Fauns and beasts spellbound, and trees; Parnassus was more delighted with it than with Phoebus, and Rhodope and Ismarus than with Orpheus (27–30); even the sky was unwilling to let night come on (86). He met the danger in part by telling the song in his own words so that Silenus'

---

39. This motif, too, connects with the poet's presentation of his pipe at the end of *Eclogue* 5.

40. Cf. Callimachus *epigram* 27P f. (*Anth.Pal.* 9.507) in praise of Aratus' *Phaenomena*, and see Pfeiffer (1968), p. 117.

technique was concealed under Virgil's. The effect is to concentrate attention on the thematic material so that the reader knows something of the themes at least of a world-stopping poem; or—to put it differently—it is equivalent to saying that great poetry can be created from a certain range of themes. It is notable how often these themes suggest themes that recur in the *Georgics*: the capture of Silenus is like the capture of Proteus; the opening of the song suggests a didactic poem and recalls Lucretius; Orpheus figures in line 30, in the Gallus-episode, and in the end of the *Georgics*; love is an important theme of the *Georgics*; and the *Georgics* is a specifically Hesiodic poem (2.176 *Ascraeum ... carmen*); and there are various other detailed thematic echoes.[41] There is no point in trying to specify a message in *Eclogue* 6, but it does seem that the unspoken field contains Virgil's reflections on themes and models that lie outside the range of pastoral. And the poem itself enacts those reflections, since the poet, having withdrawn explicitly within pastoral (6–12), composes a poem quite unlike any pastoral hitherto, containing thematic material that can accommodate not only the most elevated work of Gallus but also the future work of Virgil himself. In other words, Virgil is here exploring in the genre of pastoral the possibility of moving in a direction parallel to that of Gallus (from love-poetry to aetiological epyllion) but different from his, yet characterised by a similar relationship to the model poetry of Hesiod. But to attempt, even very sketchily, to outline the features of the unspoken field is to lapse into banalities that do no justice to the range and depth of *Eclogue* 6. The unspoken field can only be apprehended as a distant but luminous vision, and its very lack of specificity is poetically suggestive in a way that is familiar in Virgil's poetry.

In *Eclogue* 5 the primary field is constituted by the Theocritean framework; that is to be found mainly in the setting of the two songs: the introductory conversation (1–19), the dialogue that occurs between the two songs (45–55), and the concluding exchange of presents (81–90). But it is also to be found in the dependence of the topic of Daphnis' death on *Idyll* 1 of Theocritus (and, to a slight extent, on the *Epitaphios Bionos*); the dependence, however, is only general and does not (as in *Eclogue* 10) extend to details. In fact, what is really brought to attention here is the distance of the two songs, particularly of the second, from

---

41. For instance, the themes of Philomela and Orpheus are linked in *Georg.* 4.507–15.

the Greek material. That originality itself, therefore, points to the secondary field.

Here the relationship between the setting and the songs needs to be examined. It has usually been assumed that the setting and the figure of Daphnis stand in a close chronological relationship and that, for instance, Daphnis is to be understood as the 'teacher' (48, *magistrum*) of Mopsus. The basis for this assumption seems to have been the prior assumption that in some way Daphnis is connected with, even identifiable with, Julius Caesar. In its weakest form this assumption can be phrased (in the words of the latest commentator): 'It is incredible that anyone in the late 40s could have read a pastoral poem on this theme without thinking of Caesar';[42] others, however, have gone much further—for instance: 'The deified Daphnis of 5 is thus the rather thin mask of the deified Julius.'[43] To say this sort of thing is to confuse two separate issues: on the one hand, there are ideas that the poet, even if he does not express them in the actual words of the poem, intends should operate on the reader; on the other, there is material that scholarly investigation can show to have influenced the poet as he wrote (as, for instance, J. L. Lowes showed for Coleridge in *The Road to Xanadu*). It is clear that to see Daphnis as Julius Caesar simply runs counter to what the poet says about Daphnis. If the apotheosis of Julius Caesar was in Virgil's mind as he wrote the eclogue, that will add to our knowledge of Virgil's biography rather than of the poem. (In a similar way, a knowledge of Meleager's epigram *Anth.Pal.* 12.127 is interesting in the reading of *Eclogue* 2 but does not have a function in its interpretation.) However, the poet may have intended the signifiance of apotheosis in the recent Roman past to function as an index to another field of ideas, yet without drawing a specific reference to the identity of the individual Julius Caesar into the interpretation of the poem.

It is notable that, in *Idyll* 1 of Theocritus, Daphnis is not of the least concern personally to either shepherd except as a subject for song; he lived in the remote mythological past. Is it different with *Eclogue* 5? The difficulty involved in assuming that it is can be seen in Conington's note on line 58: 'We must understand Menalcas as describing a state which is just beginning or about to begin: but this will hardly excuse

42. Coleman (1977), p. 173.
43. Otis (1963), p. 135.

the impropriety of representing two such different scenes as both belonging to present time, and thus compelling us to think of each as existing only in the minds of the two shepherds.' But, as in Theocritus, the two shepherds concentrate on each other's poetic skill and exchange gifts as if Daphnis had no real or immediately personal connexion with them. The only apparent exception to this seems to be in the words of Menalcas after he has praised Mopsus' song (48–55):

> nec calamis solum aequiperas, sed voce magistrum:
> fortunate puer, tu nunc eris alter ab illo.
> nos tamen haec quocumque modo tibi nostra vicissim
> dicemus, Daphninque tuum tollemus ad astra;
> Daphnin ad astra feremus: amavit nos quoque Daphnis.
> *Mopsus.*
> an quicquam nobis tali sit munere maius?
> et puer ipse fuit cantari dignus, et ista
> iampridem Stimichon laudavit carmina nobis.

'"Not only with your pipe but with your voice you are now the equal of your teacher: young man, you are smiled on by fortune and will take second place to him. Still I shall now in turn sing this song of mine as best I can and I shall exalt your Daphnis to the stars; I shall bear Daphnis to the stars: I too have been loved by Daphnis."
Mopsus. "Could any reward be greater to me than that? He was a young man worthy to be the subject of song, and also Stimichon has long praised those songs of yours to me."'

Commentators are here content to say (as the latest does): 'As there is no hint that Mopsus is Menalcas' pupil, this must be Daphnis.'[44] But the eclogue opened with this exchange (1–4):

> *Menalcas.*
> Cur non, Mopse, boni quoniam convenimus ambo,
> tu calamos inflare leves, ego dicere versus,
> hic corylis mixtas inter consedimus ulmos?
> *Mopsus.*
> tu maior: tibi me est aequum parere, Menalca.

'*Men.* "Why, Mopsus, since we have met, both of us skilled, you to play on the fragile pipes, I to sing verses, are we not seated here where elms and

44. Coleman (1977), on lines 48–49.

hazels intermingle?" *Mopsus.* "You are the greater: it is right that I should obey you, Menalcas." '

Mopsus then goes on to say that Amyntas is his only local rival (8). Both statements are modified by lines 48–49: Mopsus is now declared equal to Menalcas in the respect in which Menalcas was superior (*voce*) and so his successor as a singer (thus outdoing Amyntas). The word (4) *maior* is ambiguous between age and skill, but the respectful obedience of Mopsus draws it to the sense of (48) *magistrum*. In that case, Menalcas modestly (modesty is his characteristic) refers to himself in the third person, just as Virgil does when he thanks the Muses after his song in *Eclogue* 10 (70–71) *haec sat erit, divae, vestrum cecinisse poetam, / dum sedet et gracili fiscellam texit hibisco.* This little scene is then picked up after Menalcas' song, and the succession of Mopsus is symbolised in his receiving the gift of the pipes that taught Menalcas *Eclogues* 2 and 3 (85–87). So, when Menalcas speaks of (51) *Daphnique tuum* he means 'Daphnis, the subject (or, inspiration) of your song'.

It is notable that, when Menalcas suggests various conventional topics as possible subjects for Mopsus' song (10–12), Mopsus rejects them in favour of a song that he has actually carved on elm, and he is confident that it will outdo Amyntas. The song turns out to be based on *Idyll* 1 of Theocritus and the song there about the death of Daphnis; but what is striking is that the only thematic connexion with Theocritus lies in the lamentation which opens the song (20–28), thereafter all is new. If one asks what authority the singer has for this novelty of poetic invention, the answer is given in the song itself (41) *mandat fieri sibi talia Daphnis*—Daphnis has given an injunction: that is, the singer has been inspired to these themes by Daphnis.

The song of Menalcas is an impromptu composition (since—by the rules of this type of song-contest—he could not know in advance what Mopsus would sing about), and he starts from a sort of pun that originates in Mopsus' words (42) *hinc usque ad sidera notus* 'famous from here to the stars'. Menalcas will 'exalt Daphnis to the stars', he will 'bear him to the stars', in both literal and metaphorical senses. From this apparently accidental but fortunate verbal echo springs the originality of Menalcas' song; and if we again ask about his authority for what he says, he too has supplied the answer in the words (52) *amavit nos quoque Daphnis*: for *amare* is used as is φιλεῖν in Greek (for instance, Theocritus *Id.* 5.80–82) to mean 'inspire', as in *Eclogue* 3.59–

63. Daphnis, then, is the source of inspiration for both singer-poets. But in the case of Menalcas that inspiration is transformed into something personal to him in the message that only he can hear echoing in the world of nature (64) *deus, deus ille, Menalca*!

That question of authority and inspiration directs attention to a remarkable (and original) feature in Mopsus' account of Daphnis: he introduced the orgiastic rites of Bacchus (29–31). This is a metonymy not merely for the introduction of poetry (Daphnis was, in some accounts, the inventor of pastoral music), but for the institutionalizing, as it were, of poetic inspiration: for the orgies of Bacchus were used—outstandingly by Horace in *Odes* 3.25–as a metonymy for the reception of poetic inspiration. That connexion with poetry is one pole of Daphnis' being in both songs. The other pole is his relationship with nature and particularly his symbiosis with all aspects of agriculture (32–39 and 58–71). The two poles are represented by (35) Pales and Apollo, by the *lustratio agri* and the Nymphs (75), by Bacchus and Ceres (79), and, most remarkably, by the contrasted gift-giving—the pipes of Menalcas being poetic (85–87), the staff, *pedum* (88), of Mopsus being agricultural. The two poles of his being constitute that close relationship between nature and poetry that is the essence of pastoral: in the one sphere he is the source of inspiration, in the other, of the harmony between man and nature that brings fruitfulness (and the conditions for poetry). In the song of Menalcas, Daphnis becomes a Roman type of agricultural deity, with winter and harvest festivals (67–75). The important features of the two poles are distributed between the two songs: Mopsus tells of Daphnis' introduction of Bacchic orgies, while Menalcas tells of the agricultural festivals instituted in Daphnis' honour.

The primary field is here constituted by the Greek elements—the shepherds, the locality, the songs, and the exchange of gifts; also by the allusions to *Idyll* 1 of Theocritus, and to *Idyll* 7 in the gift of Mopsus and the name Antigenes (89). This is the easily recognisable world of Theocritean pastoral. One index of proportionality to a secondary field is provided by the gift of Menalcas which, in appearing to identify Menalcas with the author of the *Eclogues*, functions, like the entrance of Cornelius Gallus in *Eclogue* 6, so as to break the pastoral illusion. That is the only index that appears in the setting; the others occur in the two songs, conspicuously in the Roman elements of (35) Pales, the (75) *lustratio agri*, (79) Ceres, and the characteristically Roman commercial attitude to worship (79–80). More striking indexes are the surprising detail of Daphnis' introduction of Bacchic orgies and the even more surprising apotheosis of Daphnis which recalls the recent apotheosis of Julius Caesar.

The secondary field to which these indexes point is as difficult to define as in *Eclogue* 6. It has to do with poetry and sources of inspiration. The two songs obey the rules for pastoral amoebean contests: the second responds to and 'caps' the first. It is as if the poet were posing and solving the problem: how can lamentation be poetically transformed into celebration? That was the problem that Milton, too, faced in *Lycidas* and solved by using Christian concepts of eternal life. Seen from one point of view and taking into account the echo with the apotheosis of Julius Caesar, the song of Menalcas is an assertion of the poet's power to confer divine immortality; hence the very personal nature of Menalcas' vision is stressed by him (64). But Daphnis is also a figure for the ideal poet, deeply in harmony with his natural surroundings (so his pastoral activities are stressed). Mopsus laments his death and expresses the idea of a loss that extends from mortals and nature right to the gods themselves; Menalcas celebrates his eternal life and his function as a source of inspiration. Though the commentary of Junius Philargyrius was mainly influenced by the false interpretation of (48) *magistrum* as Daphnis, yet it also has some sense of this aspect of Daphnis in asserting that Daphnis is a figure for Theocritus (also briefly asserted in the Servian commentary). Mopsus bases his song on Theocritean material and goes beyond it; but it is that material which Menalcas totally transcends in his song and then explicitly abandons in giving to Mopsus the pipes that taught him *Eclogues* 2 and 3. As it were, Menalcas takes the figure of Daphnis and transforms it into something inconceivable in Theocritean terms, using a suggestive idea from the world of contemporary Roman reality to extend the range of a traditional theme far beyond even the point to which it had been extended in the song of Mopsus (and that is impressive enough). But the complexity of relationships in which Daphnis is involved in both songs can also be viewed more generally in terms of the relationship between poetry and life. It is striking how many aspects of Daphnis and the ideas he inspires are relevant to the view of poetry that Horace put forward some twenty-five years later in *Epistles* 2.1.118–38: the poet is useful to the state in educating the young, in consolation, in prayers for help from the gods, in obtaining peace and fruitfulness and conditions that favour agriculture, and in placating the gods both of the heavens and of the under-world. Both in the epistle and in the eclogue a close relationship is asserted between poetry and the real life of the poet's world. And both poems show that relationship inherent in the very origins of poetry: for just as the eclogue asserts this in the figure of the mythological Daphnis, so Horace goes on, in the immediately following lines, to derive poetry from all kinds of country festivals.

Eclogue 10, too, is dominated by reflections on poetry and life. In this poem the primary field, by contrast, is constituted by events and relationships that belong to real life. Here belongs the curious, almost triangular, relationship on the one hand between C. Cornelius Gallus and Volumnia Cytheris (or Lycoris as she appears in the poem, because that was what Gallus called her in his poetry), and, on the other, between P. Vergilius Maro and C. Cornelius Gallus: the former relationship is characterised by the passion that can kill (10, *peribat*), the latter by the affection (73, *amor*, in the Catullan sense of *pietas*) that calmly grows in intensity with time—the sort of growth that Gallus imagines his love for Lycoris would enjoy if only he could live in Arcadia (52–53); but with that last idea we have really transferred to the secondary field. This situation is constituted by exactly corresponding opening and closing passages (1–8 and 70–77), in which the pastoral poet speaks in the modest character of a goatherd, explicitly marking this as his last pastoral poem and his farewell to bucolic poetry; here, too, as in *Eclogue* 6, the poet momentarily looks forward to the themes of the *Georgics* (76, *nocent et frugibus umbrae*, where *umbrae*, the delight of the pastoral poet, are the bane of the farmer—cf. *Georg.* 1.121). This calm surrounding frame encloses, with the same structure as in Catullus 68,[45] a poem about Gallus and his unrequited love (10, *indigno ... amore*) for Lycoris. This is transposed into the Theocritean framework of the death of Daphnis, based on the first *Idyll* of Theocritus. The enclosing introduction (1–8) and ending (70–77) can be seen to provide an index of proportionality to a secondary field which is there formulated in terms of a pastoral poet confronted with the need to write a poem for Gallus such that Lycoris can read it too (2): that is, the required poem must be written in such a way that Lycoris will be benefitted by it and behave lovingly again towards Gallus. The ending declares that purpose to have been accomplished, and it is accomplished by the pastoral

45. See Williams (1968), pp. 233–39.

poet's showing Gallus attempting—and failing—to transpose Lycoris into Arcadia. In the primary field that means that Gallus declares his elegiac devotion to Lycoris to be inescapable.

The enclosed poem opens with an almost verbatim quotation translated from Theocritus *Idyll* 1.65–69, asking the nymphs where they were when Gallus was dying. The aspect of the song in the Theocritean *Idyll* is past, for, as the poet goes on to list Daphnis' visitors, Daphnis is said to be dead (72). It is, however, only clear from the enclosing frame that Gallus is still alive—and from these lines (16–18):

> stant et oves circum: nostri nec paenitet illas,
> nec te paeniteat pecoris, divine poeta—
> et formosus ovis ad flumina pavit Adonis.

'And the sheep are standing round about: I feel no discontent with them, so you, divine poet, must not feel discontented with a flock—even the beautiful Adonis pastured his sheep along a river's side.'

These lines break out of the Theocritean framework both in their present tenses (the preceding and following verbs are past) and in the fact that the purpose of the corresponding motif in Theocritus (74–75) was to present the herd as having mourned the death of Daphnis. The present tense in Virgil represents the herd as simply standing ready (if sadly, that is not explicit). But ready for what? Ready for Gallus to tend them, like Adonis. These lines then are marked out as another index of proportionality to an unspoken field; and they modify the preceding index in the opening (1–8) in such a way as to suggest that the unspoken field is that of the relationship between the poetic genres of pastoral and love-elegy. But it soon becomes clear that such a formulation is too narrow and technical. What is involved is an aspect of the relationship between poetry and life, presented in the form of an exploration of the way in which the two literary genres treat similar themes— particularly the theme of love, which the poet represents Gallus as transposing into the pastoral mode (or, rather, trying to), but finding the exigencies of his experience driving him back to elegy: pastoral will not accommodate that destructive passion. Corresponding to the Theocritean contrast between the singer Thyrsis, blandly objective toward the sufferings of Daphnis and concentrating complacently on his own skill and on the prize he deserves, there is the striking contrast between the melodramatic agony of Gallus and the calm air of the containing poem (1–8 and 70–77), where the goatherd placidly executes his humble tasks. This part of the poem also expresses the love the goatherd-poet feels for Gallus, a love that corresponds with what Gallus envisages his passion for Lycoris might become (53–54 with 73–74) if only he could live in Arcadia—that is, if only he could become a pastoral poet: the forms of expression here suggest that the two types of love are being presented as genre-differentiated. The contrast between the two poetic genres, located in the unspoken field, is taken up in these lines (50–51):

> ibo et Chalcidico quae sunt mihi condita versu
> carmina pastoris Siculi modulabor avena.

'I shall go and tune the poems that I composed in Chalcidic verse to the pipe of a Sicilian shepherd.'

The two poets are here identified not by their own poetry but by that of their Greek models, Euphorion of Chalcis and Theocritus. Gallus, instead of being a follower of Euphorion, will join Virgil as an imitator of Theocritus. The choice of Euphorion as Gallus' model (no less than the address as *divine poeta* in line 17) suggests that Virgil here regards Gallus' transumption (*Eclogue* 6.64–73) as a fait accompli, and that Gallus is not only writing love-elegy but also the genre of Alexandrian epyllion or aetiological poem; his themes cannot be contained within pastoral, and Virgil himself is proposing to move out of that cramping genre, following the example of his distinguished friend.

At this point we must go back to the beginning of the enclosed poem. In most of the *Eclogues* the difficult problem lies in deciding the constitution of the secondary field; the primary field is generally clear enough. That is not so with *Eclogue* 10. For instance, Theocritean elements are normally used to constitute the primary field; but in *Eclogue* 10 the Theocritean lament for Daphnis is used as a framework for the secondary field. However, there is a more serious difficulty which I suspect is due to our ignorance of certain facts that would have been known to the poet's envisaged readers. Even Servius knew enough —as we do not—to note, in his usual imprecise way, against line 46: 'All these lines belong to Gallus and are transferred from his own poems'.

So actual elegiac poems of Gallus are closely alluded to, almost quoted, in this *Eclogue*; their existence as objective poems in elegiac metre belongs to the primary field, in that they constitute a real element in the relationship between Gallus and Lycoris. What other realities should the intended reader have known about? The opening of the enclosed poem is based on Theocritus but is also curiously different (9–15):

> quae nemora aut qui vos saltus habuere, puellae
> Naiades, indigno cum Gallus amore peribat?
> nam neque Parnasi vobis iuga, nam neque Pindi
> ulla moram fecere, neque Aonie Aganippe.
> illum etiam lauri, etiam flevere myricae,
> pinifer illum etiam sola sub rupe iacentem
> Maenalus et gelidi fleverunt saxa Lycaei.

'What groves or what glades detained you, Naid maidens, when Gallus lay dying of unrequited love? For neither did the ridges of Parnassus nor did those of Pindus give you any cause for delay, nor did Aonian Aganippe. Even laurel-trees, even tamarisks wept for him, even pine-bearing Maenalus and the rocks of cold Lycaeus wept over him as he lay beneath a lonely crag.'

At the corresponding point in Theocritus, the singer says (66–69): 'Where were you when Daphnis was wasting away, where were you, Nymphs? In the lovely vales of Peneius or of Pindus? For you certainly were not by the great stream of river Anapus, nor the high peak of Aetna, nor the sacred spring of Acis'. Here the singer's authority for asserting where the nymphs were not lies in his knowledge that Daphnis died and that therefore the nymphs must have been elsewhere. In *Eclogue* 10 the verbal phrase 'did not give you cause for delay' can only mean 'your presence was not required there', in any of the three places mentioned. But what authority could the poet have for saying that? I can see only one answer: the poet knew that Gallus might be supposed to be in a region poetically served, as it were, by Parnassus, Pindus, and Boeotia, and, in denying that Gallus could have been looking for poetic inspiration in that region (and so 'delaying' the nymphs), he is envisaging his own transference of Gallus to Arcadia in the central Peloponnese. A guess is needed here. Gallus' only political connexion that we know of before 44 B.C. is with Pollio (he is mentioned as a friend interested in literature in a letter from Pollio to

Cicero—*ad fam.* 10.32.5). Pollio was proconsul of Macedonia (at that time co-extensive with Greece) in 39 B.C., and his operations were in the north against the Parthini (over whom he celebrated a triumph); Pindus is relevant to that region, Parnassus is the great centre of the Muses, and Aganippe is particular to the poetry of Gallus since it is the spring that is the origin of the Permessus (by which Gallus was found wandering in *Eclogue* 6.64). What more natural than that Pollio took his friend with him to his province[46] not only for entertainment but also for practical assistance? (Gallus was a sufficiently experienced commander to be put in immediate charge of Antony's forces to effect the conquest of Egypt in 30 B.C.)[47] Gallus, in fact, was an ideal combination (like Pollio himself) of poet and soldier.

If so, in the primary field of the poem, Gallus would have been known to be serving with Pollio's troops in northern Greece, and the poet has left knowledge of that fact to be triggered by metonymic association with the regions of poetic inspiration relevant to a soldier-poet on campaign in northern Greece. But in the secondary field the poet himself transfers Gallus to Arcadia so that he may become a pastoral poet; and by that transfer he constitutes the secondary field. In consequence, Gallus' visitors function already in the secondary field. All the inhabitants of Arcadia are astonished: they have never seen love like that (21)—of course they have not, since it is elegiac. Apollo comes and tells Gallus that Lycoris has gone off with another soldier to snowy regions (21–23). This is to be understood as news to Gallus, for that must be the point of making Apollo the bearer of the news. The reader now therefore knows that (10) *indigno . . . amore* was the poet's privileged comment, and that Gallus' agony, before Apollo's news arrived, was caused simply by his separation from Lycoris. Pan comes (26), and here the poet underwrites his own authority for what happened in Arcadia by asserting that he actually saw Pan himself (26, *quem vidimus ipsi*): Pan's message (28–30), expressed in a pastoral analogy, is that Gallus' elegiac response is useless, for Love only takes cruel

46. Syme (1938), p. 39 n. 3 and (1939), p. 252, speculates that Gallus may also have served with Pollio when he held Gallia Cisalpina on behalf of Antony in 42–40 B.C. There is no reason, however, to believe Syme (1939), p. 253: 'Gallus had probably gone eastwards with Antonius soon after the Pact of Brundisium'. There is no evidence to connect Gallus with Antony at all.

47. Rice Holmes (1928), pp. 146, 162; Syme (1939), pp. 298–99.

pleasure in tears. Gallus now (31–34) says that he will die at peace if pastoral poetry is written about him (that theme connects with the introduction where the poet has been asked for just such a poem). But then he imagines himself also an Arcadian and even Lycoris sharing the pastoral life with him (35–43).

At this point unwelcome reality breaks in, resulting from Apollo's news, to shatter the Arcadian framework (44–49): as it is (*nunc*) Gallus is serving with the army and Lycoris has gone off with another to the Alps, so he turns away from the pastoral dream (which is also the writing of pastoral poetry). But immediately he turns back again, resolving to transpose his elegiac poetry into pastoral (50–51). (Here I would conjecture that Gallus had written an elegiac poem in Greece in which Apollo appeared to him and told him of Lycoris' desertion and that this is the basis of Servius' remarks.) Gallus is now in the pastoral dream again: he will compose love-poetry (*amores*) in pastoral style (52–54) and engage in pastoral activities (that is, write pastoral poetry); the dream goes into a dramatic overrun of a single dactyl (60) before Gallus suddenly realises that it is hopeless: even if he engages in pastoral activities in utmost extremes of heat and cold (65–68), Love will not submit—he must submit to Love (also in the sense of writing elegiac love-poetry). Here the secondary field, constituted by the confrontation between pastoral poetry and elegiac love-poetry, reaches a climax in the failure of pastoral to accommodate the theme of tragic love: Pan was right, but also wrong—Arcadia has nothing to offer in this predicament; submission to the cruelty of Love is the only possibility. The only way in which Gallus can come to terms with his passion for Lycoris is through the medium of elegiac love-poetry. Gallus' finding pastoral poetry inadequate for the purpose just precedes the poet Virgil's own declaration that he is abandoning it (75–78).

Eclogue 4[48] also raises the question of the poet's authority: for it is he who declares that the final age of the Sibylline oracle has come (4) and it is he who asserts the special importance of the child (8–10); neither assertion—and certainly not the latter—is predicated on the Sibyl's authority. The poet only obliquely reveals his authority when he says (10) *tuus iam regnat Apollo.*[49] It is also the poet himself who describes the coming of a Golden Age in three installments (18–45).

---

48. For interpretation, see Williams (1968), pp. 274–84, and (1974), pp. 31–46.
49. On the question of authority, see Williams (1974), pp. 33–35.

His authority for that, again, only appears obliquely after the account when he uses a near-quotation from Catullus 64 to suggest that it was the Fates who delivered the prophecy. This primary field of the poem is constituted in the opening words as Theocritean but slightly more elevated than usual (1–3): to it belong the details of the Golden Age (as many as possible taken from Theocritus), the response of the universe to the child's coming as to the epiphany of a god (50–52), and the pastoral form in which the poet looks forward to the child's life as an inspiration to epic (53–59). There is only one index of proportionality to the secondary field: it is the address (spoken aside) to Pollio (11–14) which fixes the date, suggests a marriage (by reference to a gestation), and points to the Peace of Brundisium in 40 B.C. That index then functions to trigger the introduction of the concept of a marriage into the secondary field by means of various references to Catullus 64 and especially to the song of the Fates.

Thus the secondary field is the Roman political situation in 40 B.C., and each feature of the primary field has another life in the secondary field. Commentators make remarks such as: 'It would be rash indeed to celebrate a marriage by eulogizing an offspring from it that might not—and as it happened did not—materialize', or 'One may ask whether [Virgil] would have risked having his prophecy nullified by future events'.[50] Such judgments allow the poem only a literal meaning and deny the existence of a secondary field. For in the secondary field the child functions as a product of the Peace of Brundisium and symbolises the expected result of that treaty. In the same way one can see that the Golden Age also has a function that is close to allegory: at the infant's birth (as might be expected in a pastoral poem) nature itself responds and converts itself into a pastoral ideal, and the suggestion here is of something close to the *laudes Italiae* in *Georgics* 2.136–176; when the child is about eleven, he learns Roman history, nature gives some help to mankind in general, but characteristics of the Iron Age remain (31–36) that are the results of the long civil wars and will demand military action for some time to come (one should think, for instance, of Parthia and Spain and Gaul and Britain); when the child reaches manhood, men will be enabled to give up all activities that foster greed, ambition, violence, exploitation, and deceit—this will be a time of complete moral regeneration when (31) *priscae*

---

50. Coleman (1977), p. 151.

vestigiae fraudis will disappear. When the poem is viewed in this way, it can be seen to predict with some accuracy the general movement of events over the following twenty-five years. The poet's own anticipation of an inspiration to a generically more elevated type of poetry (53–59) was also not to be disappointed. I should not be inclined to deny that Virgil himself had at this time fairly concrete plans for his own future poetic activity over that same period.

In *Eclogue* 1[51] the primary field is constituted by a generic framework created from echoes of *Idyll* 1 in the opening lines. That framework is then ruptured by various Roman details of land-confiscation, a picture of Rome itself, slavery, and civil war. These elements of contemporary reality are indexes of proportionality to a secondary field that concerns civil war and its effects, particularly on the poet. Tityrus is an elderly slave who has been threatened with confiscation, but miraculously he has obtained both his freedom and tenure of his property; he can therefore continue happily with his poetry (1–5). He owes his tenure to a divine youth who, in his divinity and in the worship offered him on his monthly birthday, is Greek and belongs to the primary field of Theocritean Greek unreality. But the indexes of proportionality provide a means of locating him also in the secondary field as an analogue of the young Octavian. His arbitrary act of grace, as remote and unfeeling as a god's (44–45), has been the salvation of Tityrus. But his friend Meliboeus is a more interesting and significant character. He too is a Greek shepherd in the primary field, but there is no sign that he had ever been under the stigma of slavery. He, however, is going into exile (4 and 64–71), and the comment that he makes in lines 71–72, *en quo discordia cives / produxit miseros* ('see the depth to which discord has brought us wretched citizens') is surprising in two ways: first, like the exile, it ruptures the Theocritean framework and so provides an index to another field; secondly, it is an illogical comment if just directed to land-confiscation, for that had for a very long time been the normal means of paying off veterans, civil war or no.

Meliboeus' comment shows that he regards the confiscation of his property as a penalty, and so it goes with his exile to create an unexpected and disturbing picture. The proscriptions of 43/42 B.C. that preceded Philippi and the land-confiscations that followed the battle were one continuous process: the latter were provided for by

51. See Williams (1968), pp. 307–12.

the former so that, not only were eighteen cities in Italy designated for confiscation in 43 B.C.,[52] but the individuals proscribed—and so automatically designated for death or exile—were selected to provide property and capital. This is the figure that Meliboeus cuts in the secondary field: in the primary he is a mere Greek shepherd and the depreciatory description of his own property accords with that (67–69); but in the secondary field he is a Roman landowner, with valuable property (70–72, *impius haec tam culta novalia miles habebit, | barbarus has segetes ... his nos consevimus agros*), compelled to save his life by abandoning his property and going into exile. Like the poet Horace and even more like many earlier Republicans, Meliboeus had been on the wrong side and was caught up in the proscriptions and their aftermath. Tityrus, like many others at the time, went to Rome to appeal,[53] and the arbitrary whim of the all-powerful Octavian saved him; that course was not open to the more important (and politically compromised) Meliboeus, whose only solace is the brief hospitality that Tityrus offers—prudence and self-preservation dictate that it can only be for one night. For Meliboeus, unlike Tityrus, poetry is a thing of the past: (77) *carmina nulla canam*; civil war and its consequences have destroyed it.

In the closely related *Eclogue* 9[54] the primary field is constituted by the poem's explicit relationship, indicated in the opening lines, with *Idyll* 7 of Theocritus. Again there are details that rupture the Greek framework: land-confiscations with absentee landlords (2–6), and fighting between veteran soldiers and civilians (11–16) such as Cassius Dio (48.9) describes as constant in the year 41 B.C. in regions where questions of land-tenure arose. There are also four quotations from the poet Menalcas, who does not appear: two of these (23–25 and 39–43) belong to the primary field and are fairly close translations of passages of Theocritus (they are from *Idylls*, whose influence is especially strong in the *Eclogues*); the other two (27–29 and 46–50) are Roman: the first is an appeal to P. Alfenus Varus, *cos. suff.* 39 B.C., a distinguished jurist from Cremona, not to confiscate land from Mantua (Virgil's birthplace); the second is a celebration of the appearance of Halley's comet in 44 B.C., taken as a sign of the apotheosis of

52. Rice Holmes (1928), p. 70; Syme (1939), p. 196.
53. Appian *BC* 5.12.49. Rice Holmes (1928), p. 93; Syme (1939), p. 207.
54. See Williams (1968), pp. 313–28.

Julius Caesar and accompanied by explicit optimism for Roman agriculture. Thus these two quotations, the second dated on its own evidence to 44 B.C., the first similarly to 41 B.C., encapsulate the destruction of this region of the Roman pastoral / agricultural world in the space of three years. The secondary field therefore concerns the relationship of poetry to contemporary politics and the possibility that the poet could actually exert an influence by means of his poetry. The pessimism is deep and complete: the poet is of no significance. He is figured in Menalcas, the mysterious absent poet; the speakers painfully recall *disiecti membra poetae*, and the fragments they recall tell the story that lies behind the poem and constitute the prime indexes of proportionality between the primary and secondary fields. But fragments are all they can recall, and in the case of the appeal to Varus the poem itself was never completed (26). They look forward—with little conviction, it seems—to Menalcas' coming and to the possibility of poetry again, which, from being their hope of salvation (10–16), has now become a mere means of consolation (17–18) in their desperate troubles.

The primary field of *Eclogue* 2[55] also is constituted by a Theocritean framework, based mainly on *Idylls* 3 and 11: it concerns the relationship between Corydon, the tragic lover, and Alexis. The technique here is close to that of dramatic monologue as it was analysed above. This, however, is not a dramatic monologue, since the poet introduces the lover's soliloquy in words that explain his emotional situation and emphasise that the scene which the poem embodies, far from being unique, is repeated every day. The indexes of proportionality have to be inferred by the reader from hints in the poet's introduction and in the soliloquy: they are that both Corydon and Alexis are slaves, that Alexis lives in the (remote) town-house and is the beloved of the master-owner of both slaves. It is an index of the same type as in *Eclogues* 1 and 9: it measures the distance between Theocritean make-believe and a harsh Roman reality. The secondary field here is like that of *Eclogue* 10: it concerns the relationship between the theme of tragic love and the way it can be treated in pastoral poetry. In this way unexpected new life is given to a series of Theocritean themes, for the indexes of proportionality reveal Corydon as a poet who knows his generic themes but who uses them in such a way as to

55. See ibid., pp. 303–07.

enforce an ironic interpretation. The effect is to add to the sense of depth through a literary dimension, and to dismiss the easy Theocritean assertion (*Idyll* 11.1–18 and 80–81) that poetry is a remedy for love. A more convincing view emerges of the relationship between poetry and life: poetry is born out of suffering. The tragedy and destructiveness of human love was a theme to which Virgil often returned; but here in his earliest poetry it is already given memorable expression within the narrow limits of a cramping genre by means of the objective framework. And the paradoxical feature that was noticed in the technique of dramatic monologue—that the more specific the setting the more readily could the ideas be referred to a general view of the human condition—is seen here too.

It is hard to regard *Eclogues* 3 and 7 as more than light-hearted Theocritean jeux d'esprit. In *Eclogue* 3 there is a feature in the introduction of the index of proportionality that was seen in *Eclogue* 6: its effect is parallel to that of breaking the dramatic illusion. In the centre of their singing-contest the two shepherds refer flatteringly to Pollio, his pre-eminence as a poet, and his value as a patron-critic. In *Eclogue* 7 the index is provided by the setting: the shepherds are Arcadians (4), but they are singing by the river Mincius. In both *Eclogues* the index should be taken to be not so much an actual measurement of the proportionality of two related fields as a measurement of a deliberated distance from Theocritus. The index points to the Romanization of a typically Greek genre, with a specifically Greek background; and thus the poet claims value for the singing-contests within the contemporary Roman poetic scene. In both *Eclogues* poetry is viewed as the application of a practised technique to given material, though there is also room for thematic invention in various quite modest ways. Theocritean material is always signalled, but it is also varied. The actual form of the contest is, as it were, a challenge accepted by the poet Virgil: there is a high degree of polish, deft syntactical adaptations, and extreme metrical variety. The poems deliberately exemplify the ways in which a Greek genre can be taken over and adapted to Roman poetical ideals.

Eclogue 8 is of the same form as *Eclogue* 5: the contest consists of two lengthy songs (17–61 and 64–109), precisely balancing one another in amoebean style. Both songs are on the theme of tragic love,[56] and

56. On the ending of the second song, see ibid., p. 304.

the singer casts himself as the unhappy lover, male in the first, female in the second. The first owes little except a couple of echoes to Theocritus; the second is closely modelled on *Idyll* 2. There is no attempt in either song to individualize or characterize, and direct expression of emotion is avoided; instead there are two brief lyrical expressions of emotion in secondary language: in the first there is the memory of a first childhood meeting (37–41); in the second there is the simile, based on Lucretius, of the heifer searching hopelessly for her mate (85–89)—this simile, which exactly suits the girl's situation, is what she wishes on her perfidious lover, and here there is bitter dramatic irony in the sexual inappropriateness. Emotion is expressed in both songs by an interesting use of an objective correlative: in the first it is the repeated use of the reversal of nature, mirroring the unnatural desertion of the lover by his *coniunx* Nysa; in the second it is the details of magical ritual that provide an alternative upside-down world of unreality to an unbearable reality.

Here the poet tells of the singing-contest in his own person as if he himself had been present; the first five lines set a scene of Orphic magic, expressed in the type of incantatory repetition that is one of the generic markers of pastoral.[57] Then the poet turns aside in a parenthesis (6–13) to address Pollio.[58] This address is deliberately set inside the pastoral account, and the effect is twofold: first to separate the persona of the shepherd from that of the author, stressing both (the shepherd's by the details of magic in nature, and the author's by the abrupt movement to the dimension of poetic craft in the real contemporary world—a movement repeated in lines 62–63 where the poet in his own person appeals for inspiration between his report of the two songs); secondly, to create a contemporary Roman connexion to a Roman world of reality. This is a clear index of proportionality, and it is picked up by Roman details in both songs: the first envisages a marriage and in Roman terms; the second contains references to Roman fears of spells on crops (forbidden in the *Twelve Tables*) and to Roman ideas of *perfidia* and the deposit of a pledge (*pignus*). In this *Eclogue* the secondary field concerns itself with the Roman poet's treatment of traditional pastoral themes of unhappy love; or, to put it crudely but more truly, the problem of expressing the dilemma of

---

57. See Williams (1974), pp. 42–43.
58. For explanation of the unnamed addressee, see Williams (1978), p. 130.

unhappy love using the traditional themes of pastoral poetry. Virgil, as it were, shows his shepherds solving that problem in one particular way that still leaves each song a moving poetic statement in itself.

This is all highly self-conscious poetry, and the poet constantly reflects on his own activity; but, by using the technique of the objective framework, he never loses touch with the real world in which he lives. By this technique he has transcended the essential artificiality of Theocritus, who, as a poet, had a tenuous grip on the real world, and who, with the poets of his circle, viewed literary activity as a sort of complicated and learned game whose rules had been laid down in the half-millennium before him. What Virgil does is to drag that type of poetic composition into immediate confrontation with the real Roman world of about 40 B.C., so that both are comprehended in the focus of his *Eclogues*. It is the function of the index in the *Eclogues*, roughly speaking, to provide a bridge between those two worlds.

That is done in several ways that are now worth defining. All of the *Eclogues*, with the exception of the un-pastoral 4, 6, and 10, mention a herdsman of one sort or another in the first line,[59] and each of these characters has a clearly Greek name. That device serves to create an expectation of a Theocritean bucolic setting, with a geographical location in Sicily (or Cos) and a location in time that normally admits of no historical identification. The poet of the *Eclogues* then proceeds to shatter that expectation by rupturing either the illusion of the geographical setting or of the timelessness or of both. The former is done in most of the *Eclogues* by mention of Roman realities of place or culture—these have been briefly indicated in the analyses above: *Eclogue* 7, for instance, is typical, where the speaker Meliboeus identifies the two herdsmen as *Arcades ambo* (4), and then reports one of them as naming the river by which they are sitting as the Mincius. The illusion of time is variously ruptured in the *Eclogues* that create Theocritean expectation: in 1 and 9 it is by the early references that fix the setting in the land-confiscations of 42–40 B.C.; in *Eclogue* 3, by the centrally placed praises of Pollio on the part of the two herdsmen (84–91); in *Eclogue* 5, by the poet's surprising entry in his own bucolic persona into the dramatic scene of the poem (85–87). In *Eclogue* 8 it is done by the lengthy dedication to Pollio, which not only fixes the time precisely as 39 B.C. but is marked as spoken within

59. See Coleman (1977) on *Eclogue* 1.1.

the dramatic illusion of the poem by the fact that the poet describes the pastoral setting in five lines before turning aside to address Pollio. The effect would have been different if that address had opened the poem, since the poet could then be seen to move out from reality into poetic fantasy; instead, he draws reality deliberately into the pastoral fantasy. But the most surprising shattering of the illusion of time is the appearance of Gallus in the non-Theocritean *Eclogue* 6, among the mythical characters in the song of Silenus. In *Eclogue* 10 the illusions both of place and time are shattered by the historical reality of Gallus, not only in the enclosing sections of the poem, but also in the central Theocritean section based on *Idyll* 1.

But the non-Theocritean *Eclogues* also display a rupturing element that occurs occasionally in the Theocritean *Eclogues*. This can be seen in the gift-motif in *Eclogue* 5: the effect of that motif is to create a gap between the poet as a pastoral poet of a Theocritean type, and as an undefined type of poet which he will become and which is somehow adumbrated in the preceding song about the apotheosis of Daphnis. That gap is then taken up in the opening of *Eclogue* 6 in the form of a distance established between the humble genre of the pastoral poet and the higher aspirations of the poet Virgil. (That gap had already appeared in a similar form in the opening of *Eclogue* 4.) That is also the function of the address to Pollio in *Eclogue* 8, and there it measures the distance between the pastoral poet's relationship with Theocritus and Virgil's with distinguished contemporary poets. A corresponding gap is uniquely explored in *Eclogue* 10; there the distance is precisely defined between the persona of the pastoral poet and the real Virgil, not only by means of the contrast between his activity as a goatherd and his real relationship with Gallus in the real world, but also by means of the contrast between the real Gallus and the Gallus who appears in the persona of a tragic lover in his own poetry. In *Eclogue* 10 that gap permits the poet to take leave of pastoral poetry and suggest his movement forward to a different type of poetry. A literary gap of a somewhat different type, but explored in a similarly self-conscious way, will recur as a constant feature of the *Georgics*. This interest in regarding his own poetic activity from a detached viewpoint is as much a characteristic of the *Georgics* as it is of the *Eclogues*.

It was observed above that one effect of the blending of Greek and Roman elements in the *Odes* of Horace was to create an unresolved tension between these elements that provided immediate support to the index of proportionality, since that very tension created the sense of something beyond the ostensible field of the poem. The same effect can be seen in the very similar blending of Greek and Roman elements in the *Eclogues*; in them the tension is an indicator of the gap to be bridged between Theocritean make-believe and another many-faceted field that includes a whole range of features from contemporary reality to poetic ideals. Later imitators and interpreters of Virgil's *Eclogues* simply did not understand the function of the technique and supposed the whole style of composition to be a combination of pretty fantasy with a variable element of allegory or roman à clef. This led easily to Samuel Johnson's harsh judgment on pastoral when he wrote of *Lycidas* in his *Life of Milton*: 'In this poem there is no nature, for there is nothing new. Its form is that of a pastoral, easy, vulgar, and therefore disgusting; whatever images it can supply are long ago exhausted, and its inherent improbability always forces dissatisfaction on the mind'. But the essence of the Virgilian technique lies in the creation of a sense of a gap between an ostensible field and an unspoken field, and the provision of poetic bridges to span it.

What is strikingly original in this respect in the *Eclogues* is the poet's constant exploration and play on that gap; it is the single most imaginatively exciting feature of the *Eclogues*. That constitution of a gap between an apparently simple ostensible field and another field of wide-ranging complexity is also a central feature of the composition of the *Georgics*; and, as in the *Eclogues*, the poet constantly focusses his attention on that gap. Analysis here must concentrate simply on this particular feature of the *Georgics*, and every other aspect of this immensely rich poem will be ignored.

The scale of the *Georgics* required a more complex adaptation of the technique. Traditional analysis has regarded the poem as a work on agriculture, with other topics treated in a series of digressions, more or less tenuously related to the technical subject-matter. The poem can, however, be regarded as composed by means of the technique of the objective framework. The ostensible field of the poem concerns the relationship of the poet-as-teacher with his subject-matter, with the problems of agriculture in Italy, and with his addressees, Italian farmers. The unspoken field is the synecdochically related field of mankind (and the poet) in his relationship with the universe as a whole, in its temporal, geographical, religious, cultural, political, and moral extensions. Constantly recurring indexes of proportionality keep the secondary field in view as a background, in such a way that many details of the primary field are immediately referable to a location also within the secondary field.

The genre of didactic poetry, a branch of epic, had long previously established a persona for the didactic poet: he was a teacher addressing his pupils from the fullness of his own knowledge. Lucretius had added to that the capacity of the author to reflect self-consciously as poet on his poetic activity as he wrestled with recalcitrant material to make it palatable and suited to poetry. Virgil extended that capacity for self-conscious reflection widely in constantly recurring passages throughout the work, so that the feature is transformed to become a suggestive index of proportionality to the secondary field. This begins with the great invocation in Book 1. There Maecenas is addressed (2), as the poet announces the various aspects of his subject-matter. This list (1–4), though intentionally bald, already contains an important feature: (4) *apibus quanta experientia parcis*, 'what experience is needed for keeping thrifty bees'. Here the adjective *parcis*, with its sense of a virtue admired by Romans, creates an unexpected moral dimension, not in the pupil but in the object of his labours. Also the word *experientia* is used by Virgil only once elsewhere—as he begins (316) the account of *bougonia* that occupies the second half of Book 4. (This suggestion of a ring-composition between Books 1 and 4 will be explored further below.)

The poet then calls on a series of deities for help: the sun and moon, Bacchus, Ceres, Fauns, Dryads, Neptune, Aristaeus, Pan, Minerva, Triptolemus, Silvanus, and all gods and goddesses who have to do with farming (5–23). He then adds an address (24–42) to one who is destined to become a god, Caesar, asking him to act as if he were a god already and to give his blessing to the poet (40). The address to the various gods and the address to Caesar are almost exactly equal in length. This latter address does not, of course, in any way clash with that to Maecenas, since Octavian is addressed in the special capacity of a prospective deity. But the unexpected address to the living ruler of the Roman world, contrasting strongly with the preceding Greek deities, has a threefold effect. First, it introduces a Roman political dimension, since this man is addressed in virtue both of his relationship to Julius Caesar and of his own achievements that have brought him to pre-eminence in Rome (though this is latent and will only become explicit later in the poem). Second, Caesar is invested with potential authority in all regions of the universe. This allows the poet to survey the earth (both cities and countryside), the sea, the heavens, and (with a deprecation) the underworld, so suggesting a field that is coterminous with the universe itself. In various ways all these regions of the universe will figure in the poem. Thirdly, the appeal to Caesar suggests a modification of the announced subject-matter (1–4), for the poet says (40–42):

> da facilem cursum atque audacibus adnue coeptis,
> ignarosque viae mecum miseratus agrestis
> ingredere et votis iam nunc adsuesce vocari.

'Make easy my course for me and give your assent to my audacious plans, and, joining me in pity for farmers who do not know the path, begin and accustom yourself even now to be called upon in prayer.'

The request for 'an easy course' and the description of his plans as 'audacious' suggest an undertaking far more wide-ranging than the modest list of topics outlined in lines 1–4. This suggestion is underlined by the echo of a famous phrase of Lucretius in line 41. In *de rerum natura* 2.7–16 Lucretius says:

> sed nil dulcius est bene quam munita tenere
> edita doctrina sapientum templa serena,
> despicere unde queas alios passimque videre
> errare atque viam palantis quaerere vitae,
> certare ingenio, contendere nobilitate,
> noctes atque dies niti praestante labore
> ad summas emergere opes rerumque potiri.
> o miseras hominum mentis, o pectora caeca!
> qualibus in tenebris vitae quantisque periclis
> degitur hoc aevi quodcumque est!

'But nothing is more enjoyable than to dwell in elevated regions that are fortified by the calm teachings of the wise, from which you can look down and see the others wandering about everywhere and going astray as they search for the path of life, vying with each other on grounds of ability or fame, night and day struggling with extraordinary effort to reach the height of wealth and possess the world. O wretched minds of men! O blind hearts! In what darkness of life and in what dangers is passed this little span of our time here!'

That passage supplies the background and tone of Virgil's phrase. It will be taken up again later in the famous passage at the end of Book 2 (458–59):

> o fortunatos nimium, sua si bona norint,
> agricolas!

'O farmers, blessed and more than blessed—if only they should come to realise their advantages!'

The poet has in mind something more than the technical problems of agriculture; it is something that can only be expressed by saying that the life of the farmer represents an ideal form of the relationship between man and the universe in which he finds himself. It is a task of the poet to make that relationship known to men who do not understand it. In fact, the whole of this address to Caesar establishes, right at the beginning of the poem, a clear index of proportionality to a field that is far greater than that of the ostensible subject-matter. The poet's task is one that can encompass the ruler of the Roman world and every region of the universe. The passage is no mere flattery of Octavian added at a late stage. It not only functions as an index; it also anticipates later themes throughout the *Georgics*, but especially in Book 4. There is a clear ring-composition with the *sphragis* (4.559–66), where it becomes explicit that Octavian is making his way to the heavens (562, *viamque adfectat Olympo*) not in virtue of his relationship to Julius Caesar, but through the victories he is winning against Rome's external enemies. That theme is also conspicuous in the beginning of Book 3. The negative treatment of the underworld also anticipates the theme of Orpheus' visit there in Book 4 (467–515), and the name of Proserpina recurs there (1.39 and 4.487). This ring-composition is underlined by what can only be treated as a whimsical *jeu d'esprit*. Maecenas is addressed four times in the *Georgics* at the beginning of each book: in Books 2 and 3 the address comes at line 41, while in Books 1 and 4 the address comes in line 2.

A different type of index of proportionality, but one that also derives from the poet's self-conscious reflection on his own activity, occurs at *Georgics* 1.176–86. There he introduces instructions on how to treat mice and moles and toads and weevils and ants, in these words (176–77):

possum multa tibi veterum praecepta referre,
ni refugis tenuisque piget cognoscere curas.

'I am able to recall for you many rules of the ancients, unless you are rushing away and feeling bored at learning of such trivial cares.'

Having thus established the distance between these tiny creatures and the human world (while apparently simply indulging a traditional formula of politeness), the poet goes on to treat them in human terms, with fine mock-heroic humour. The importance of this is that it refers all living things to one scale, on which there are differences of size and constitution, but it makes those differences essentially irrelevant to the poet's eye. This is therefore another index of proportionality to the secondary field. It will be important in Book 2, where trees and plants are treated as having human qualities, and it will be vital in creating not only the scenes of love's power at work in the universe in Book 3, but also the tragedy caused by disease at the end of the same book.

The prooemium to Book 2 only begins after the poet is well started on his theme. The book opens with a prayer to Bacchus (1–8), and then (the reverse of the procedure in Book 1) the poet calls on farmers to learn the cultivation of trees and especially of the vine and the olive (35–38); then he appeals to Maecenas (39–46):

tuque ades inceptumque una decurre laborem,
o decus, o famae merito pars maxima nostrae,   40
Maecenas, pelagoque volans da vela patenti.
non ego cuncta meis amplecti versibus opto,
non, mihi si linguae centum sint oraque centum,
ferrea vox. ades et primi lege litoris oram;
in manibus terrae. non hic te carmine ficto   45
atque per ambages et longa exorsa tenebo.

'And you, please be present to help and skim with me over the task I have undertaken, Maecenas, my glory and properly the greatest part of my fame (40);[60] and, flying along, set all sail for the open sea. My intention is not to include everything in my poetry, not if I had a hundred tongues, a

60. This address to Maecenas is imitated by Propertius in 2.1.73–4: see p. 172 above.

hundred mouths, a voice of steel. Be present and skirt the shore of the nearby coast: the land will be close at hand. In this I shall not detain you with mythic poetry (45) and digressions and tedious preludes.'

Conington's comment on line 41 was: 'however understood, it clashes with the imagery of vv. 44, 45'; and Peerlkamp reversed the order of lines 41 and 42 in order to bring the reference to the open sea under the influence of *non*. But the sea is 'open' as distinct from the harbour from which the journey starts; its openness also serves to make a claim to originality that is not made explicitly before the end of the great passage in praise of Italy (174–76) and then in the opening of Book 3. The real emphasis falls on *volans* and *da vela*. The keynote is speed of movement and certainty of course (guaranteed by keeping the shoreline in sight). This is important because it is a measure both of the vastness of the subject and of the poet's capacity to control it. The poet's selectivity is analogous to the skill of a mariner. The climax of this prooemium functions as an index of proportionality to the secondary field in a novel way. The denial of mythical themes will recur in the prologue to Book 3, but the importance of the denial of digressions lies in the fact that it follows closely on what commentators regard as the major digression which ends Book 1 (463–514) and precedes the extensive 'digression' (458–542) at the end of Book 2— not to mention the passage on the praises of Italy (136–74). The denial in effect affirms that these so-called digressions are integral to the poem and its subject-matter, and that they are what I have called indexes of proportionality to the secondary field. What the poet asserts by implication in these words is the essential interlocking of the primary (or ostensible) and the secondary fields.

This interdependence of the two fields is asserted at the end of Book 2, in an autobiographical passage (475–94) inserted in the great 'digression' on the moral quality of the farmer's life (458–542). There the poet prays that the Muses may reveal to him the secrets of the universe (475–82). If, however, a defect of intellect in him prevents that (483–84), then he would live in the country amid rivers and woods, without fame. He sums up his view in the famous contrast (490–94):

> felix qui potuit rerum cognoscere causas
> atque metus omnis et inexorabile fatum

subiecit pedibus strepitumque Acherontis avari:
fortunatus et ille deos qui novit agrestis
Panaque Silvanumque senem Nymphasque sorores.

'Happy the man who has been able to learn the causes of things and has
trampled under his feet all fear and inexorable Fate and the roar of greedy
Acheron: blessed also is he who knows the gods of the country—Pan and the
aged Silvanus and the sister nymphs.'

All commentators seem to understand that Virgil is regretting his
inability to be a Lucretius, and opting for a second-best which is still
highly desirable. But all that is in the poet's words is a desire to understand the universe and a frank acknowledgment of the extreme difficulty
of the task (together with a note of scepticism about its possibility);
this is accompanied by an assertion that life in the country and knowledge of it is open to any man who has the will. What is missing,
however, is exactly the will; and the reason why it is missing is that
men do not understand. What the poet strives for is that understanding
—(458) *sua si bona norint*: it is difficult and analogous to the achievement
of Lucretius, but, by implication, the poet hopes to attain it and pass
it on. But there is also here a disturbing note of deep pessimism that,
because of some defect in himself, he may fail in his hopes (483–84);
and this is a note that will recur later in other contexts. The whole
passage should be read as another original and unobtrusive index of
proportionality to the secondary field. In effect, the relative treatment
given by the poet to the two areas of experience enacts the relationship
in his own poem between the primary (technical) and the secondary
(Lucretian) fields. The poet is not abandoning the hope of a Lucretian
achievement; his worry concerns his success in the endeavour.

Book 3 opens with a very elaborate prooemium which, according
to the usual interpretation, would blatantly contradict the poet's
denial of (2.46) *longa exorsa*. The first two lines address Pales and
Apollo and Pan—appropriately, since the subject of the book is livestock. With a surprising turn, the poet then dismisses 'all other themes'
as hackneyed (3–4); he lists Eurystheus, Busiris, Hylas, Delos, Hippodamia, and Pelops. The poet must find a new path to fame (8–9);
if he lives, he will bring the Muses in triumph (11, *deducam*) to Italy.
He will be the first to bring Palestinian palms to Mantua (12), and
there, by the Mincius, he will build a marble temple (13–15). Caesar

will be its occupying deity (16), and, in his honour, the poet will race a hundred chariots victoriously along the river (17–18). All Greece will abandon Olympia and Nemea, and will come to contest with the poet in races and boxing (19–20). The poet will win (21–22),[61] and already looks forward to processions and sacrifices and dramatic performances (21–25). In the temple will be represented all the triumphs of Caesar (25–33), but also his Trojan ancestors (34–36). Envy will be shown to be in fear of the tortures of the underworld (37–39). Meanwhile, however, the poet calls on Maecenas to help him continue the *Georgics* (40–45). Then he says (46–48):

> mox tamen ardentis accingar dicere pugnas
> Caesaris et nomen fama tot ferre per annos,
> Tithoni prima quot abest ab origine Caesar.

'Soon, however, I shall gird myself to sing the blazing battles of Caesar and bear aloft his name in fame through as many years as Caesar himself is distant from his earliest ancestor, Tithonus.'

In this prooemium, the words (3) *cetera quae vacuas tenuissent carmine mentes / omnia iam vulgata* 'all other themes that might have charmed idle minds in poetry—they are all of them hackneyed', both constitute an implicit claim to originality for the *Georgics* and also make way for a metonymic transfer to a new field—that of epic— with a list of Greek mythological themes. When the poet then says that he also must find a path to fame, he is not excluding the *Georgics* (he had already made a claim for them in 2.174–76, will make another in 3.291–93, and yet another in 4.6–7), but his eyes are fixed on the new field. His originality in epic will come from combining Greek and Roman themes. On the epithet (12) *Idumaeas*, applied to the palms of victory, the comment of Conington is typical: '*Idumaeas* would be otiose if applied only to palms: it is worse than otiose, as drawing a contrast between *palmas* and *Mantua*'. But the epithet's function is to support the picture of the poet celebrating a Roman triumph over external foes in the Eastern empire. The ideas proceed by a combination of metonymic and metaphoric modes. The triumph is metonymically related to the temple built to celebrate it and to

---

61. This is left to be understood in the gap between the games and the poet's extensive celebration.

the games instituted to commemorate its foundation. But the triumph, temple, and games themselves form an elaborate Pindaric metaphor[62] for the composition of an epic poem. At that point there is another metonymic connexion with the list of Greek myths (4–8): all Greece will abandon Olympia (founded by Pelops) and Nemea (founded by Hercules)—the Pythian games are not mentioned but are suggested in the mention of (6) *Latonia Delos*. And there is a further, latent, connexion in the Greek myths: Hercules, the saviour-god, figures in the first three of them, and Augustan poets often used him as a symbol of Augustus. The poet's own triumph fades into the theme which the temple will celebrate: the military triumphs of Octavian. It will also celebrate the Trojan ancestors, and it will threaten with the torments of the underworld those who enviously oppose Octavian (37, *Invidia*). Here the poet turns aside again to return to the *Georgics*. That poem presents no mean task (41, *haud mollia iussa*); but, with Maecenas' help, the poet will achieve something *altum* (42). The poet feels the inspiration, the call of his subject (43–45). Soon he will celebrate Caesar in an epic beginning from Troy.

If—as commentators seem to assume—the poet is anxiously assuring Octavian that his turn for celebration will come, why does this appear in the *Georgics*, and why at this point? A letter would have discharged so irrelevant a task more appropriately. Commentators go on to ask how this promise relates to the *Aeneid* as we have it. Conington's comment on line 48 is again typical: 'The promise here given, or rather repeated, was fulfilled in the composition of the *Aeneid*; but the manner of its performance was very different from anything sketched here; indeed the method proposed was exactly reversed in practice, the mythical ancestors of Rome and the Julian family being made the central figures, and Augustus and his exploits only accessory.' It certainly seems clear that a plan for the *Aeneid* was in the poet's mind as he wrote this passage (just as a plan for the *Georgics* was in his mind as he wrote *Eclogue* 6). But why irrelevantly spill it out here, and, in any case, why not get it right? The prime relevance of this passage must be to the *Georgics*, and that purpose must have conditioned the shape and emphasis which the poet gave to his thoughts about the *Aeneid* here.

Interpretation may start from an earlier passage (2.167–76) that provides a clear index of proportionality to the secondary field of the *Georgics*:

62. See especially Wilkinson (1969), pp. 167–68.

haec genus acre virum, Marsos pubemque Sabellam
adsuetumque malo Ligurem Volscosque verutos
extulit, haec Decios Marios magnosque Camillos,
Scipiadas duros bello et te, maxime Caesar,   170
qui nunc extremis Asiae iam victor in oris
imbellem avertis Romanis arcibus Indum.
salve, magna parens frugum, Saturnia tellus,
magna virum: tibi res antiquae laudis et artem
ingredior sanctos ausus recludere fontis,   175
Ascraeumque cano Romana per oppida carmen.

'This land [Italy] has raised a fierce breed of men, Marsians, young Sabine men, Ligurians inured to hardship, and Volscians armed with darts; it has produced men like Decius, or Marius, or the great Camillus, or Scipio unyielding in war, and it has produced you, greatest Caesar (170), who now, victorious on the farthest shores of Asia, beat the Indian, not bred for war, back from the citadels of Rome. Hail, great mother of harvests, land of Saturn, mother of men: in your honour I begin on themes of old glory and skill, bold to open up springs of inspiration (175), and through Roman towns I sing a Hesiodic song.'

A series of statements is made here. First, using Lucretian language (1.927), the poet claims originality for the *Georgics*, but in a characteristically modest way (175). The second statement is made only here, and it is surprising: the poem is being composed in honour of Italy. The climax of the whole passage on the pre-eminence of Italy (136 ff.) treats Italy as mother of great men, and it is in honour of her in this historical aspect, at least as much as in her agricultural aspect, that the poem is said to be composed. The Italians celebrated are all warriors, and the climax to this historical view of Italy is the picture of Caesar defeating Rome's external enemies. This takes up and corrects, as it were, the pessimistic view, expressed at the end of Book 1, of war raging all round the Roman empire and of things out of control (1.509–14)—unless the gods allow Octavian to continue living on earth. It is an index of proportionality to that part of the secondary field of the *Georgics* which comprises a historical view of Italy culminating in the achievements of Octavian.

That theme is taken to greater heights in the prooemium to Book 3 (and it will recur in the *sphragis* of Book 4); but since it is a theme that belongs only to the secondary field of the *Georgics*, the poet devises an index of proportionality on each occasion. In Book 3 the index is provided by the poet's looking forward in review to his next work—from the originality of the *Georgics* to the originality of the *Aeneid*, both similarly original in combining Greek and Roman elements. But the act of looking forward to the *Aeneid* does not deny that historical theme to the *Georgics*. On the contrary, the poet's self-conscious reflection on his own poetic activity is intended to provide an index of proportionality to the Roman and historical aspect of the secondary field of the *Georgics*, and that is why such an odd and inaccurate preview of the *Aeneid* is given. Even the theme of the underworld is adapted to this purpose. At the end of Book 1, it was the envy (504, *invidet*) of the gods that was a danger to Rome's possession of Octavian; in 3.37 it is the envy of possible rivals of Octavian's power that the poet will represent as threatened by tortures in the underworld. This theme of the underworld, like that of Caesar's triumphs, is a connecting link in the *Georgics* and, like the triumphs too, is an element only of the secondary field, requiring an index of proportionality in 1.36–39, 3.37–39, and 4.467–506. This is not the underworld as it will appear in *Aeneid* 6, any more than the metaphor of the temple in honour of Octavian adequately represents the way the *Aeneid* treats contemporary history; both themes are shaped to serve their purpose as an index to the unspoken field of the *Georgics*, and show the poet's mind occupied with that field as he is engaged on composing the *Georgics*, under the guise of reflecting on a real, projected future work. What is said is, as often, metonymically related to what is not said: what is said about the future work is to be applied also to the present work, which is in no way suggested to be second-best. But there is nevertheless an unmistakable suggestion, merely in the poet's looking forward to the next work to achieve something which is also a part of the present work, that he is conscious of possible failure. The optimism invested in the future and the resolve to try to achieve fame for himself (8–9) suggests a present and disturbing pessimism, as if the task may, in some way, be beyond the poet's powers.

Further self-conscious reflection on the poet's own activity provides another index later in the book, 3.284–94:

> sed fugit interea, fugit inreparabile tempus,
> singula dum capti circumvectamur amore.   285
> hoc satis armentis: superat pars altera curae,

lanigeros agitare greges hirtasque capellas;
hic labor, hinc laudem fortes sperate coloni.
nec sum animi dubius verbis ea vincere magnum
quam sit, et angustis hunc addere rebus honorem;   290
sed me Parnasi deserta per ardua dulcis
raptat amor; iuvat ire iugis, qua nulla priorum
Castaliam molli devertitur orbita clivo.
nunc, veneranda Pales, magno nunc ore sonandum.

'But meanwhile time runs away, time that cannot be made up again, while, captivated by love, we keep circling around single details (285). That is enough on large livestock: there remains the second part of the work, to deal with wool-bearing flocks and shaggy goats; here is toil, from this, sturdy farmers, look for glory. And my mind is in no doubt how mighty a task it is to master those themes in words and add poetic distinction to narrow topics (290). But sweet love compels me to traverse deserted heights of Parnassus: it is my delight to scale ridges where no path of a predecessor turns aside to Castalia by an easy slope. Now, divine Pales, now must I speak with a loftier sound.'

The poet has just been describing the ravages of *amor* in the world; the same emotion tempts him to spoil the proportions of his work and, that resisted, now inspires him to tackle a very difficult area. The claim to originality is the most explicit in the *Georgics*, but it is modestly undercut by being placed at the opening of what is admitted to be a testing section: the poet does not claim success; he prays for it. The passage serves—in the use of the word *amor*—as an index of proportionality to connect the previous section on the destructive power of love to the secondary field and to open up a cosmic view of the power of love. But there is another feature here. The poet speaks as if the problem of treating sheep and goats were merely a question of how to make them poetic. Yet he talks of his inspiration in high poetic terms and of the style needed in terms of epic (294, *magno nunc ore sonandum*). There is here a gap between subject-matter and treatment that is measurably the same as the gap that was noticed between the poet's listing of his subject-matter in 1.1–4 and his later reference to it in 1.40–41. The reason for the gap is the same in both cases: it measures the distance between the primary and the secondary fields. Sheep and goats belong to the most sheerly technical part of the poet's material, yet they too will establish their claim to a place in the secondary field: they are not just objects of agricultural technique, but share a place with human beings in the universe as a whole. The poet's self-conscious reflection here establishes an index of proportionality to two striking passages that follow: in the first (339–83) the poet's vision widens to take in the condition of humans and animals in two opposite regions: in the scorching land of Libya, and in the icebound snowfields of Scythia; both are portraits of great imagination and feeling. In the second, which ends the book (478–566), the poet describes the epidemic in Noricum in tones of universal tragedy (*magno nunc ore sonandum*) that regards animals and human beings as not essentially different.

A similar gap can be seen in the prooemium to Book 4 between the bees (3, *levium spectacula rerum*) and the way the poet speaks of them (4–5):

> magnanimosque duces totiusque ordine gentis
> mores et studia et populos et proelia dicam.

'I shall tell in order of great-hearted commanders and of the character of the whole nation and of their peoples and of their battles.'

That gap is then translated into the self-conscious poet's terms (6–7):

> in tenui labor: at tenuis non gloria, si quem
> numina laeva sinunt auditque vocatus Apollo.

'My labour is on trivial things; but not trivial is the glory if adverse deities allow and Apollo hears a poet's prayer.'

Here, too, the gap measures the distance between the primary and the secondary fields, and is an index of proportionality to the participation of the bees in the secondary field: *sub specie aeternitatis* the bees can be seen behaving not only as human beings but as Romans, and even in some ways—notably in their lack of sexual drive, which frees them for total patriotic devotion of their lives (197–209)—as superior to Romans.[63]

63. There is clearly an echo here of the sort of idealising that formed the background to Augustus' moral legislation; but fear of the destructive power of sexual love recurs constantly in all Virgil's writing.

The same gap, spanning the distance between the two fields of the poem, appears finally in the *sphragis*. The poet contrasts the activity of Caesar, warring victoriously against external foes and imposing Roman civilisation on a grateful world, with his own life in Naples, devoted 'to the pursuits of inglorious inactivity'. The poet, as mere teacher, is inactive and inglorious in contrast to his subject-matter which, in the primary field, concerns 'the cultivation of fields and herds and trees' (559–60); but he is at an even greater remove from the activity of his secondary field which, in the aspect stressed here, concerns the destiny of the Roman state in the world. The shape given here to the latter field is designed to take it up as a theme that has permeated the whole poem and to add the final touch to it: the divine immortality which the poet foresaw for Rome's ruler at the beginning of the poem will be no more than the due reward for his own efforts and achievements— (562) *viamque adfectat Olympo*. The primary field—(1.168) *divini gloria ruris*—and the secondary field—Rome's proper destiny in the world— are united in the last words of the poem in a contrast with the inactivity of the poet, whose fame, in contrast to that of the farmer or of Caesar, is as nothing (the *Eclogues*, with a mention of which he signs off, being dismissed as a mere *lusus*): the poet's is an *otium* that wins no fame.[64] The idea, with an underlying note of pessimism (after all allowances for self-depreciating humour and irony), takes up the same note of pessimism that was implicit in the prooemium to Book 3 and explicit in 2.486 *flumina amem silvasque inglorius*.

To these passages of self-conscious reflection by the poet on his own activity could be added 4.116–48, where he regrets that, since he is 'drawing in his sails and hastening to turn the prow towards the land', he is unable to talk about gardens. With a neat *praeteritio*, he lists what he has to omit (119–24), and allows this to remind him of an ideal garden he once saw near Tarentum, worked by an old pirate out of recalcitrant land. Here the gap between the poet's wishes and the exigencies of the work allows him to bridge that other gap between the technical details of the subject and the ideal of human existence, in a portrait that draws together themes from Books 1 and 2 of physical work as a condition of human life, of Italy as the ideal agent of Nature and product of toil, and of the ideal life of the farmer. The two fields of the poem are here approximated swiftly and unobtrusively, with the secondary field

---

64. Cf. 2.486, *flumina amem silvasque inglorius*.

apprehended through the thematic connexions with earlier passages of the poem.

The recurring self-conscious reflections of the poet on his own activity that constitute indexes of proportionality excite constant awareness of the secondary field, and that sense of its omnipresence in the background gives significance and depth to all the poet's technical instructions on agriculture. The secondary field is continuously alive in the poet's mind, as, for instance, in the frequent metaphor of the farmer as a Roman soldier fighting and subduing the fields (e.g. 1.99, *imperat arvis*), or in the vision of young plants as young people (2.270, *adeo in teneris consuescere multum est*). It was consequently open to him to transfer to the secondary field at will, without making any but tenuous connexions with the primary field—hence the great series of so-called digressions, at least two to each book. In the first book (118–59) the poet establishes the proposition that Juppiter made toil the fundamental condition of the moral life, on which all progress and happiness depend, by giving a novel account of the fall from the Golden Age. In the great ending to that book (463–514), in which he portrays the peril of the Roman world beleaguered by wars, the connexion to the primary field is made by occasional motifs: Eridanus floods and carries away woods and cattle together with the stables (481–82); the time will come when farmers will plough up weapons and bones in the fields of Philippi (493–97); and the general proposition, which is not stated in so many words but underlies the viewpoint, that agricultural prosperity is the fundamental symbol of Peace. The praise of Italy (2.136–76) begins with agricultural considerations but soon takes wing deep into the historical aspect of the secondary field. The great passage with which Book 2 ends (458–540) begins with a concrete valuation of the farmer's life as against life in the city; then it swerves into the poet's reflections on his poetry and returns to equate the virtues of country life, not only with absence of the miseries associated with ambition, but also with absence of civil war; and, positively, with existence as it was in the far, ideal past of Rome; and, finally, with the Golden Age itself. The implication of the passage is that this ideal state can be restored.

The grim view of Book 1, with man fighting against Nature and the Roman against himself and the world, gives way in Book 2 to a vision of Nature's co-operation with man and of man's finding ideal happiness in a life lived close to Nature. These two contrasted aspects correspond, as it were, to the two poles of life: toil and celebration. But the poet uses this opportunity, created in the primary field, also to move from political pessimism (modified, however, by a clear hope) to political optimism, and that optimism grows steadily to its climax in the *sphragis* (which means, incidentally, that political views cannot be used to distinguish between passages of the *Georgics* as composed at earlier or later times, since that growth of optimism must have been part of the artistic design). But the universe itself contains, as a constituent element, seeds of tragedy, and it is this, not the political state of man, that darkens Book 3, which, apart from its prooemium, is the least political of the four books; consequently the movement between the two fields is at is simplest in this book. The three great set pieces of Book 3—passages on the destructive force of passion (242–83), on the life of herdsmen in Libya and Scythia (339–83), and on the destructive force of disease (478–566)—all take their origin in obvious ways from the primary field, but gather force and depth from the universalizing dimensions of the secondary field.

The most difficult of all the passages that move out into the secondary field is the last; it is the climax to the whole poem. It is a myth, and from its excess of adequacy to the immediate context (where it purports to be an aetiology of *bougonia*), it can be inferred that its meaning is greater than appears at first sight. It is constructed on the pattern of poem 64 of Catullus: it contains a myth within a myth. The myth of Aristaeus' discovery of how to create a swarm of bees contains within it the myth of Orpheus and Eurydice. In fact, the whole passage functions in the manner of the myth of Laudamia and Protesilaus in Catullus 68: the myths take the place of statements in primary language and require that the reader's imagination work in co-operation with the poet's to apprehend, rather than reconstruct in discursive prose, the gist of the propositions for which the myths have been substituted. The structural character of the whole passage as a digression is carefully marked by the poet's repetition (in largely different words) at the end of the passage (548–58) of the subject-matter that led into the myths (295–314).[65]

The passage notably treats a number of themes that have occurred earlier in the poem, but that have either had an apparently local significance only in their own contexts, or else have had only a distant,

65. On this structural feature, see p. 101 above.

often figurative, significance for the main subject-matter of the poem. For instance, the theme of the sea runs through the poem, but it is not really central to the subject-matter; it is used in metaphors and similes and comparisions. In this final passage it plays a central part, together with Neptune and Proteus and sea-nymphs. Again, the destructive nature of love's power was the subject of a set piece in Book 3; here it recurs memorably, not only in the figure of Orpheus and his relationship with Eurydice, but also in his death at the hands of Ciconian matrons and in Aristaeus' pursuit of Eurydice that caused her death. It also recurs here as the subject-matter of Clymene's song (345–47), showing even the gods subject to its disruptive force. The underworld was deliberately introduced by the poet into his invocation of Caesar at the beginning of the poem, with specific mention of Proserpina (36–39). Here the theme returns on an extended scale (467–506), and Proserpina plays a central part in the drama (487). The theme had also been used as part of the poet's wish to master the universe (2.490–91) and in the prooemium to Book 3 (37–39). It is also into an underworld —but a very different underworld—that Aristaeus descends to meet his mother (357–73). There are also many minor thematic connexions. For instance, Apollo, father of Aristaeus (323), makes a link with the prooemia to Books 3 and 4. The rivers Tiber and Eridanus were conspicuous at the end of Book 1 (499, 482); Aristaeus sees their sources beneath the earth (4.369, 372). Rhodope appeared at 1.332 and 3.351 and 462; it reappears in 4.461. The Getae appeared in 3.462 and now reappear in 4.463. The land of the Hyperboreans was mentioned in 3.196 and 381; now again in 4.517. Riphaeus, too, occurred in 1.240 and 3.382; it recurs in 4.518. Most striking here is the occurrence together of Hyperboreans and Riphaeus in the memorable passage on herdsmen of the Northlands, which is repeated in the picture of the desolate Orpheus. These thematic connexions not only create a technical poetic unity; they also create a unity of time, place, and action, a universe that is defined and familiar, the same for the whole range of actors.

On the face of it the whole passage is an extended excursion into the secondary field of the *Georgics*: its themes concern the universe rather than the farm. But indexes of proportionality that provide a bridge back to the subject-matter of agriculture are as clear to see here as in the passage on Rome at the end of Book 1. Here the theme of bees provides an immediate link to the subject-matter of Book 4.

Further, Aristaeus is not merely, or even primarily, a bee-keeper; he is also a shepherd and farmer (326–32). Again, Proteus is portrayed as a shepherd, and a simile comparing him to a mountain herdsman underlines the thematic link (425–36): Proteus is the equivalent at sea of the farmer-shepherd on land.

As with Catullus 64, the contrasts between the two myths are more conspicuous than their connexions. The greatest contrast is that Aristaeus brings his bees back to life again, as it were, while Orpheus fails to bring Eurydice up from the underworld. It has already been said that Orpheus and Aristaeus both descend to underworlds, but they are very different underworlds, as are also the rivers they both see (363–73 and 478–80); and Aristaeus listens to music there, but Orpheus' music is his one means of obtaining a hearing from the grim powers. Orpheus goes with great daring (467–70); Aristaeus has the right of a god to go (358–59). Orpheus wrests a concession from powers that heed no human prayers (470, *nesciaque humanis precibus mansuescere corda*), and when he makes a small mistake there is no forgiveness: (489) *ignoscenda quidem—scirent si ignoscere Manes*. But Aristaeus, who has committed a considerable sin, pays a small penalty and his crime is easily expiated (453–56). And, while the powers of the underworld are adamant against Orpheus, the nymphs are only too ready to hear Aristaeus, forgive him, and make amends (534–36). In fact, Orpheus is subject to all the frailties of the human condition faced with the fact of death, while Aristaeus is not only divine himself but all the gods are on his side, and he is a being in harmony with the whole of the universe (except for his crime—that turns out to be so venial).

Such are the contrasts, and what is important here is that these contrasts are not the accidental product of the myths in themselves; it was exactly the poet's own alterations of the traditional myths that produced these specific contrasts. For Virgil invented the connexion between Aristaeus and Eurydice, the part played by Proteus, and, most important, the failure of Orpheus to bring Eurydice up from the underworld. There is a further contrast which is the result of stylistic deliberation. The enclosing narrative of Aristaeus' visit to Clymene, her various speeches, and the capture of Proteus are all characterised throughout by the pretty rococo narrative-technique of Hellenistic poets. This contrasts equally strongly with the deeply emotional, tragic tones of the story of Orpheus,[66] as with the starkly realistic

---

66. See Otis (1963), pp. 194–201, though he does not use these terms.

descriptions of bees produced from rotting carcases which precede and end the whole passage. This stylistic contrast is closely parallel to that between the pretty story of Silenus' capture in *Eclogue* 6 and the highly emotional tale, for instance, of Pasiphae.

These various contrasts can be summed up and explained by the hypothesis that Aristaeus is a mythic symbol of the farmer deeply in harmony with the world in which he lives, subject, indeed, to loss and destruction, but capable of recovery by hard work and willingness to undertake unpleasant tasks. Knowledge is the great key to mastery of his condition. On the other hand, Orpheus is, on this hypothesis, the mythic symbol of the poet, who, however great his powers, fights a hostile or, at least, an alien world and is subject to total unexpected and irreversible failure at the last moment. His powers to influence others remain, as those of Orpheus remained after he returned from Hades so that tigers lay at his feet and oak trees followed him (509–10), but he fails to accomplish what he most wanted, though it seemed at one time wholly within his powers. His knowledge and his powers do not help him against irrational, inexplicable failure. This contrast takes up the contrast expressed by the poet at the end of Book 2 between the joys of understanding the universe on the one hand and of living in the country on the other. In fact, the figure of Orpheus gathers together themes expressed in the series of passages throughout the poem where the poet reflected self-consciously on his own activity. The pessimism expressed in Book 4, however, goes further than that inherent in the contrast at the end of Book 2 or in the prooemium to Book 3, and seems to bring out into the open doubts felt by the poet who, engaged on the *Georgics*, yet in Book 3 looked forward to the *Aeneid* as in some way capable of treating themes that the *Georgics* dealt with only inadequately and of guaranteeing the poet immortal fame. Another form of the contrast is expressed in the *sphragis* that follows the myths of Aristaeus and Orpheus: there it is put in the form of a distinction between the victorious leader who can change the world for the better and gains immortality in that way, and the poet devoted to the pursuits of inglorious inactivity.

The secondary field of the *Georgics* comprises the relationship between man and the universe, as it can be exemplified in various aspects of that relationship, and one of these is that of the poet and his subject-matter. *Eclogue* 9 posed the problem of the power of poetry as a force in the real world; it turned out that poetry had no such power—it simply has the capacity to comfort the distressed. In the

Georgics the very capacity of the poet to achieve the task he set himself seems called into question, and in this respect the poet is contrasted not only with the ruler of the Roman people, but with the practical, hard-working farmer. Both Caesar and the farmer (*divini gloria ruris*) have fame within their grasp: it eludes the poet. This is the tone (however self-depreciating it also is) of the *sphragis*: 'an inactivity that wins no fame' must recall (3.8–9) *temptanda via est qua me quoque possim / tollere humo*; that *me quoque* is recalled in the *sphragis*, no less than the hopes for victory that the poet, in the same context, pinned on his next work (3.9, *victorque virum volitare per ora*).

In the *Eclogues* the relationship between the ostensible and the unspoken fields was often suggested by the poet's self-consciously exploring a gap between a literal dependence on Theocritean make-believe and the poet's own world of about 40 B.C. That exploration was sometimes literary, in the sense that it involved a contrast between the persona of a herdsman in a Theocritean world and a real poet wrestling with, and reflecting upon, poetic problems in the Roman world of 40 B.C. But the persistent identity of the didactic poet's persona in the *Georgics* permitted a more consistent technique. The gap between the ostensible and the unspoken fields is there always measured in terms of the poet's self-conscious reflection on his own activity. In the opening to Book 1 it is the gap between the technical subject-matter (and farmers who are the addressees) and mankind's place in the universe as a whole. Later in that book it is the gap between the poet's need to concentrate on tiny animals and man's general reluctance to concern himself with things he regards as trivial and far beneath him; what emerges is that there can be no real gap between such creatures and mankind. At the beginning of Book 2 the gap is again that between the narrowly technical subject-matter and the extensiveness of the unspoken field. At the end of that Book, the gap is converted into the tension between the technical subject-matter and the poet's Lucretian ambitions to explain and dominate the universe. That same gap is explored at the beginning of Book 3 in terms of the composition of the *Georgics* and is contrasted with the poet's plans for the projected epic on Aeneas: one aspect of the poet's aim in the unspoken field of the *Georgics* is illumined by the poet's anticipation of the way he will fulfil that aim in the *Aeneid*. Later in Book 3 and at the beginning of Book 4 the gap is measured in terms of the contrast between the humble material, concerned with sheep or bees, and the grand style that is needed to make poetry out of it. Later in Book 4, in the description of the Corycian *senex*, the gap is presented in terms of the exigencies of the work, which pull in one direction, and the poet's wishes, which draw him in another. The *sphragis* finally represents the gap as one that exists between the humble, ingloriously inactive poet on the one hand and the ruler of the Roman world on the other (together with the Italian farmers who can win glory for themselves by work).

All of these various ways of viewing the gap are indexes that allow the reader to sense the proportionality between the ostensible field and the multi-faceted unspoken field: the poet as the teacher of a specified subject is also aware simply as a poet of a complex series of relations that constitute the unspoken field, and that field also includes within its boundaries his own activity as a poet. This complex system of relations is taken up at the end of Book 4 and unified in a detailed mythic contrast that measures the gap between the tragic poet on the one hand and the divine farmer Aristaeus on the other. That myth stands in a relationship to the poem as a whole which combines elements that are synecdochic (requiring extensive reconstruction by the reader) with elements that are metaphoric. Like the myth of Laudamia in Catullus 68, it takes the place of a discursive statement by the poet: it transforms the didactic relationship between the technically knowledgeable teacher and the pupil-farmer into a confrontation between the poet as such and the enormity of the unspoken field that he has throughout felt compelled to draw into his work.

The central difference between the techniques of the *Eclogues* and of the *Georgics* can be focused by an attempt to define the two fields in both cases. In the *Eclogues* they are shepherds and the make-believe world of Theocritus on the one hand and the poet and his contemporary Roman world on the other. In the *Georgics* they are Italian farmers and the problems of farming on the one hand, and, on the other, mankind in relation to the universe. It quickly becomes clear, however, that the formulation offered for the fields of the *Georgics* is incomplete, for it ignores the position of the poet. In the *Eclogues* that presented no problem, for, with the exception, for instance, of the enclosing sections of *Eclogue* 10 or of the opening of *Eclogues* 6 and 8, the poet does not make an entrance into the *Eclogues* in his own person; and in two of those entrances he dramatises himself as a herdsman. However, not only did the nature of didactic poetry thrust the poet into the foreground, but Virgil in the *Georgics* chose to emphasise that aspect of his poem.

The result was to provide him with a ready means (only occasionally available to him in the *Eclogues*) of relating the two fields to one another; for his own decision to use the technique of the objective framework in the composition of the *Georgics* inevitably posed exactly the sort of poetic problems that provided opportunities for self-conscious reflection on his poetic activity. So it comes about that at every point where he reflects on his own poetic activity he is also providing an index of proportionality between the two fields of the poem. Thus the indexes are concentrated on the gap that spans the relationship between the didactic persona addressing Italian farmers on technicalities and the real-life poet Virgil, endlessly concerned with the relationship between poetry and reality (for that is also the relationship between man and the world in which he lives).

So far certain relevant aspects (but no more) of both *Eclogues* and *Georgics* have been analysed in terms of the technique of the objective framework. It may be said (very much in passing) that the *Aeneid* is also susceptible to similar analysis; but that work needs treatment on a scale which would be inappropriate here and must await a later occasion. Meanwhile we can turn to the so-called *Ars Poetica* of Horace, for it was certainly Virgil's highly original use of the technique in the *Georgics* that pointed the way to Horace when he was composing his didactic work.

The primary field of the *Epistula ad Pisones* is that of the poet as teacher in relationship to his pupils who are to be taught how to write poetry.[67] The secondary field is that of the contemporary poet's relationship to the age in which he lives; and that relationship covers technique, subject-matter (which is life itself), and function. The various ways in which Horace, writing about the primary field, makes the reader apprehend the secondary field are reminiscent of Virgil's procedure in the *Georgics*; it becomes clear to a reader of both works that this was the result of conscious imitation on the part of Horace. In the *Georgics* the poet assumed the appropriate didactic role of teacher, and so often spoke in the first person to a pupil or pupils who were addressed in the second person. But beside this there was a series of self-conscious reflections on his own poetic activity in the first person,

67. A more widely ranging analysis of the *Ars Poetica* can be found in Williams (1968), pp. 329–57, and reference to the fuller discussion of details there will be assumed in what follows.

and these were used by Virgil as indexes of proportionality to the secondary field. Horace makes use of exactly this framework in the *Ars Poetica*. In addition to the didactic persona as such which Horace adopts throughout the work, he also appears in the guise of an ordinary member of the public, a playgoer, a critic, and a reader of poems (42, 101 ff., 153, 188, 244, 270 ff., 317, 351 ff., 357 ff., 388, 409 ff., and 463–64); all of these are easy and useful extensions of the didactic role. At a late stage in the work this role is explicitly linked with another role into which the poet had transferred himself without explanation on half-a-dozen conspicuous occasions. In those passages (24–26, 55 ff., 86 ff., 234 ff., 240 ff., and 265 ff.) the poet spoke not as a teacher, but as a practising poet whom the reader could recognise as Q. Horatius Flaccus, the author of the *Satires*, the *Epodes*, three books of *Odes*, and one book of *Epistles*. In lines 295 ff. he explains that ever since Democritus judged natural genius superior to art and denied sane men the name of poet, a large proportion of would-be poets stopped going to the barber or washing or taking the cure for insanity. He continues (301–07):

> o ego laevus,
> qui purgor bilem sub verni temporis horam—
> non alius faceret meliora poemata: verum
> nil tanti est. ergo fungar vice cotis, acutum
> reddere quae ferrum valet exsors ipsa secandi: 305
> munus et officium nil scribens ipse docebo,
> unde parentur opes . . .

'O unlucky that I am, I purge the bile from my system every springtime— yet no one else could have written better poems: but it is just not worth while. So I shall fulfil the function of a whetstone that can make steel sharp without itself being able to cut: writing nothing myself, I shall teach the duty and function ⟨of a poet⟩, where to find material. . . . '

The self-mockery—the idea that if he were prepared to be insane he would be a better poet than any—is unmistakable; but, beneath that, the reader is being given an index of the relationship between the two fields, in one of which the poet is a teacher (and the *Ars Poetica* is not poetry), but in the other of which he is the man who has had the past of Q. Horatius Flaccus. The passage shows how the ostensible (didactic) purpose of the work legitimates the primary field, but it also measures the distance to the secondary field by the claim to have given up poetry-writing. This is a man who, whatever appears to be the nature of the present work, can speak with the authority of a great poet. The subtle and teasing postponement to a late stage of that vital piece of information is characteristic of the meditative (as distinct from rhetorical) nature of Horace's writing: it colours in retrospect, suggesting that the reader will not look in vain for the great poet under the guise of the teacher of young boys. Some of the other examples of the teacher speaking as practising poet will be examined below.

On a number of occasions in the *Georgics* there appeared a gap that could be interpreted as measuring the distance between the primary and secondary fields. A similar gap can be seen in the *Ars Poetica*. The problem of the style appropriate to a particular subject-matter (which had already been interpreted in terms of a distinction of genres defined by metres in lines 73–85) is discussed with reference to the contrasting genres of fifth-century Athenian tragedy and New Comedy (86–111). After that, the relation between style and character is discussed in terms again of fifth-century Athenian tragedy and of Homeric epic (114–27). Then follows a discussion of composition in terms of Homer and the cyclic poets (128–52). The discussion then returns to drama, and a series of rules for the composition of drama are derived (179–201) by means of Aristotle's *Poetics* from fifth-century Athenian drama—with the exception of the one rule for which the fifth-century material was recalcitrant and forced even Aristotle into a vague and complicated analysis. This was the rule that established the proper length of a play by counting its constituent parts: here Horace abandoned tragedy and based his influential five-act rule on New Comedy.

He goes on to discuss (202–19) the question of music in terms (used by Plato and Aristotle) of its effect on an audience and of its impact on their taste and judgment; but, for the purpose, he uses a change in the nature of music which had been brought about in the last quarter of the fifth century B.C. The tone of the discussion is moralising in the Platonic manner and looks back regretfully to the earlier fifth century before the change had taken place. This is followed by an analysis of the stylistic problem presented by satyr-plays (220–50); but the problem is posed in terms of the early fifth century, in which the satyr-play was closely related thematically to the immediately preceding tragic trilogy and shared some of the leading characters. After this there is a discussion of metre (251–74) in terms of the iambic trimeter and senarius which bridges the gap between Greece and Rome, for the first time in the technical discussion in terms of literary composition rather than the audience. This leads to a swift history of drama (275–91) which, like the preceding discussion of metre, gets as far as the dramatists of the second century B.C. in Rome and stops there.

Thus most of the discussion of technical problems is conducted in terms of Greek literature of the fifth century or earlier; only when it becomes unavoidable does the poet descend further, and then only to New Comedy. When problems of metre and the history of drama are used to make the bridge to Rome, the analysis stops before the end of the second century B.C. There are three occasions where the bridge to Rome is made by other means. After the discussion of style, the 'Roman knights and infantry' (112–13) are wittily seen laughing at a dramatist who has misjudged his stylistic proprieties. At lines 153–57 the poet introduces his prescriptions for the composition of drama by imagining himself seated among the people as a member of a Roman audience, ready to stay and listen (or not) till the final appeal for applause. Then, after the discussion of satyr-drama, he again uses a Roman audience (248–50) to establish norms for success or failure. In each case the movement to Rome is made by means of an audience at a Roman drama, and in Horace's time the plays that were presented to such audiences were virtually all revivals of plays written in the second century B.C. Thus, by the end of the technical discussion of literary composition, the only territory other than early Greek literature that the poet has set his foot in has been Greek New Comedy and early Roman drama.

But there are two important indexes of proportionality to the secondary field of the contemporary literary scene, one preceding and one concluding the technical discussion. In his remarks on choice of words, the poet recommends a modest licence in the invention of new words, especially if they are derived from Greek. He then asks indignantly (53–58):

> quid autem
> Caecilio Plautoque dabit Romanus ademptum
> Vergilio Varioque? ego cur, acquirere pauca
> si possum, invideor, cum lingua Catonis et Enni
> sermonem patrium ditaverit et nova rerum
> nomina protulerit?

'Yet why will you find Romans allowing to Caecilius and Plautus what they deny to Virgil and Varius? And I—why am I grudged the capacity to acquire a few words, when the tongue of Cato and of Ennius lavishly enriched their ancestral language and produced new names for things?'

The gap between the early second century B.C. (represented by its major literary figures, Plautus, Cato, Ennius, and Caecilius) and the present day is closed by the poet's naming his friends Virgil and Varius. The point is underlined by the poet's naming himself also; and, lest an unwitting reader be tempted to hear only the teacher's casual tones, he illustrates the principle he is defending by basing a linguistic novelty on Greek in the use of (56) *invideor*. The reader will easily recognise what is in fact an outstanding characteristic of the poetic practice of Horace himself (the invention of syntactical novelties based on Greek).

The other index is less explicit. It ends the technical section of the poem and follows the poet's assertion that Rome would be as famous for literature as for military prowess if only poets did not lack care and polish. Then he addresses his young pupils (291–94):

> vos, o
> Pompilius sanguis, carmen reprehendite quod non
> multa dies et multa litura coercuit atque
> praesectum decies non castigavit ad unguem.

'O you descendants from the blood of Numa, you must criticise a poem that has not been brought into line by many a day and many a blotting-out, and that has not been ten times corrected as if it were a most polished piece of sculpture.'

Here the word *carmen*, after the poet has reached the present day by the generalising statement about Roman arms, naturally refers not to drama but to poetry intended to be read—that is, poetry in the sense in which Horace used the word *carmen* of his *Odes*. The proportionality between the concentrated attention on the far past, on the one hand, and the poet's own present day, on the other, is here presented for the reader's apprehension: what has been said by the teacher about drama of the second century B.C. is referable, *mutatis mutandis*, to the field of the poet in relation to his own age by means of a critical procedure (outlined in 292–94) that was unknown in the earlier period. Soon after this (301–08) comes the index that established the relationship between the figures of the teacher and of the practising poet, which, at this deliberately late stage, serves to locate in the secondary field the various moments so far where the poet has spoken as if he were a practitioner, and has referred instructions, mostly derived from the far Greek past or from early Roman drama, for critical illustration to the theoretical possibility of his actually practising them himself, exactly as he had formulated them (so 24–26, 55–58, 86–88, 234–43, and 265–69). But they need, of course, to be translated, not just transferred, into that field. A further index to span the gap follows in lines 341–46:

> centuriae seniorum agitant expertia frugis,
> celsi praetereunt austera poemata Ramnes:
> omne tulit punctum qui miscuit utile dulci,
> lectorem delectando pariterque monendo;
> hic meret aera liber Sosiis; hic et mare transit   345
> et longum noto scriptori prorogat aevum.

'The centuries of the elders expel poetry that is without moral profit: lofty young aristocrats pass over poems that are austere. The poet who has mixed the profitable with the pleasurable has always won every vote, by delighting his reader at the same time as he instructs him. That is the book that earns money for booksellers: it both travels overseas (345) and extends the life of its famous author far into the future.'

This starts with a picture that suggests drama, both because of the numbers of the elders, massed together, and the verb (341) *agitant* (meaning 'drive off, hiss off the stage'); but then the poet moves into a clear picture of young aristocrats reading books—a picture that is then made explicit in (344) *lectorem* and in the name of the Sosii, the famous contemporary Roman booksellers. This is contemporary Rome, with its book-trade, its growing audience overseas, and its famous writers that combine pleasure with serious thinking.

When Horace moves at line 295 from the technical discussion of poetic composition to discussion of the poet, his training, his material, his aims, and his relation to his own society, he chooses his exemplary material from Greek sources that extend from Homer (and earlier) down to third-century Alexandria and from Roman sources that are contemporary with himself. The greater ease of generalisation here, that is, permits him to draw the primary and secondary fields together, and this linking of the fields is indexed by the linking of the two personae of the teacher and of the poet near the beginning of this final section of the *Ars Poetica* (301–08). The poem ends with an excursion into secondary language (453–76) which has a function analogous to that of the myth of Aristaeus and Orpheus at the end of the *Georgics*. This ending forms a ring-composition with the picture of poetic madness with which the section opened (where the madness links Greece and Rome, with Helicon, Democritus, and Anticyra balanced by the Roman barber Licinus). The final portrait is amusing and fantastic, and, just as the poet refused poetry at the price of madness in the earlier passage, here he enters his own picture as an ordinary citizen, urging his fellows not to rescue the mad poet from the well on the ground that maybe he wanted to commit suicide and in any case ought to be allowed the option. But the portrait is not just funny: it takes the place of a primary statement about the poet's relation with his own society, which the reader must reconstruct.

This portrait is immediately preceded by another (438–52), an attractive portrait of the ideal critic. That theme was anticipated (the *Ars Poetica* is tightly bound together by the technique of thematic anticipation)[68] fifty lines earlier (386–90):

> si quid tamen olim
> scripseris, in Maeci descendat iudicis auris
> et patris et nostras, nonumque prematur in annum,
> membranis intus positis. delere licebit
> quod non edideris: nescit vox missa reverti.

If, however, you compose something at some time, let it descend into the ears of the critic Maecius and your father's and mine, and let it be suppressed for nine years, the draft locked up in your house. You will be able to delete what you have not published: the word once broadcast knows no return.'

Spurius Maecius Tarpa was an earlier contemporary of Horace's and certainly of advanced years at the time of writing; with him Horace associates the father of the Pisones and also himself. The theme of criticism returns in the picture of the false friend as critic (419–37) who will praise everything lavishly. Then comes the detailed portrait of the true critic in the person of the poet's recently dead friend, Quintilius Varus, and the imperfect tenses, signifying that death,

68. See Williams (1968), pp. 352–56.

answer in advance a reader's question why the poet did not mention Quintilius instead of Maecius earlier. The actual portrait of Quintilius ends with the splendid epigram (442–44):

> si defendere delictum quam vertere malles,
> nullum ultra verbum aut operam insumebat inanem
> quin sine rivali teque et tua solus amares.

'If you preferred to defend your error rather than alter it, not another word used he to waste or any vain effort to prevent your being your own and your poetry's lover, alone and without rival.'

Then he draws conclusions from the portrait. The good, sensible man will responsibly censure error of every kind, and (450–52):

> fiet Aristarchus, nec dicet 'cur ego amicum
> offendam in nugis?' hae nugae seria ducent
> in mala derisum semel exceptumque sinistre.

'He will be a very Aristarchus, and he will not say "Why should I hurt my friend over things that do not matter?" These things that do not matter will draw him into serious trouble if he is once mocked and received unfavourably.'

These passages all talk ostensibly about criticism, but they also function as an index of the writer's view of the seriousness of poetry, and they serve to draw poetry within the ethical framework of society. The poet had earlier made the point that, since poetry belongs, not to the necessary arts (like judicial oratory), but to the 'fine' or superfluous arts that man can live without, its only justification for existence is that it should be excellent: (372–73) *mediocribus esse poetis | non homines, non di, non concessere columnae*, 'neither men nor gods nor booksellers have given sanction for poets to be mediocre'. In the later passage (450–52) it becomes clear that the poet is involved in his society in such a way that his relationship with it is injured if his poetry is bad. This is an important index to the way the final portrait of the mad poet should be understood. A further index is provided by another favourite theme of Horace's: poetry should not only be pleasurable; it should be socially useful too. The theme is illustrated by a historical sketch of poetry (391–407), showing that it has always played an essential role in society and especially in helping to bring about social reforms;

it is consequently an activity to be regarded with pride (406–07). It was with this aspect of poetry in mind that the writer had advised the young poet to find material in (310) *Socraticae chartae*—philosophical works devoted to moral theory. A serious moral interest pervades Horace's own poetry, and it was this attitude that enabled him to deal so effectively with contemporary political themes. That ideal is expressed explicitly, but in an unobtrusive and modestly generalised way, in the letter to Augustus (*Epist.* 2.1.118–38). In the *Ars Poetica*, however, the theme belongs to the secondary field and must be apprehended by a series of indexes.

The indexes of proportionality to the secondary field in the technical part of the *Ars Poetica* (1–294) are based on the supposition that the writer is himself a practising poet (the denial of that does not come till lines 301–08), but they are often obscured by some negative feature in their formulation. The first, for instance, is made with a grand address to Piso and his sons (24, *pater et iuvenes patre digni*) and is concerned with the fact that 'most of us poets are led astray by the semblance of what is right: I try to be brief, but turn out obscure. . . .' But there the autobiographical formulation ends and the other examples of attempts to achieve particular stylistic excellence that go wrong are expressed in the third person. However, not only has the poet imitated or, rather, exemplified the virtue of brevity in his formulation of the idea, but such brevity is also a conspicuous characteristic of Horace's poetry. When, in lines 55–58, the writer complains that he is grudged a licence that is allowed to Cato and Ennius, again the licence in question (to produce linguistic inventions) is particularly characteristic of Horace's poetry. But the autobiographical impact is deliberately weakened by the preceding association of Virgil and Varius with the same licence. In lines 86–88, after a section on metre which explained historically how particular areas of subject-matter had become appropriated to particular metres, the poet says (86–88):

> descriptas servare vices operumque colores
> cur ego si nequeo ignoroque poeta salutor?
> cur nescire pudens prave quam discere malo?

'If I am unable to observe the established variations and styles of each type of work and am ignorant of them, why should I be saluted as a poet? Why, with false shame, should I prefer to remain ignorant than to learn?'

The lines are transitional: (86) *descriptas vices* refers back to the metrical genre-distinctions, and *operumque colores* forward to the next problem—that of the style appropriate to each genre. This again was a problem of the greatest interest to the poet Horace, and not only did he compose a wide range of different works in different metres, but even within the same work he shows the greatest inventiveness and sensitivity in changes of tone by stylistic means. In lines 263–69, in the technical discussion on the way the iambic trimeter migrated to Rome and was there treated with unseemly carelessness, he says:

> non quivis videt immodulata poemata iudex,
> et data Romanis venia est indigna poetis.
> idcircone vager scribamque licenter? an omnis   265
> visuros peccata putem mea, tutus et intra
> spem veniae cautus? vitavi denique culpam,
> non laudem merui. vos exemplaria Graeca
> nocturna versate manu, versate diurna.

'Not every critic can spot unrhythmical verses, and indulgence has been shown to Roman poets that is unworthy of poets. Am I, then, for that reason to be undisciplined and write lawlessly? Or am I to suppose that everyone will spot my faults, and so protect myself and be cautious ⟨keeping⟩ within hope of indulgence. In that case, I have escaped censure, but I have not merited praise. You must thumb the Greek models by night and by day.'

Here the poet (as often) illustrates his topic of metrical irregularity in a line (263) of irregular metrical form. But again the problem was clearly one of the greatest interest to the poet Horace, and the way in which he poses it—in terms of two equally unacceptable extremes—emphasises the artisic originality that is so characteristic of him: a readiness to experiment is needed, but it must be controlled by a judgment that has been formed by careful study not of Roman predecessors but of Greek exemplars.

Each of these passages is an index of proportionality in the sense that it shows how to approach the secondary field through the apparently irrelevant discussion of drama and epic and iambic trimeters. One index, however, has been omitted and must now be considered. With the introduction of the topic of stylistic appropriateness in 89 ff., the exemplary genre becomes drama (mainly tragedy) until line 250; this sequence is broken by a brief excursion into epic, in lines 128–52, to illustrate how to achieve originality in traditional subject-matter. There is only one index of proportionality in all this long discussion, and it comes at the climax in connexion with the most irrelevant genre of all. The discussion of music (202–19) results in the poet's condemnation of the 'new' style in music that came into vogue in Athens towards the end of the fifth century B.C., and the poet concludes by characterising the stylistic licence which came into poetry that was accompanied by the 'new' music. That theme of style now leads into the discussion of satyr-plays (220–50), and this topic is further connected thematically with the section on music by the drunken licentiousness of the audience (209, 224). The reason for discussing satyr-drama is not that Horace thought it a viable literary genre in Augustan Rome, but because it offered a means of posing a particular type of stylistic problem, while still keeping within the genres traditional to literary criticism. This interpretation is clinched by the fact that the poet has chosen the most primitive form of satyr-drama, practised by the early fifth-century tragedians, because in that form the stylistic problem could be formulated in the sharpest and most arresting terms. The problem is how to follow three tragedies, themselves thematically linked, with a satyr-play in which there is a strong element of farce yet also some of the same characters who appeared in the tragedies; and how to render stylistically the farcical element without either descending into vulgarity or, in an attempt to avoid the earthy, soaring into cloudy inanities (229–30). Then follows the most extensive autobiographical entrance in the *Ars Poetica* (234–50):

> non ego inornata et dominantia nomina solum
> verbaque, Pisones, Satyrorum scriptor amabo;   235
> nec sic enitar tragico differre colori
> ut nihil intersit Davusne loquatur et audax
> Pythias emuncto lucrata Simone talentum,
> an custos famulusque dei Silenus alumni.
> ex noto fictum carmen sequar, ut sibi quivis   240
> speret idem, sudet multum frustraque laboret
> ausus idem: tantum series iuncturaque pollet,
> tantum de medio sumptis accedit honoris.
> silvis deducti caveant, me iudice, Fauni
> ne velut innati triviis ac paene forenses   245
> aut nimium teneris iuvenentur versibus umquam,
> aut immunda crepent ignominiosaque dicta.

offenduntur enim quibus est equus et pater et res,
nec, si quid fricti ciceris probat et nucis emptor,
aequis accipiunt animis donantve corona.   250

'As a writer of satyr-plays, Pisones, I shall not cling to unadorned and everyday words and phrases only (235); nor yet shall I so struggle to create a distinction from tragic style that it makes no difference whether a slave is speaking— a Davus and a brazen Pythias who has just wiped old Simo's nose and raked in a talent—or Silenus, the guardian and attendant of the god who was his ward (239). My aim will be a poem created from what is familiar in such a way that anyone might hope to achieve the same, but in daring it sweat much and toil in vain: so very important are order and combination, so much distinction is added to things drawn from the common stock. In my judgment, the Fauns, when brought out of the woods, should be careful not to appear natives of the streets and even of the Forum (245), nor yet play the precious young man with over-sentimental verses, nor crack coarse and disgraceful jokes. For those who possess horse, father, and property are offended, nor do they, just because the roast-bean and chestnut buyers approve ⟨the play⟩, accept it gladly and reward it with the prize.'

In the *Ars Poetica* Horace often uses ring-composition to mark a section, as in lines 29–30 (with 1 ff.), or in lines 273–74 (where the order of topics, derived from 270–71, *et numeros et . . . sales*, is reversed to obtain the ring-composition with 251 ff.), or in lines 453 ff. (with 295 ff.). Here, too, the poet uses the principle of ring-composition, but with the additional feature, at the close of the section, of translating satyr-plays into Roman terms and of bringing them before a Roman audience. This is accompanied by a shift also in the writer's persona from being a poet of satyr-plays (235, *satyrorum scriptor*) to being a critic (244, *me iudice*) offering helpful advice to pupils who might write a satyr-play for the Roman stage (and here the stylistic characterisation of the extremes to be avoided is also a translation into Roman terms of what had been more universally expressed in lines 229–30). All of this serves to emphasise the remarkable passage where the writer poses as a poet of satyr-plays and talks about the stylistic difficulty in technical language that formulates the problem first in terms of drama (234–39); but this is then translated into general terms (assisted, as was noticed also in line 292, by the word 240, *carmen*) that are quite easily applicable to Horace's own *Odes*. This formulation, in fact, amounts to a claim —that ought readily to be conceded—to a particular kind of originality in Horace's own writing, apparently simple but really most difficult to attain; and it constitutes one of the most important indexes of proportionality in the *Ars Poetica* to the secondary field of the contemporary poet and the relationship of style and subject-matter. The situation envisaged is that of the poet who uses both language and themes that are familiar, but in such a way, by careful arrangement and use of figures, that stylistic effects are achieved which range within the limits of high poetry on the one hand and low comedy on the other. Satyr-drama is the exemplary genre that calls for such stylistic flexibility, and that is why a most important index to the secondary field is attached to a discussion of this otherwise totally irrelevant genre. Its stylistic problems happened to coincide in an exemplary way more or less with those posed by the tonal range of Horace's *Odes*.

The index here is to problems of tonal flexibility treated in terms of style, and the primary emphasis is on the consequent stylistic problems; but it is clear, both from the phrasing and from the very fact of posing the problem in terms of the most antique type of satyr-drama, that the poet fully realised that, in such cases at least, the distinction between style and content was most difficult to hold. Thus, although attention is primarily concentrated on style, the wording (especially in 240, *ex noto fictum*, and 243, *de medio sumptis*) expands to acknowledge the interdependence of style and subject-matter. It is that recognition particularly, with its consequent emphasis on a tonal flexibility, responding to variations in subject-matter and observing *decorum*, that now recalls (*e sequentibus praecedentia*) an earlier discussion of style which, at first sight, is interested only in the narrowly compositional aspects.

It is worth considering this passage in detail (45–72):

in verbis etiam tenuis cautusque serendis	46
hoc amet, hoc spernat promissi carminis auctor.	45
dixeris egregie notum si callida verbum	
reddiderit iunctura novum. si forte necesse est	
indiciis monstrare recentibus abdita rerum,	
fingere cinctutis non exaudita Cethegis	50
continget, dabiturque licentia sumpta pudenter;	
et nova fictaque nuper habebunt verba fidem si	
Graeco fonte cadent, parce detorta. quid autem	
Caecilio Plautoque dabit Romanus ademptum	
Vergilio Varioque? ego cur, acquirere pauca	55

si possum, invideor, cum lingua Catonis et Enni
sermonem patrium ditaverit et nova rerum
nomina protulerit? licuit semperque licebit
signatum praesente nota producere nomen.
ut silvae foliis pronos mutantur in annos,   60
prima cadunt: ita verborum vetus interit aetas
et iuvenum ritu florent modo nata vigentque.
(debemur morti nos nostraque; sive receptus
terra Neptunus classis aquilonibus arcet,
regis opus, sterilisve diu palus aptaque remis   65
vicinas urbis alit et grave sentit aratrum,
seu cursum mutavit iniquum frugibus amnis
doctus iter melius—mortalia facta peribunt,
nedum sermonum stet honos et gratia vivax.)
multa renascentur quae iam cecidere, cadentque   70
quae nunc sunt in honore vocabula, si volet usus,
quem penes arbitrium est et ius et norma loquendi.

'Also in sowing words the composer of our promised poem should be sparing and careful, taking joy in this one, rejecting that. You will find that you write with distinction if a clever connexion shall render a familiar word new. If it happens to be necessary to point to abstruse things by means of new indicators, it will fall to you to invent words that were not heard by the girdled Cethegi (50), and licence will be conceded if it is used in moderation; new and recently invented words will gain acceptance if they shall flow from a Greek spring, sparingly channelled off. For why shall Romans allow to Caecilius and Plautus what is denied to Virgil and Varius? Why am I (55) grudged the capacity to make a few acquisitions, when the tongue of Cato and of Ennius enriched their ancestral language and created new names for things? It has always been permissible, and always will be, to give currency to words stamped in the mint of the present day. Year after plunging year, as the forests change leaf (60), the previous leaves keep falling: in the same way the older generation of words keeps perishing, and like young men the newly born flourish and are strong. (We are a debt to death—we and all our works: whether the ocean, received into the land, guards fleets from northern gales, a work worthy of a king, or whether a marsh, long sterile and suited for oars (65), now feeds neighbouring cities and suffers the weight of the plough, or whether a river has altered a course that was destructive to cultivation, now taught a better path—the works of mortals shall perish: far less shall the splendour and charm of language live on and on.) Many words shall be born again that now have perished, and they shall perish (70) that are now highly honoured, if Necessity shall wish it, in whose hands is the power of decision and the jurisdiction and the command over speech.'

It is often remarked with astonishment that Horace, writing a work about poetry, does not mention figures, especially metaphor. That remark is only made because the originality of the first four lines of the passage above is missed. Commentators discuss with sackfuls of parallels what (46) *verba serere* could mean. But the phrase has no parallel in fact because it is a metaphor ('to sow words'), and the adjectives *tenuis cautusque* are chosen in the interest of that metaphor. The poet is thinking particularly of a famous passage of Virgil's *Georgics* (1.193–203) in which careful selection of seed is enjoined because everything tends to decline and the balance can only be held, with the utmost effort, by rigorous selection of the best. No more than the farmer his seed does the poet scatter his words broadcast and unselected. Then again (48) *iunctura* is an invention of Horace's in this sense. What happens here is that Horace has invented a formula— *notum si callida verbum | reddiderit iunctura novum*—to cover all types of linguistic originality that involve juxtaposition of words. And metaphor can be regarded simply as a new juxtaposition of a familiar word. The poet has just illustrated the process by juxtaposing *verba* and *serere*—to the puzzlement of commentators. He then goes on to discuss two further types of linguistic procedure that are important to his own poetic composition: coinage and the use of archaisms. With coinage is explicitly included another favourite procedure of Horace's: the use of a Latin word by analogy with a Greek syntactical structure (illustrated here by his use of 56, *invideor*). The principles that govern all these procedures are artistic necessity (48) and good judgment (51, 53); the latter principle is clear enough, but the former is original and will be taken up again. He then illustrates his assertion of a universal licence to coin words (58–59) by a different type of *callida iunctura* that is also entirely original. This is the following *iunctura* of *folia* and *verba*, whereby the famous Homeric simile (*Iliad* 6.146–49), comparing the generations of men to leaves (which inspired many later imitations), is for the first time applied to language. The simile is also given a novel structure, with novel locutions (like *pronos . . . in annos*),[69] and the element of the leaves growing again is suppressed (to be understood retrospectively). The simile adds the novel idea that old words die and so new words must be created, drawing the analogy of the processes of nature.

69. On this structure, see Williams *CR* 24 (1974): 55–56.

The theme of death now leads metonymically to the idea of the universality of death. The status of lines 63–69 as a parenthesis is shown by the thematic connexion of line 70 with lines 61–62. This parenthesis is another *callida iunctura*. An epigram attributed to Simonides (*Anth.Pal.* 10.105) runs: 'A certain Theodorus is glad that I am dead. Another shall rejoice over him—we are all owed to death.' The new *iunctura* consists in extending *nos* by *nostraque* and, in a surprise conclusion, associating *nostra* with language by an argument a fortiori. It is a passage whose tone also contrasts with the immediate context: the parenthesis is deeply pessimistic (in a very Horatian way), whereas the simile expresses the optimism of new generations. But the parenthesis serves another purpose also: it insulates the simile from an idea which the poet now wants to express, but which cannot, without contradiction, be extracted directly from the simile. This is the novel idea of linguistic metempsychosis: under certain conditions old dead words will come to life again, and what have become κύρια ὀνόματα will die. Now, since this cannot, except by a grossly circular argument, be accomplished by usage, (71) *usus* must mean the necessity of the literary artist (taking up 48, *necesse est* by the familiar process of ring-composition). 'Usage' is a descriptive term that bases itself on things that have happened: that is, it legitimates ex post facto; it does not create. What is new here is not only the idea that archaisms come to life a second time, but that the words that die are not now regarded as (61) *verborum . . . vetus aetas* (which are old-fashioned words but not archaisms), but as current vocabulary. What the poet is asserting, then, is that there are two ways in which words die: old age and rejection. The novel idea that he is putting forward is that, as far as the poet is concerned (and the poet is not like ordinary men, nor is he concerned with ordinary speech), the important principle is artistic necessity. Such artistic necessity is parallel to the process of nature in the simile (60–62): the poet is the arbiter of the generations of words; his choice and his decision spell death or rebirth for words.

Understood like this, the passage becomes an important index of proportionality to the secondary field of the *Ars Poetica* in two ways. First, at one level it presents the teacher giving instruction on language; but, at another, it shows the poet reflecting deeply and self-consciously on his own procedures as a poet. Secondly, it shows the poet, purporting to be a teacher, yet exemplifying the essence of poetic composition by practising it as he pretends to teach. The same procedure can be seen many times in the *Ars Poetica*, most conspicuously in the discussion of character (153–78), where Aristotle's logical organisation into three periods has been altered by Horace into the four seasons of human life.[70] A further feature emerges from the passage on poetic language. The poet demonstrates—what must always be true for poets—that a distinction between language and subject-matter is artificial, and that when procedures which are apparently characteristic of linguistic manipulation are discussed, those procedures are in fact also applicable to the manipulation of ideas. That is shown by the way Horace gave material he derived from Homer and from Simonides a new life, but using the same process of *callida iunctura* on them as he used on single words.

That theme of how to give originality to inherited material is specifically taken up in lines 128 ff., but disguised within the objective framework that the poet invented for the *Ars Poetica*: it is a discussion of how to give originality to traditional epic material, and the transition to this topic from the preceding discussion of linguistic propriety in drama is made by the observation that it is better to use the *Iliad* for dramatic material than to attempt to devise a completely original plot. Finally, the discussion of satyr-drama (225–50) leads to a generalising of the problem involved in that type of composition, which serves to emphasise the fact that poets must draw on a common pool not only of words but also of ideas (240–43). The purpose of that emphasis is to pose the problem of poetic originality in the sharpest form possible. The answer to the problem is provided by the central concept of the earlier passage (45 ff.), now formulated deliberately in a way that recalls that passage—(242) *tantum series iuncturaque pollet*. It is an answer constantly illustrated by the poetry of Horace himself, of Virgil, of Propertius, and of Catullus: it is that the rhetorical figures provide a means for creative renewal not only of language, but also, as this book has argued, of ideas; and that the poetic process essentially consists (so Horace's formulation runs) in inspired combinations both of words and ideas that were well known before, but in quite different combinations. That formulation is too simple to be useful in itself as an analytical tool because it is also too general, but its poetic simplicity is an exciting revelation of the basic process of poetic composition as it was caught by the vision of a supreme practitioner.

70. On this, see Williams (1968), pp. 331–33.

REFERENCES

The following abbreviations are used:

AJP	*American Journal of Philology*
CP	*Classical Philology*
CQ	*Classical Quarterly*
CR	*Classical Review*
G&R	*Greece and Rome*
JRS	*Journal of Roman Studies*
Mnemos.	*Mnemosyne*
PCPS	*Proceedings of the Cambridge Philological Society*
RhM	*Rheinisches Museum*
SO	*Symbolae Osloenses*

Anderson, W. S. 'Horace *Carm.* 1.14: What kind of ship?' *CP* 61 (1966): 84–98.

Booth, Wayne. *The Rhetoric of Fiction*. Chicago, 1961.

Brunt, P. A., and Moore, J. M. *Res Gestae Divi Augusti*. Oxford, 1967.

Butler, H. E., and Barber, E. A. *The Elegies of Propertius*. Oxford, 1933.

Cairns, Francis. 'Propertius 2.30 A and B'. *CQ* 65 (1971): 204–13.

———. *Generic Composition in Greek and Roman Poetry*. Edinburgh, 1972.

Camps, W. A. *Propertius Elegies Books 1–4*. 4 vols. Cambridge, 1961–67.

Canter, H. V. 'The mythological paradigm in Greek and Latin poetry'. *AJP* 54 (1933): 201–24.

Coleman, Robert. *Vergil: Eclogues*. Cambridge, 1977.

Commager, Steele. 'Horace *Carmina* I.2'. *AJP* 80 (1959): 37–55.

———. *A Prolegomenon to Propertius*. Lectures in memory of Louise Taft Semple, 3d series. Cincinnati, Ohio: University of Cincinnati, 1974.

Eliot, T. S. *Selected Essays*. London, 1951.

Fordyce, C. J. *Catullus*. Oxford, 1961.

Fraenkel, Eduard. *Horace*. Oxford, 1957.

Galinsky, Karl. 'Some emendations and non-emendations in the third edition of *Corpus Tibullianum*'. *Mnemos.* 26 (1973): 160–69.

Gow, A. S. F., and Page, D. L. *The Greek Anthology: Hellenistic Epigrams.* Cambridge, 1965.

Hubbard, Margaret. *Propertius.* London, 1974.

———. 'The capture of Silenus'. *PCPS* 21 (1975): 53–62.

Jakobson, Roman. *Fundamentals of Language.* New York, 1956.

Judge, E. A. '"Res publica restituta": A modern illusion?' In *Polis and Imperium: Studies in Honour of E. T. Salmon,* edited by J. A. S. Evans. Toronto, 1974. pp. 279–311.

Kroll, Wilhelm. *C. Valerius Catullus.* Leipzig and Berlin, 1929.

Lausberg, Heinrich. *Handbuch der literarischen Rhetorik.* Munich, 1960.

Luck, Georg. 'Beiträge zum Text der römischen Elegiker'. *RhM* 105 (1962): 337–51.

Macleod, C. W. 'Parody and personalities in Catullus.' *CQ* 23 (1973): 294–303.

———. 'Propertius 2.26'. *SO* 51 (1976): 131–36.

Millar, Fergus. 'Triumvirate and Principate'. *JRS* 63 (1973): 50–67.

Nisbet, R. G. M., and Hubbard, Margaret. *A Commentary on Horace: Odes Book 1.* Oxford, 1970.

Otis, Brooks. *Virgil: A Study in Civilized Poetry.* Oxford, 1963.

Otto, A. *Die Sprichwörter und sprichwörtlichen Redensarten der Römer.* Leipzig, 1890.

Page, Denys. *Sappho and Alcaeus.* Oxford, 1955.

———. *Poetae Melici Graeci.* Oxford, 1962.

Pfeiffer, Rudolf. *History of Classical Scholarship: From the Beginnings to the End of the Hellenistic Age.* Oxford, 1968.

Pöschl, Viktor. *Horazische Lyrik.* Heidelberg, 1970.

Reitzenstein, Richard. 'Zur Sprache der lateinischen Erotik'. *Sitzungsb. der Heidelberger Akad. d. Wissenschaften* 12 (1912): 1–36.

Rice Holmes, T. *The Architect of the Roman Empire (44–27 B.C.).* Oxford, 1928.

Russell, D. A. *'Longinus' On the Sublime.* Oxford, 1964.

———. 'Rhetoric and criticism'. *G&R* 14 (1967): 130–44.

Shackleton Bailey, D. R. *Propertiana.* Cambridge, 1956.

Smith, Kirby Flower. *The Elegies of Albius Tibullus.* New York, 1913.

Syme, Ronald. 'The origin of Cornelius Gallus'. *CQ* 32 (1938): 39–44.

———. *The Roman Revolution.* Oxford, 1939.

Vahlen, Johannes. 'Über die Paetus-Elegie des Propertius'. *Sitzungsb. der königl. preuss. Akad. d. Wissenschaften zu Berlin* (1883), pp. 69–90.

Weinstock, Stefan. *Divus Julius.* Oxford, 1971.

West, David. *Reading Horace.* Edinburgh, 1967.

Wilkinson, L. P. 'The continuity of Propertius ii.13'. *CR* 16 (1966): 141–44.
———. *The Georgics of Virgil*. Cambridge, 1969.
Williams, Gordon. 'Review and discussion of Shackleton Bailey *Propertiana*, Cambridge 1956' *JRS* 47 (1957): 240–47.
———. 'Some aspects of Roman marriage ceremonies and ideals'. *JRS* 48 (1958): 16–29.
———. *Tradition and Originality in Roman Poetry*. Oxford, 1968.
———. *The Third Book of Horace's 'Odes'*. Oxford, 1969.
———. 'Horace *Odes* i.12 and the succession to Augustus'. *Hermathena* 118 (1974): 147–55.
———. 'A version of pastoral: Virgil *Eclogue* 4'. In *Quality and Pleasure in Latin Poetry*, edited by Woodman and West. Cambridge 1974. pp. 31–46.
———. *Change and Decline: Roman Literature in the Early Empire*. Berkeley: University of California Press, 1978.
Wiseman, T. P. *Cinna the Poet and other Roman Essays*. Leicester, Eng.: Leicester University Press, 1974.

INDEX OF PASSAGES
DISCUSSED

GENERAL INDEX

Abrupt changes of addressee: in Propertius, 126, 129, 131, 135–36, 140, 145, 153, 167, 198,

Alcaeus, 26–27

Allegory: as extended metaphor, 25–27; as substitution of related fields, 28; distinguished from objective framework, 189, 190–91; types of, in *Eclogue* 4, 237

amare: in sense of 'inspire' in pastoral, 228–29

amicitia and *amor,* 60, 214–17

Amoebean contests in pastoral, 228, 230, 241

Antonomasia, 25

Apostrophe, 42–43, 47, 55, 126, 131, 153

Apotheosis, theme of: in *Eclogue* 5, 226–30

Arbitrary assertion of similarity, xii, 62–64; defined, 51, 63–64; in Catullus, 50–61; in Propertius, 64–69, 71–77, 79–91; in Horace, 70–71, 77–79; in Tibullus, 91–94

Aristotle, 28, 268

Ars Poetica of Horace: primary and secondary fields of, defined, 226–67, 270–72; self-conscious reflection on his own activity, used as an index in, 267, 271–72, 274, 277, 281–82; personae of poet in, 267; exemplary use of fifth-century Greek poetry in, 268–69; problem of stylistic flexibility discussed, 276–78; satyr-plays in, 276–78; claim to originality in, 277–78; are figures considered in . . . ?, 280–81

Ars Rhetorica: falsely attributed to Dionysius of Halicarnassus, 7, 191

Artificiality of Theocritus transcended in *Eclogues,* 243

Artistic necessity, principle of, in Horace, 280–81

Association of ideas, xii, 21, 28–29, 93, 94, 138, 169, 235; by opposites, 147

Atreus, 3–5

auctor ad Herennium, 23

Augustus: as avenger of Julius Caesar, 11; ideology of, 12–13, 15–19, 136, 159, 186–88, 211, 257; his plans for his own succession, 15; treated as a god, 124–25, 246–47; opposition to his moral programme, 187–88

Authority, problem of poet's and speaker's: in pastoral, 228–29, 234–35, 236–37

Bacchus, rites of: metonymy for poetry and inspiration, 229

Biography of poet rather than interpretation of poem, material relevant to, 226

Blending of Greek and Roman elements, effects of, 122, 208–09, 244–45

callida iunctura, 280–81, 282

Callimachus, 47, 124, 127, 221–22, 223

Cato. *See* Porcius Cato

Catullus: as innovator, 45–61, 123; his poem 34, official composition of 53 B.C.?, 209; homosexual themes in, 212–16; views Lesbia as wife and *amica,* 60, 216–17; poem 64 as background to *Eclogue* 4, 237

Cicero, 23, 28, 33, 96, 154–55, 159, 214–16, 220

Civil war: as a theme of Augustan poetry, 10–13, 26–27, 115–18, 160–61, 165–66, 237, 238–39

Close repetition: as poetic linking device, 50, 124

Q6